Film, Drama and the Break-Up of Britain

Steve Blandford

Dedication

This book is dedicated with much love to my ever-generous partner, Mitch Winfield, my adorable children, Sam and Beth, and my parents, Ron and Gwen Blandford. Thank you all so much.

Film, Drama and the Break-Up of Britain

Steve Blandford

intellect Bristol, UK / Chicago, USA

First Published in the UK in 2007 by
Intellect Books, PO Box 862, Bristol BS99 1DE, UK

First published in the USA in 2007 by
Intellect Books, The University of Chicago Press, 1427 E. 60th Street, Chicago,
IL 60637, USA

A catalogue record for this book is available from the British Library.

Cover Design: Gabriel Solomons
Copy Editor: Holly Spradling
Typesetting: Mac Style, Nafferton, E. Yorkshire

ISBN 978–1-84150–150–5

Printed and bound by Gutenberg Press Ltd, Malta

CONTENTS

Acknowledgements   6

Chapter 1   Introduction   7

Chapter 2   Last Orders in Wonderland: England and Cinema   19

Chapter 3   Beyond 'Priests, Pigs and Poverty': Ireland and Cinema   47

Chapter 4   'We Can't Even Pick a Decent Country to be Colonised By': Scotland
             and Cinema   65

Chapter 5   'A Beautiful Mistake': Wales and Cinema   87

Chapter 6   'An Evaporation of Certainty': England and Theatre   105

Chapter 7   'Protestants Don't Write Plays, You See': Ireland and Theatre   125

Chapter 8   No More 'Cultural Cringe': Scotland and Theatre   145

Chapter 9   Behind 'the Façade of Cool Cymru': Wales and Theatre   163

Bibliography   181

Index   191

ACKNOWLEDGEMENTS

I would very much like to acknowledge the support and encouragement of all my colleagues at the University of Glamorgan, past and present; particularly Mary Traynor, Andy Cole, Ieuan Morris, Sam Boardman Jacobs, Daryl Perrins, Mark Woods, Richard Hand, Hamish Fyfe, Stephen Lacey, Michael Carklin, Michael Wilson, Katja Krebs, Inga Burrows, Rea Dennis, Wyn Mason, Ceri Sherlock, Heike Roms, Michael Connolly, Maggy McNorton, Alan Jones, Jeff Wallace, Rod Jones, Lisa Lewis, Mark Jenkins, David Barlow, Jesse Schwenk, Sara Jolly, Diana Brand, Jane Aaron and Chris Williams. I would also like to thank all the students of Theatre, Film and Television at Glamorgan, who I have enjoyed teaching and working with so much over the years.

I have also received generous assistance with interviews and discussions of various kinds from Ed Thomas, Marc Evans, Fizzy Oppe, Amma Asante, Kevin Jackson, Dai Smith, Peter Stead, Julian Upton, Peter Edwards, Jim Hillier and Phil Clark.

As will be evident from the bibliography, I am deeply indebted to the excellent work already done on the national cinemas and theatre and performance cultures of Britain and Ireland; particularly that by Dave Berry, Duncan Petrie, Martin McLoone, John Hill, Margaret Llewellyn-Jones, Jen Harvie and Ruth Barton

Most of all, though, I have to thank Mitch, Sam and Beth to whom this book is dedicated.

ORDERING INFORMATION

Orders from the U.S.A. and Canada:

The University of Chicago Press
Order Department
11030 South Langley Avenue
Chicago, Illinois 60628
U.S.A.

Telephone: 1-800-621-2736 (U.S.A. only);
(773) 568-1550
Facsimile: 1-800-621-8476 (U.S.A. only);
(773) 660-2235
Pubnet @ 202-5280
WWW: http://www.press.uchicago.edu

Orders from the United Kingdom and Europe:

The University of Chicago Press
c/o John Wiley & Sons Ltd.
Distribution Centre
1 Oldlands Way
Bognor Regis, West Sussex PO22 9SA
UNITED KINGDOM
Telephone: (0) 1243 779777
Facsimile: (0) 1243 820250
Internet: cs-books@wiley.co.uk
WWW:
http://www.wiley.com/WorldWide/Europe.html

Orders from Japan:

Booksellers' orders should be
placed with our agent:
United Publishers' Services, Ltd.
Kenkyu-sha Building
9, Kanda Surugadai 2-chome
Chiyoda-ku, Tokyo
JAPAN
Telephone: (03) 3291-4541
Facsimile: (03) 3293-3484
Libraries and individuals should place their
orders with local booksellers.

Orders from Australia, New Zealand, South Pacific, Africa, the Middle East, China (P.R.C.), Southeast Asia, India, Mexico, Central and South America:

The University of Chicago Press
International Sales Manager
1427 E. 60th Street
Chicago, Illinois 60637
U.S.A.
Telephone: (773) 702-7740
Facsimile: (773) 702-9756
Internet: dblobaum@press.uchicago.edu

Orders from Korea, Hong Kong, and Taiwan, R.O.C.:

The American University Press Group
3-21-18-206 Higashi Shinagawa
Shinagawa-ku, Tokyo, 140
JAPAN
Telephone: (03) 3450-2857
Facsimile: (03) 3472-9706
Internet: andishig@po.iijnet.or.jp

1

Introduction

As I am sure will be clear to many, the title of this book makes direct reference to Tom Nairn's highly influential *The Break-Up of Britain: Crisis and Neo-nationalism* (1977). Nairn's book predicted, rather too prematurely as it turned out, the end of Britain via the aspirations to independence of Scotland and Wales, and his work has become a key reference point for those seeking to re-examine the future of 'Britain' both as an idea and a political reality since the devolution of power to the Scottish Parliament and the Welsh Assembly in the late 1990s.

The aim of this book is more modest than Nairn's and those of the other historians and social scientists that have followed him in attempting to understand and predict the shape of Britain's constitutional future. It essentially sets out to trace and examine some of the ways that film and theatre in this country have begun to reflect and contribute to a Britain that is changing so rapidly in its sense of itself that, many would argue, it amounts to a break-up of the very idea of there being a meaningful British identity at all.

Working in Wales during the 1990s clearly offered the opportunity to experience at close quarters both the political climate that led to devolution and the work of those working in film and drama in Wales, who were responding to the changing sense of the nation that such a climate was producing. However, it quickly becomes obvious to anyone that considers the question that devolution for Scotland and Wales is only one, albeit important, dimension to the notion that the 'idea' of Britain is 'breaking up'. It is arguable, of course, whether a truly cohesive idea of Britain ever existed at all, but the last two decades have brought open debate over the fractured nature of modern British identity much more firmly into the realm of popular consciousness. Whilst devolution for Scotland and Wales has been one powerful factor in this profound and important change in the way that the British think of themselves, there are many others, and I would like to start by briefly discussing those that appear to have been the most significant for British dramatic and cinematic culture during this time.

To begin with the most obvious, the Peace Process in Ireland has radically altered, yet again, the relationship between the UK and the Republic and of course the political status of the north of Ireland. The Good Friday agreement's plans for newly devolved powers, inter-governmental committees and power-sharing arrangements, though they have been fraught with practical difficulty, have radically altered the sense of the role of all parts of Ireland in the future of British identity. This in turn has to be seen in the context of the emergence of the 'Celtic Tiger' economy in the Republic with all the consequent shifts in the way that 'Irish' identity as a generality is viewed by the British. For this book, this has meant that consideration has had to be given to cinema and theatre with roots on both sides of the Irish border in order to properly tackle the complexities of their contributions to the overall question of British national identity itself.

In more modest ways the post-1997 New Labour government has also sought to extend the idea of political devolution to parts of England through the concepts of regional assemblies and elected mayors. Even though this has had mixed success, to say the least, the very act of introducing the idea has refreshed the concept of regional and, indeed, English identity to the point of spawning a rash of publications on the subject including those with a populist bent such as Jeremy Paxman's *The English* (1998).

It is also not entirely true that there is no appetite for any form of English regional devolution. In London, for example, Ken Livingstone has remerged as a political figure of some force and influence through his role as mayor, whilst under his influence London has pursued transport, culture and infrastructural policies that declare the independence of its thinking from the rest of the UK. By 2005, twelve other British towns and cities had also opted to choose a mayor through direct elections. Though this has to be weighed against the huge majority against the idea of a North-East regional assembly in the 2004 referendum, there is evidence through a wide variety of campaign groups that devolution in Scotland, Wales and Northern Ireland has raised profound questions in the minds of many about the future constitutional status of England.

This book argues that in turn this has been reflected in a previously non-existent interest in the idea of there being a distinctively English cinema and theatre culture. It is by no means clear that such a thing yet exists, but in both art forms there has emerged work that raises questions about the idea of an enduring England and, more commonly, of a Britain within which England and the metropolis at its centre automatically hold sway.

On a much larger scale, the expansion of the EU and the endless conversation around Britain's relationship to the rest of Europe have become ever more significant influences on any primitive sense of an older British identity that was forged out of a sense of isolation and an island fortress imagination. Such influences, of course, have to compete both with the fluctuating status of this country's relationship with the United States, an issue that has, of course, taken on a much sharper focus during recent years, and the overwhelming sense of the end of empire given public expression through such public acts as the handing over of Hong Kong to China in 1997.

In the last decade the influence of the EU on British national identity has proved to be extremely complex and needs to be seen in the context of a resurgence of nationalism across Europe that has taken many forms. As a French commentator in 1999 spelt out, what might be termed the devolutionary spirit has by no means been confined to Britain:

Although nationalism was discredited by the appalling slaughter that took place in Europe in the course of two world wars, attachment to the nation is making a powerful comeback. The up-surge of micro-nationalisms within established nation-states of Western Europe probably reflects a belief that reconstituting the state on the basis of a more 'authentic' nation will better protect the rights and interests of citizens – especially where the territory of the would-be nation has strong economic potential. (Thiesse 1996)

If one corollary of the spread of the EU is the resurgence of the nation state in Europe, then it is ironic how often the artists of the resurgent British nations help to define themselves by referring to the 'European' nature of their work. Again and again it is possible to find writers and film-makers from Scotland and Wales seeking to distance themselves from a 'British' identity by locating their work in what they see as a European context. This is partly, of course, in order to be rid of the situation that compels identity to be defined in opposition to England and emerges as possibly the most clearly defined way in which membership of the EU is reflected in the way that artists have dealt with national identity.

This latter tendency is perhaps most visible in the way that theatre-makers have worked in traditions that are in opposition to the dominant British literary tradition. The last two decades in particular have seen a spectacular growth in British theatre companies that have drawn on physical performance traditions, which whilst not exclusively European (there has also been an enormous growth in the influence of work from the Far East and Africa), tend to draw on the work of practitioners with their roots in mainland Europe. In film as well there has been a strong tendency for younger independent film-makers to look to smaller European film cultures for inspiration, something which is discussed particularly in this volume's chapter on Scottish film.

Ironically, of course, such developments take place against the backdrop of what is popularly perceived as an enduring British suspicion of all things 'European' and, in particular, all things connected to the EU. This tension can be seen to typify one of the functions of art in the continuing process of the imagining of national and other identities. Work for theatre and film that reads against the grain of what is seen (often through the vested interests of sections of the media) as popular opinion becomes part of the process of suggesting hybrid identities, something which is of particular relevance and importance at a time of particularly marked changes to British identity itself.

Perhaps even more directly apparent, at least in the last five years, is the way that dramatic fictions have dealt with the increasingly contentious relationship between Britain and the United States and its ramifications for national identity. This has been at its clearest in work that has dealt not only with the Iraq war itself (such as David Hare's *Stuff Happens* for the Royal National Theatre in 2004), but also with the perceived identity of Britain, inextricably linked now to the United States in the wider Islamic world.

Finally, of course (and linked in some respects to the issue of Britain's alliance with the United States), there is the highly topical question of the impact on British identity of its highly diverse ethnic populations. It would be foolish to think of this as a 'new' question – much of Britain's cultural strength and energy have always come from successive waves of immigration. However, there are strong arguments for suggesting that the current situation is of a different order. Just as devolution has come as the natural expression of a desire to more accurately reflect the genuine diversity of Britain, so too has there been more confident assertions of difference from second and third generations of British families who originally emigrated to Britain. Alongside these questions with a direct relationship to Britain's colonial past, the reconfiguration of Europe continues to broaden the range of both those who are able to live and work in Britain as of right and those who must seek to negotiate an ever more labyrinthine asylum and refugee process.

These welcome additions to the already highly diverse ways in which it is possible to be British have, of course, often been caught up in the ugly politics of nationalism and other kinds of cultural identity. From irresponsible politicians seeking to make cheap electoral capital out of irrational fears of asylum seekers, to the horrifying reminders in July 2005 of the way that disaffection with mainstream British identity can be exploited to deadly effect, there are endless ways in which xenophobia can be fostered and the desire for a return to an essentialist notion of what it is to be British kindled in the unsuspecting. The much parodied 'cricket test' first proposed by Norman Tebbitt in the 1980s has now become the citizenship test that we must take more seriously as it appears to be government policy rather than the mere musings of a notorious xenophobe.

On the positive side, the last ten years have seen the rise of a large number of black and Asian artists working in both film and theatre, though, as the book discusses there remain serious inequalities with respect to positions of real power in both industries. However, there has undoubtedly been a great deal of recent work emerging from all the British nations and by artists from a variety of backgrounds that seeks to explore in positive ways the complex questions of identity that arise from Britain's changing ethnic mix. As was acknowledged above this is not a new question, but perhaps one given sharper focus by the changing face of world politics and to some extent by the changing internal politics of the United Kingdom. In 2004, an article in *The Guardian* discussed a 'museum for migrants' though it concluded that

> Maybe we need more than a museum – we need a redefinition of what the words British and immigrants mean. We look back at those once unwelcome migrants – the Romans, Norse and Anglo-Saxons to define what the first Britain was. Only when we weave in the French, the forgotten Dutch, the Germans, the Jews, the Irish, the Indians, the Afro-Caribbeans, the Chinese, the Turks, the Russians, the Africans and everyone right down to the last Albanian who came to Britain clinging to the undercarriage of a Eurostar train, will we see the carpet of many colours that a New Britain will become. (Gibbons 2003 a.)

In all the chapters of this volume, work is discussed that either attempts to imagine what such a new British or Irish or Scottish or Welsh identity might become, or, at least, raises the difficult questions that take such a debate forward. Arguably, this is the most important sense in which an older idea of Britain needs to be dismantled forever, and it is partly the role of artists to produce work that assists in such a process.

Inevitably one of the key critical frameworks for this discussion has tended to be the complex and often problematic way in which postcolonial criticism has been applied to Britain's internal 'colonies'. The last ten years especially have seen a number of attempts to raise questions about the usefulness, or otherwise, of the considerable body of work grouped under the banner of postcolonial studies to an internal British context.

In turn there has been a much broader movement within film, theatre and performance studies that has seen a fundamental shift in the dominant critical tendency towards (some would say 'back towards') the specificity of contexts for the production of works of art. This has resulted in, among many other things, a resurgent interest in the idea of national cinemas and theatres. As Mette Hjort and Scott Mackenzie put it:

> More specifically, the influential critical vocabulary associated with deconstruction and psychoanalytic semiology must compete with a new set of terms: 'hybridity', 'multiculturalism', 'transnationalism', 'nationalism', 'internationalism', 'globalisation', 'cosmopolitanism', 'exile', 'postcolonialism', to mention but some of the salient terms.' (Hjort and Mackenzie 2000: 1)

To a large extent, this loose summary of the 'critical vocabulary' that has dominated recent critical discussion of the national in relation to forms of cultural production is also a summary of the conceptual framework within which this discussion of the 'break-up' of Britain takes place. Just as the framework has been used globally in order to raise questions about the idea of the nation and its relationship to art and culture, here it is used in the micro context of Britain in order to examine the ways that film and theatre in the four British nations have responded to the idea of a much more ambiguous sense of a British nation.

In many ways it has been surprising to see, during the course of writing the book, the extent to which the idea of Britain in the discourse surrounding the nation in relation to cinema and theatre has remained unproblematic. In a critical world in which the concepts outlined above by Hjort and Mackenzie have been prominent for the best part of two decades, it is only relatively recently that the idea of a monolithic 'British' cinema or theatre has been rendered profoundly problematic. To take just one example, one had to wait until the second edition of Robert Murphy's influential *The British Cinema Book* before the inclusion of Martin McLoone's very useful chapter entitled 'Internal Decolonisation? British Cinema in the Celtic Fringe' which ends with the following assertion:

> The re-imagining that is taking place in Scotland, Wales and Northern Ireland involves a reworking of national or regional tropes and stereotypes. If many of these are the inventions of the metropolitan centre, nevertheless, their reinterpretation impacts on a concept of Britishness, which is already under pressure. The multicultural nature of English society has begun to erase singular definitions of national identity and British cinema has begun to explore the bewildering concatenation of local, regional, national, ethnic and racial identities. Film-making in Britain's Celtic periphery suggests that a process of internal decolonisation is well underway and that peripherality has moved towards the cutting edge of contemporary debate. (McLoone 2001: 190)

McLoone's very welcome intervention in the context of a widely circulated and influential collection remains, nevertheless, a comparatively rare example of work that applies such conceptual frameworks across the British nations. Whilst there is excellent work, to differing extents, on national cinemas in Scotland and Ireland in particular (McLoone 2000 and Petrie 2000), there has been, to date, little work that looks comparatively at all four nations, and almost nothing on the idea of England and cinema.

In the field of theatre and performance Jen Harvie's recent book *Staging the UK* is an excellent attempt to apply some of the thinking around the idea of the nation to its 'performance', particularly in relation to some examples of difference between the UK's constituent nations. Harvie's work does not attempt to be comprehensive in its coverage of contemporary practices, but rather uses tightly focused case studies in order to explore what she sees as highly distinctive practices that have recently emerged. In setting out her own critical framework, Harvie asserts the centrality of Benedict Anderson (and those that have developed his work) to both her own ideas and to most recent work on the relationships between cultural practices and identity:

> A founding principle here is that national identities are neither biologically nor territorially given; rather, they are creatively produced or staged. I am not arguing, wilfully, that political acts, legislation and the material conditions of geography have no influence on national identities. But it is necessary in this context to distinguish between a state and a nation. A state is a political authority that asserts power; but a nation is a *sense* that people share a culture, a culture that may or may not be coterminus with the state's borders. As Benedict Anderson proposed most influentially in his book *Imagined Communities: Reflections on the Origin and Spread of Nationalism*, a person's sense of his or her nation is based largely on participation in shared cultural practices such as reading newspapers, listening to the radio, watching television and reading novels... Through their cultural activities people will imagine their communities. And one of the ways they will do so is through performance. (Harvie 2005: 2)

As they are for Harvie, Anderson's ideas on nation and community are inevitably vital throughout this discussion. Though they have rightly been debated and challenged throughout the two decades since he originally produced them, Anderson's central tenets remain at the heart of most writing on the concept of the nation state and the influential role of cultural production in its formation and continual evolution. This is particularly so in a context such as that of contemporary Britain where quasi-states have recently been created and where older 'nations' have therefore been given new impetus to flourish. As Harvie goes on to point out, it is not simply that Anderson stresses the idea of the imaginary in the creation of nation states, he also insists that they exist in a process of constant flux and change:

> In this understanding, 'the UK' is not a stable, universally and timelessly agreed entity; rather, it and its meanings are constantly conceived in many different ways. For example, for Northern Irish Republicans and others, the 'UK' may be an imperialist and assimilating imposition. For others it may be a focus for national pride. (Harvie 2005: 3)

Inevitably such ideas about the inherent instability of the idea of the nation have been intelligently extended and inflected, often by those working within the broad frame of postcolonial studies during the last two decades. More recently, particularly since devolution, there have been attempts to apply such thinking to the changed British context and to use it as a vehicle to think through contemporary ideas about the nation state. This has resulted in a number of debates about the desirability of fostering new national 'projects' and related calls to embrace the 'post-national'. One example of such a debate occurs, bravely, in a single volume, *Postcolonial Wales* (2005) in which the two editors openly and honestly express their disagreements about the future direction of Wales, particularly in terms of the cultural climate that is being fostered. For the historian Chris Williams,

> Discourses of nationality operate by 'othering', by identifying borders between 'us' and 'them'. Such reactive and essentialist binarisms erect psychological barriers between peoples, excite unnecessary antagonisms towards others, and render marginal or invisible those whose characteristics do not fit those of the imagined nation... They close frontiers both internally and externally. In Wales we would do well to avoid what Said called the 'rhetoric of blame' that often exists between imperial and newly independent states, and to refrain from indulging in an anachronistic burst of nation-building, just as the nation-state finally begins to recede from its central position on the world stage. A 'post-national' Wales is a more attractive prospect. (Williams 2005: 16)

As he later admits, Williams' position is unashamedly utopian and is an attempt to use the profoundly changed political status of Wales to think through a radical position beyond the nation state. His co-editor, Jane Aaron, is however far more sceptical about the advantage to Wales of adopting such a stance, just at the moment when devolution has provided the opportunity to assert a radically different sense of Welsh cultural identity. During the course of her analysis of the way that poetry and fiction have worked as forms of resistance to an imposed colonial identity in the history of Wales, Aaron both acknowledges the attractiveness of the post-national future proposed by Williams whilst at the same time strongly opposing the unilateral adoption of such a position by Wales at this historical moment:

> Whilst the possibility of constructing human communities capable of cooperation and of maintaining a wealth of cultural diversity while eschewing nationhood may be an ideal worth working for, for contemporary Wales to give up its aspirations to nationhood surely would do little to further that cause. The post-nation people of Wales could not float in limbo in a world otherwise inhabited by nationals without being recategorized: we would all, willy-nilly, be categorized by others if not by ourselves, as 'British', as unproblematic members of the British nation-state. And in today's Britain, the default position for those who identify, or are identified, as British only, with no qualifiers, remains an unexamined English cultural identity. (Aaron 2005: 155)

Similar debates have, of course, surfaced in relation to the rest of the UK, particularly in the work of those who have examined the re-imagining of Britain by artists working in the post-devolutionary context. Berthold Schoene, for example, makes a similar case to that made by Chris Williams above in his plea for Scotland to seize the opportunity of 'post nationhood', particularly through an abandonment of traditional masculine discourse:

> Finding itself at the beginning of a new era Scotland has been given the chance to resist a re-erection of the hyperbolic self and its patriarchally organised nation state. By taking on board Ian Chambers' position the nation as a cultural and linguistic unit is not a closed history, something that has already been achieved, but is an open, malleable framework in

the making... Scotland could develop into what Catherine Hall calls a 'post-nation'.(Schoene 2002: 97)

Schoene's particular concern is the highly masculinized discourse of recent Scottish fiction, but his point is much broader and part of a wider tendency to attempt to see beyond the natural 'cultural confidence' that came with devolution. On the other hand, as suggested by Jane Aaron and others, there is a counter-tendency to embrace the opportunity to build on this confidence and to create spaces for work to emerge that is increasingly distinctive from a more generalized sense of Britishness. The tension that results from the existence of these two positions frequently informs much of the work discussed in this volume as film- and theatre-makers have responded to, often in ways that are oblique, a changing sense of what Britain and its constituent nations can become. They have responded in ways that do not automatically accept any idea of a Britain that is overwhelmingly dominated by its postcolonial position, but which nevertheless are inevitably influenced by profound political change that, at the very least, raises interesting questions that are analogous to those raised in less ambiguously postcolonial societies.

Whilst the book inevitably draws on the particularly extensive literature around the concept of 'national cinemas' and the slightly less extensive body of work on 'national theatres' it should be clear then that it does so firmly within the context of the idea of the nation (and therefore of national cinemas and theatres) having becoming ever more complex and problematic. It has long been routine for those who work in the field of national cinemas to preface anything that they write about a given culture with an extended critique of the idea of stable or fixed boundaries to the nation. Typical of such a tendency, though obviously inflected by the particular relationship of Canada to the idea of a postcolonial society, is Scott Mackenzie's description of the country at the start of a discussion on the nature of Canadian National Cinema: 'It is my contention that in relation to cultural production, in many ways, Canada is already postnational and multicultural in nature and therefore offers us insight into what shape a multicultural, postnational cinema might take.'(Mackenzie 1999) Despite such a description Mackenzie nevertheless continues to use the idea of Canadian cinema as a useful critical category, a tendency that is very common amongst those working in the field. Tom O'Regan's influential study of Australian cinema not only raises the problematics of a category called 'Australian', but also of the critical construct that is implied by the idea of the national in relation to any art form. Discussing his own thinking in relation to that of Christian Metz on the problems of using national cinema as a critical framework, O'Regan acknowledges the profound difficulties for the critic employing the category national cinema but, at the same time, is firm in his defence of the potential advantages and insights that such an approach can potentially offer:

> The hybrid analytical strategies demanded in examining national cinemas are also its strength. Significantly, national cinema writing is neither the analysis of a film text nor policy discourse; neither film industry journalism and economic analysis nor film reviewing, but a mixture of each. Because a national cinema study needs to deal with texts, technology, language, power and society, it has a chance of holding onto the multiple connections that make the cinema 'possible' and drive it forward. (O'Regan 1996: 3)

Both Mackenzie and O'Regan then manage to imply different kinds of problems with the idea of national cinema as an analytical framework whilst simultaneously asserting its continued usefulness. In this they are joined by virtually all those who have used the idea in any sustained way and, as Susan Hayward so clearly puts it, is 'fairly self-evident' that 'there will always be problems in defining "national" cinema.'(Hayward 2000: 91) Though this book is not an attempt at a piece of sustained national cinema analysis, it clearly relies upon some of its conceptual underpinning and it implicitly recognizes the problems and dilemmas identified by these and other commentators for its use as an analytical tool. For Britain, at this particular historical moment, it is arguably a category of more use than ever in that the tensions that have always been inherent in the idea of any kind of British national cinema have been highlighted and exposed, particularly by devolution, but also by the intensification of the other factors implicated in the 'break-up' of the idea of Britain.

In the case of theatre, whilst there has not been quite the sustained general interrogation (or indeed use) of the idea of the national as an analytical category, there has certainly been a sustained questioning of the problematic idea of a specifically British national theatre in the period since devolution and this volume draws heavily upon that body of work. Unsurprisingly, much of the analysis and debate has come from the newly devolved nations and has frequently focused on the desirability and potential nature of new 'national' theatre institutions proposed for Scotland and Wales. Adrienne Scullion, in her discussion of Scottish identity in the work of women playwrights, makes a point that is echoed in a number of other pieces that have appeared in the period since devolution:

> In passing, I would certainly consider that, in our post-devolution context, critics and practitioners alike might do well to interrogate and to reframe just what it is they want 'national' to mean. In a post-devolution context just what 'national' might actually mean is a key area of debate for critics and practitioners. A key indication of the new politics of Scotland is that a Labour/Liberal coalition government is prepared to be so sure about culture as a way of representing our *national* identity – when that national identity is assumed to be Scottish as opposed to British. (Scullion 2001: 389)

Whilst Scullion focuses here on the identity implied by the idea of the 'national' in Scotland, others have debated the problems inherent in the very idea of an institutional theatrical representation of the nation. Both in Scotland and Wales there have been numerous calls for radical models which are more than pale imitations of the 'British' model on the South Bank in London and, as is discussed in detail in the chapter on Scottish theatre, the early signs are that Scotland has taken some bold steps to produce a bold decentralized version of a national theatre that has the flexibility to respond to a changing, multi-faceted nation. In Wales the current signs are less optimistic and so, correspondingly, has been much of the critical debate. In an introduction to a special issue on Wales of *Studies in Theatre and Performance*, Nic Ros suggested, with what seemed a pessimistic shrug, that 'Any discussion of the need for the creation of any national theatre for Wales is redundant, because the politicians see it as part of the nation-building project.'(Ros 2004: 147) Whilst in another article in the same edition, Ceri Sherlock engages in just such a discussion, though with rather more passion:

> We *have* a national theatre and it is all around us in Wales in the performative. Again I am led to question why we are adopting concepts that have little resonance and even less meaning for us in Wales. Are we incapable of finding an appropriate frame for

understanding our theatrical tradition? The national theatre argument confuses public subsidy with patronage – although with the moral force of religion. 'It needs to exist if we are to be considered a cultured country' the argument goes... (Sherlock 2004: 158)

Particularly in Scotland and Wales then, but in different ways in both Ireland and England, the function of theatre in the creation (and evolution) of national identity has been high on the recent critical agenda, as indeed has the importance (or otherwise) of national theatres to the development of theatre within given geographical boundaries. The resultant questions form a key part of the framework for the discussion here of the part played by theatre in the recent and accelerated fracturing of a singular British national identity.

* * *

Perhaps, inevitably, the scope of this book has shifted considerably during its writing and has certainly expanded a great deal from its initial position which was to deal principally with cinema and theatre that could much more explicitly be seen as dealing with the idea of national identity in the contemporary British context. The ultimate difficulty in defining such a category has meant the inclusion of a considerable amount of work that is less obviously concerned with the idea of the nation, but which nevertheless has a bearing on it in the context of the debates about the idea of Britain that have taken place during the last ten years. This of course brings its own risks, principal of which is the sheer difficulty of selection and the problem of implying any sense of comprehensive coverage of all the work produced for either medium in the UK during the last decade. It is important therefore to state that there is no intention here to be comprehensive, but equally that there is a definite intention to include enough significant work to cover the central positions as regards national identity as it has been dealt with by theatre and cinema in Britain and Ireland in the period during which devolution has been a central focus of the reconstruction of the idea of Britishness.

This leads in turn to the limitations of an approach that structures the book around apparently tight definitions of each of the British nations and the work that has emanated from them in recent times. It must be stated that this should not be mistaken for a belief on my part that there is an unproblematic definition of what might constitute, say, Welsh theatre or Scottish cinema, let alone the chapters concerned with Ireland or England which bring their own additional complications. The rationale behind the work included in the respective chapters has in a sense been rather simpler and based more upon the kind of questions raised by the work as well as connections to the particular nation through questions of funding and the related conditions of production.

In many cases this has thrown up dilemmas and contradictions which serve mainly to emphasize the central instability of the idea of the nation that is at the heart of the book and virtually all of the theoretical work that underpins it. For example, the recent work of Ken Loach is included in the chapter on Scottish cinema for the blindingly obvious reasons that the films not only received large parts of their funding from Scottish sources, but that they deal with a Scottish social, economic and political landscape in a way that makes national identity inextricably linked to Loach's more familiar concern with class and capitalism. In turn, the films of one of Loach's most celebrated recent actors, Peter Mullan, are dealt with both in the chapters on Scotland and Ireland for similar reasons.

None of this is meant to imply that films placed in particular chapters speak only to the concerns of that respective nation. The most telling example of this dilemma is the fact that far more attention is paid in the chapters on 'England' to questions of immigration and asylum than in the chapters on the other countries. This is not in any sense to imply that these issues are not of the utmost importance in any discussion of the evolving nature of identity in Ireland, Scotland and Wales. Indeed, in all the chapters there is discussion of recent work such as *A Way of Life* (Wales 2004) or *Ae Fond Kiss* (Scotland 2003) which is directly concerned with the implications for identity of the multi-faceted question of ethnicity. However, it is inescapable that just as 'England' rather than Ireland, Scotland or Wales remains the dominant emblem of colonialism, issues of ethnicity in a postcolonial context are of more direct and telling concern at the centre of power. Thus it is the Royal National Theatre in London that has concerned itself most directly with addressing its fundamental problem of what kind of audience it addresses, and it is films that scrutinize a fading 'England' such as Pawel Pawlikowski's *The Last Resort* (England 2000) or Stephen Frears' *Dirty Pretty Things* (England 2002) that provide the bleakest meditations on the interaction of contemporary national identity and the colonial past.

It should also be admitted that the initial idea of this volume included discussion of television drama in order to provide an overarching survey of all dramatic narratives concerned with the changing idea of the nation in Britain. It quickly became clear that such an idea could simply not be managed within the space available and that, additionally, the institutional questions involved in the discussion of television are of a different order to those addressed here. Whilst the idea of 'independence' is a complex and problematic one even in the areas of theatre and cinema, within television it becomes inextricably linked to the rapidly changing issues surrounding the control and regulation of the medium that have dominated its recent history. The move from a tightly controlled analogue era of four terrestrial channels to the current time of digitally based technological convergence has been so profound as to need far more reflection on the contexts in which all dramatic narratives for television are produced than would have been possible in a book of this size.

Instead, the concentration on theatre and films made for cinema which, in a British context, are most often of a scale to allow for the emergence of a genuine authorial voice, reflects an aspiration to discuss views of the idea of the nation which have been expressed through dramatic narratives as diverse and wide ranging as possible. Whilst such an aspiration might easily encompass some work produced exclusively for television, a number of the series conceived by Paul Abbott or Russell T. Davies are clear examples; the institutional complexity of television production is such that it is the institutional context itself that tends to dominate, rather than the narrative itself.

This should not in any way imply that a consideration of television drama would not produce powerful insights into the way that dramatic fiction responds to questions of a changing national identity. The increased sense of the need for national inclusivity at the BBC, for example, is clearly reflective of a changed institutional sense of what Britain is becoming. At the same time the amount of material from each of the 'nations' that is networked by the BBC has long been a matter of debate and controversy, something which I have written about elsewhere (Blandford 2005: 166–182). Inevitably, though, questions around the individual narratives tend to be dominated by those concerning institutional power structures and whilst these are by no means absent from discussion of theatre and cinema they are of a different order. As a result, partly for pragmatic reasons, but also because of the institutional context, a discussion of television drama parallel to those presented here will have to wait for other spaces to become available.

In summary then, the book takes as its starting point the idea that the fresh impetus given to devolution by the election of a Labour government in 1997 also heralded the acceleration of other changes to the public conversation on the nature of Britishness. It therefore attempts to examine some of the key films, plays and other kinds of theatrical 'texts' of the last decade as part of an attempt to understand the diverse and, this book suggests, wholly healthy way in which any idea of a monolithic 'Britain' is indeed 'breaking up'. It stresses, of course, that this is part of a process which neither began in 1997 nor will finish at any point in the foreseeable future. Nevertheless the actual moment of devolution itself is significant enough for it be an appropriate time around which to focus this snapshot of the ways in which dramatic narratives have played a significant part in the re-imagination of the idea of Britain.

2

LAST ORDERS IN WONDERLAND: ENGLAND AND CINEMA

In May 2005 the UK general election resulted in the return of a third successive Labour government albeit with a much reduced majority. In the post-election scramble for crumbs of comfort, the leader of the Conservative Party, Michael Howard, was heard trumpeting the fact that the Conservatives actually 'won' in England with the clear subtext that if only the Celts had not been allowed to have their cake and eat it (their own Parliaments/Assemblies as well as Westminster representation), then there could have been a Conservative government. Pre-devolution such an analysis would have been less likely to surface, but in 2005 it becomes only the latest manifestation of a growing awareness of the problematics of Englishness, and this chapter will attempt an assessment of the responses of film-makers to the emergence of a new idea of the English in the age of devolution.

In the ever growing body of literature about British cinema there is even less discussion of the idea of a distinctive 'English' cinema than there is of the emergence of cinema that can, within certain limits, be defined as Scottish or Welsh. At one level the explanation for this is simple: for most people the term 'British' remains synonymous with 'English'. However, in an academic climate that has been relatively pre-occupied with the discourses of nationalism and postcolonialism, it is surprising that so few questions have emerged about the implications of devolution for an emergent English culture and therefore an English cinema.

In a comparatively rare direct reference to this debate, Peter Bradshaw, reviewing Pawel Pawlikowski's *My Summer of Love* (2004), asserts that

> If there is such a thing as English cinema as opposed to British cinema, then this new film from Pawel Pawlikowski fits the bill. It has taken a Polish-born director to respond to the exoticism of the English countryside and English mannerisms of region and class. (Bradshaw 2004 b.)

Bradshaw's point is clearly a fascinating one: that it takes a comparative outsider (though, of course, Pawlikowski has lived most of his life in Britain) to recognize the essence of our English identity and that it actually resides not at the metropolitan centre, but in the diverse manifestations of English regionalism. If anything can be said to be at the heart of English film-making in the last decade it is probably exactly that – the very different attempts to root films in English communities that themselves have distinctive and powerful characteristics and which therefore defy monolithic definitions of the English. These have variously consisted of actual geographic locations or, just as significantly, of communities defined by ethnicity or sexuality.

Of course it is only proper to remind ourselves at the beginning of such a chapter that there have also been very high-profile films made in this period which trade mercilessly on exactly the idea of quintessential Englishness which is under question. These would include the series begun by *Four Weddings and a Funeral* (1994) and continued through *Notting Hill* (1999) and *Love Actually* (2003). However, on balance, it would be fair to suggest that, while dominating at the box office, such films are less than typical and that 'English' cinema has at least partly been about creating a more complex vision of what that term can mean.

As in other chapters there is of course no false attempt to suggest that any new sense of Englishness in cinema can possibly date from the post-1997 introduction of devolution. On the contrary it is possible to suggest that such tendencies are traceable back to times well beyond the scope of this book. (Powrie 2000: 316–326, for example). For the sake of comparison, however, the chapter will first consider a highly successful example of the conscious use of an idea of Englishness that appears to be fading in the period since devolution. It will then examine the dominant idea of fragmentation that appears to have become the heart of English cinema since the mid-1990s.

As Robert Murphy put it, part of the appeal of that most stereotypical of 1990s 'English' films, *Four Weddings and a Funeral* 'came from its exploitation of an international conception of Britain as a country of odd rituals and dotty aristocrats' (Murphy 2000: 9).Whilst Murphy uses 'Britain' here it is clear that the central thrust of the film is 'English', something emphasized through the film's one excursion outside England to a wedding in a Scottish castle, complete with all the clichéd trappings of 'tartanry'. In response to such an extravagant display of fairy-tale Scottishness, Gareth (Simon Callow) inevitably exclaims 'It's *Brigadoon*, it's bloody *Brigadoon*!' further emphasizing Scotland's lack of reality for the culture which the principal characters inhabit. Scotland can exist only as a 'set' upon which the fantasies of the English characters are played out and the fact that the film displays a kind of self-knowledge through Gareth's remark does little to dissipate the sense that we are watching a theme park film with an idea of England at its core.

As Murphy says elsewhere, for all its froth, *Four Weddings* is a confident film in that it dares to offer the values and mores of a narrow class of people for our tacit approval. It assumes that an audience, especially an oversees one, will find the spectacles it offers endearing. These are essentially the values of an England post-Thatcherism and, as Murphy (2001: 298) puts it elsewhere, this is a film that, above all else, epitomizes the very short period in which the values of the Major government received any airtime at all. We are undoubtedly in the territory of spinsters, mist, evensong and cricket, even if the film makes efforts to undercut this highly conservative cultural vision with comic swearing and Richard Curtis's obligatory eccentric housemates.

Four Weddings and a Funeral will clearly not be the last film that unashamedly trades on a very narrow sense of what it is to be English and pass it off as 'British'. However, in the period since the film was made it has become increasingly difficult to sustain such ideas in the face of the forces ranged against a monolithic definition of national identity. Whilst there is a case for saying that its traditions survive in films such as *Bridget Jones's Diary* (2001), *Four Weddings* can, in many ways, be seen as the end of a particular line in terms of British film and its engagement with questions of national identity. Alongside its treatment of 'other' British nations as comically stuck in a theme park history, *Four Weddings* also seeks to elide difficult questions around class and national identity through the same character (Gareth) who is given the task of commenting on Scotland. Gareth is played by Simon Callow in a way that would have been all too familiar to audiences of a string of Merchant-Ivory films over the previous decade in which Callow's massive cod Dickensian booming presence dominates key comic scenes as he portrays a string of 'lovable' British (English) eccentrics.

In *Four Weddings* Callow's character is part of the gay couple who appear to have been admitted to the inner sanctum of the group of upper-middle-class friends whose lives are so socially dominated by the need to pair off in suitable marriages. Whilst for most of the film Gareth's social origins appear to be no different from the rest of the characters, when he dies from a heart attack at a wedding, the cut to his funeral is, one supposes, an attempt to unsettle the audience about its assumptions: in one of the few shots to stray from the comfortable/bohemian existences of the main characters we are given a wide panoramic view of the Thames estuary east of London as the M25 crosses the river and sweeps past an endless sea of post-war local authority housing and heavy industrial landscape in decline. In the middle of all this sits a tiny Victorian church dwarfed by ugly buildings that are the only visual indicators in the film that anybody in England actually has to work for a living. Inside the church, as Matthew (John Hannah), Gareth's partner, delivers his farewell speech complete with lengthy quotation from Auden, the camera sweeps around the congregation which is a model of inclusivity. For the only time in the film, we see black faces, working-class faces and most often of all the stricken faces of Gareth's elderly parents, clearly bewildered by the ceremony that will lay their son to rest.

This sudden, isolated attempt to make a bridge between the froth of most of the film and a world where the harshness of a lifetime of industrial labour is now meeting the overwhelming emotions of losing a son is fundamental to the film's aspirations to belong to a world where an older, more unified, stable sense of Britain was imaginable, if equally untenable. Such a cinema was at its peak, as John Hill says, during and immediately following the Second World War, but as Hill also says this was a 'British' cinema which, like *Four Weddings*, was English masquerading as British:

> The paradigm of British 'national cinema' is often taken to have been during the Second World War when films (such as *In Which We Serve* and *Millions Like Us*) celebrated the community pulling together to win the war. Powerful though such films are, however, their versions of the 'nation' privileged 'Englishness' (even the south of England) at the expense

of other national (Scottish, Welsh and Irish) and regional identifications within the UK. (Hill 2001: 33)

The scene at Gareth's funeral seems an attempt on the part of *Four Weddings* to join in such a tradition in the spirit of cod national unity that seemed to flourish in the aftermath of the devastation wrought by Thatcherism. Not only do weddings in glorious English churches take place, but England is also a place where someone from a south London council estate like Gareth can join in this vision of a perfect, slightly dotty existence and be passed off as one of the chosen ones (as indeed did the Brixton-born son of the circus, John Major!). In many ways *Four Weddings* has become a cheap target; much of it is amiable enough and there are moments of great craft and skill in both the writing and acting, but its biggest flaw resides in its wanting to have its cake and eat it on the key questions of class and national identity. This is a film credited with kick-starting the 1990s revival of the British film industry through its demonstration that quintessentially British films could perform at the British and American box offices, but it did this by resorting to a definition of 'British' that was English and upper middle class. In the funeral scene it attempts to avoid the charge, but in fact only succeeds in emphasizing the narrowness of its national and class vision and in the process becomes more than a little ugly and exploitative of the representations of working-class life that it gratuitously introduces for the only time in the film.

Though not radically different in their underlying appeal, the other two feature films (to date) that have been written as a kind of trilogy by Richard Curtis are different enough to offer some sense of the way that an English cinema was evolving in response to a changed sense of national identity. In a *Sight and Sound* piece to coincide with the release of *Notting Hill*, Nick James makes the film's loose connection with a changing Britain quite explicit:

> The English are redefining themselves against a background of Scots and Welsh devolution and the gradual European absorption of all the British, but *Notting Hill* enjoys only the confusion, not the potential for change. Of course comedy relies on the stereotype remaining true, but it is legitimate to ask what kind of fantasy of London, of England, of Britain we are getting. (James 1999: 22)

To attempt an answer to James's question would instructively involve a comparison with the fantasy presented in *Four Weddings*. To start with we do have a very similar central character mainly because they are both played by Hugh Grant with the same attempts at charming self-effacing awkwardness. The appeal of a particular kind of upper-middle-class educated British male is once again to the fore and again it is a glamorous American woman, this time film star, Anna Scott (Julia Roberts), who highlights the appeal by falling in love with him. Grant's character in *Notting Hill* even lives in the same kind of scruffy and eccentric flat-sharing arrangement that he had in *Four Weddings*, though this time with a man, and has also gathered around him a similar circle of friends that thrive on telling each other what failures they feel.

On the other hand, small, but significant, differences do become apparent and the most significant of these are the related ideas around money and power. Whereas in *Four Weddings* Grant's character briefly mentions work it is clearly not high on his agenda, some of his friends are almost comically wealthy and his connections are vast and aristocratic. In *Notting Hill* we are still, by most standards in a privileged world, though Grant's character is seen not only to work for a living (he runs a travel bookshop) but also to be reasonably learned (he discusses Henry James). His friends this time are far from wealthy (leading some to ask why they end up living in a chic London district, soon to be firmly associated in the popular consciousness with Peter Mandelson, the epitome of the new Labour meritocracy) and, as has already been alluded to, are given to competitions about who is the biggest social failure. As one reviewer put it, the shift in the sense of British (English) national identity between *Four Weddings* and *Notting Hill* is, on the surface, enormous:

> In *Four Weddings*, 'vulgar' America is in thrall to cultured, wealthy Britain... In *Notting Hill* there's no competition: big, bold glamorous America is on top; Britain has banana-slipped from importance to impotence. In *Four Weddings*, Hugh Grant's character knew one of the 'sixth richest men in Britain'; here all his friends are financial failures. America is shown to have a clear identity, while Britain is all at sea. (O'Sullivan 1999: 50)

Clearly, though, the reviewer has her tongue firmly in her cheek. By the end of the film the American (Julia Roberts) has bought into an escape from the world she inhabits and, in a final scene, is shown lying contentedly with her head in the lap of the financially impoverished Englishman who is reading *Captain Corelli's Mandolin*, that epitome of middlebrow cultural capital.

It would be foolish to read too many profound lessons about shifts in national identity into a single film like *Notting Hill*. On the other hand it is impossible to ignore an attempt to extend the 'franchise' of one of the most successful British films of all time (particularly at the American box office). Whilst the old-fashioned appeal to braying, confident English aristocratic eccentricity has gone, we are now offered the masquerade of a self-effacing Englishness that is learning new ways to sell its image in the world market. Perhaps there is a hint of identity crisis, but it is one that is able to be commodified and sold as part of the package.

Finally, in case we are in doubt that this is an English, as opposed to British, film, we are given the comic but wise Welshman in the shape of Spike (Rhys Ifans). Ifans's portrayal of Spike was justifiably singled out for critical praise and it has launched him on a prolific career that has often seemed to parallel the rocky road of British film-making since *Notting Hill*'s release. However, it is surely significant that Ifans's virtuoso comic turn serves to heighten the film's exclusivity which is based on class and racial and national identity. Andrew Anthony writing in the *Observer* commented on the criticism of the film's lack of ethnic representation when it is based in an area traditionally thought of as ethnically diverse, partly through the extensive historical coverage of the Notting Hill carnival:

> Much has already been made, a month before its release, of the whiteness of the film. The Portuguese and Jamaican aspects of the social mix don't get so much as a walk-on part. But that is neither a plot weakness nor particularly inaccurate. The truth is gentrification has priced out most of the area's multiculturalism and it is common for members of the white middle-class – Curtis's milieu – to maintain the ethnic community as an exotic, but distant backdrop to their lives. This guilty situation has untold comic possibilities, but, alas, they remain untold in *Notting Hill*. (Anthony 1999)

This is not the place to unpack the precision of these observations about the changing socio-economic make-up of this rather overexposed part of the UK. The point remains, however, that the film peddles a version of Englishness which, whilst affecting to be self-deprecating, is enormously self-satisfied and highly exclusive. Perhaps, were it not for its own foregrounding of national identity as a key ingredient in its narrative then it would be barely worth discussing in the context. However, this, coupled with the massive marketing campaign that makes much of its Britishness, means that its contribution to the evolution of a new national sensibility cannot be entirely overlooked.

The final film in the trilogy, *Love Actually*, extended Curtis's auteur grip as he directed for the first time as well as writing the screenplay. The critical consensus on the film appeared to be that the genre had run out of steam and was in danger of unintentional self-parody. This prompted a number of articles that not only looked at this film as popular cinema, but which assessed, often quite savagely, Curtis's overall contribution to the debate about national identity. In one, admittedly light-hearted, example, this pointedly examined 'Curtis Britain' in the context of Anglo-American relations, Europe and a post-devolutionary sense of national identity:

> The Americans you see in Curtis films are not like the Americans in your hometown in America. They are thin, have passports and tend to speak perfect idiomatic British English with American accents. This is a different breed of American; they actually come from a little island in the mid-Atlantic with special diplomatic status, which is why no one ever gives them a hard time about US foreign policy at dinner parties...

> In Britain people prefer to form tight social clusters, rather than large networks, choosing close friends from a wide variety of social backgrounds. The largest proportion will naturally have gone to either Oxford or Cambridge, in keeping with the fact that approximately 70% of the population attended one or the other. Each grouping will also contain a representative from Scotland or Wales, plus a single minority or a differently abled person, but not both: there simply aren't enough to go round. The exact balance is governed by complex legislation...

> English people rarely go into work, and if they do they generally carry out their jobs with an endearing incompetence. They just happen to believe there are more important things in life, like swearing and snow... Most Britons appear to be rich and live in large town houses or cool flats, even though none seem to have proper jobs... (Dowling 2003)

Ironically, *Love Actually* does attempt a kind of superficial social inclusivity that is absent from the first two films, but the problem is that the film is so relentlessly one-dimensional that the attempt appears patronizing in the same way as the isolated moment of Gareth's funeral in *Four Weddings*.

If it appears heavy-handed to subject this series of films to such scrutiny on questions of national definition then it is worth looking at one of *Love Actually*'s worst moments for evidence that, actually, Curtis and his collaborators do want to be taken seriously. Hugh Grant in the role of 'David the Prime Minister' reminds us in the course of a speech on Anglo-American relations that all the phone messages sent from the hijacked planes on September 11, 2001 were of love, not hate. This rather mawkish attempt to situate itself in a post-9/11 zeitgeist is surely evidence that this film (and by extension the whole trilogy) asks us to take some of its ideas about the efficacy of the best of British values seriously. The blindingly obvious fact that these are very narrowly based, upper-middle-class English values has, therefore, to be stated as often as possible.

Curtis's other major involvement in feature films of this period has, of course, been as co-screenwriter on both *Bridget Jones's Diary* (2001) and *Bridget Jones: The Edge of Reason* (2004). On the whole their version of Britain/England does little to radically alter or extend the one discussed above in relation to his other work, with confusion and self-deprecation to the fore and little to suggest a life outside the metropolis and the home counties where one's parents live. A mildly interesting twist on the obsessive post-colonial saga of defining British national identity in relation to the United States was provided by the casting of the Texan Renee Zellweger as Bridget Jones rather than one of the hundreds of very suitable British actresses. For most critics, Zellweger was excellent in the role, even resorting to a De Niro-like programme of weight gain to give her physical appearance some authenticity. However, the resort to the traditional casting of an established American star was a strong reminder of what is all too obviously still the most powerful factor in creating British national identity, even in an age where that has become a more interesting subject for debate and re-definition.

After *Four Weddings and a Funeral* the next most dramatically popular box office success to emerge from British cinema was *The Full Monty* (1997), which can reasonably be seen as the cornerstone of a tendency within English cinema that was radically different from the vision dominated by the work of Richard Curtis above. As Moya Luckett put it:

> ... many 90's films stabilise their representations of regional difference within the UK by articulating the north/south divide in terms borrowed from 1960's cinema. While the 1960's also witnessed changing and uncertain national identity, the passage of three decades has reshaped its images to connote a distinct, recognisable image of nation. (Luckett 2000: 94)

Along with *Brassed Off* (1996), *Up 'n' Under* (1997), some of the work of Ken Loach (principally discussed in the chapter on Cinema in Scotland) and work emerging from Scotland, Wales, and Northern Ireland (also discussed elsewhere in this volume), *The Full Monty* appears to represent a tendency within 1990s cinema to re-assert the centrality of regional and class difference in any discussion of national identity, whilst at the same time creating problematic paradigms around questions of gender and, to a lesser extent, race.

The opening of *The Full Monty* is perhaps indicative of this group of film's tendency to implicitly undermine facile attempts to create mythic identities. It uses a short film from the 1970s, presumably made in order to sell Sheffield's economic attractiveness, entitled *Sheffield: City on the Move*. This glib vision of a prosperous 'modern' city founded upon the steel industry then cuts to the Sheffield of the mid-1990s and the large areas of blighted, post-industrial landscape that dominated the city. It is against the backdrop of this landscape that we see played out the tragic-comic drama of a group of unemployed men who eventually turn to stripping as a means not so much of genuine economic survival, but of rediscovering a sense of personal identity and purpose.

Interestingly *The Full Monty*'s presentation of a Britain all but on its knees after decades of economic decline and Conservative neglect of public services came just before the launch of New Labour's 'makeover' of the national image. Despite its comically upbeat ending, it is clear that *The Full Monty* has nothing of 'Cool Britannia' about it, though it has subsequently been appropriated for a range of related purposes including, most bizarrely, the recreation of the dole queue dance scene at a party to celebrate the birthday of Prince Charles. (http://news.bbc.co.uk/1/hi/uk/213484.stm, 13 November 1998) The national image it recreates is dominated by cultural icons that are a long way from the 'Britpop' and 'Britart' so favoured by the Blair government in its bid to re-brand Britain.

Despite this there has certainly been a critical tendency to equate *The Full Monty* with the post-1997 political mood, typified by the following assertion on the BFI website: 'Championed by the incoming post-welfare New Labour, *The Full Monty* (1997) came to epitomise a new and entertaining conception of British social realism' (Armstrong 2005). By contrast it is possible to find Geoff Mulgan, one of the founders of *Demos* (the think tank at the heart of New Labour) using the film quite explicitly as a benchmark for everything that the re-branding of Britain would seek to expunge from the national psyche, what Mulgan referred to as 'the Full Monty picture of unemployment, with a few riots thrown in.' (Quoted in Pink 1999)

By the same token *The Full Monty*'s surprise world-wide box office success, as well as its release in the same year as the election of a New Labour government, have made it something of a site of ideological contention over the way that it treats issues of gender. Claire Monk, for example, has argued that the film marks less of a shift in national identity from the self-satisfied revelling in old England of *Four Weddings*, and more of a transference of the general crisis in masculinity from Hugh Grant's upper-middle-class bumbling uncertainty to 'northern unemployed labour' (Monk 2000 a.: 161), a point that she makes not only about *The Full Monty* but also *Brassed Off*.

The point is clearly an interesting one which puts a crisis of masculinity at the heart of films which came to be seen as at least partly concerned with shifts in national identity. This is of course entirely consistent with the idea of a developing uncertainty over the nature of English identity in particular. However, there is sense in which this over simplifies and, by implication, dismisses *The Full Monty* far too easily. As John Hill has pointed out, the group of men that come together to form the group of strippers in *The Full Monty* can hardly be seen as simply representative of a dying breed of resentful working-class heroes:

> ... the group that is forged in *The Full Monty* cannot be regarded as fully traditional. It is significant, for example, that two of the men – Lomper (Steve Huison) and Guy (Hugo Speer) – are revealed as gay... While this may have a certain air of contrivance about it, it also begins to re-imagine the traditionally heterosexual world of the northern working-class community... The inclusion of the black character Horse in the group also establishes a degree of difference from the male working-class community as traditionally imagined. Although there were complaints that the film had, in conception, been more multi-cultural in character, it is still significant that the black character, and his relatives, are simply accepted as part of the drama without it becoming an issue or a problem. (Hill 2000: 186)

In addition the attitude to women in the film is far from being entirely unified. Monk declares the film's misogyny unambiguously as a given, going on to relate this fact to 'the widespread and powerful appeal of these films for male audiences'. (Monk 2000 a.: 162) However, as Hill has argued, *The Full Monty* also enjoyed a huge following amongst women:

> One of the striking characteristics of the cinema audience for the film (particularly in the UK) was the high proportion of women (who often attended in groups). So, while at a diegetic level, the film may be read as being about the re-empowering of men, it was nonetheless enjoyed by female audiences because of the degree of role reversal as well as the incongruity and just plain silliness involved in the men's actions. (Hill 2000: 185)

Of course, if popularity with female audiences were an automatic guarantee that a film was not misogynistic then the cinema would be an altogether healthier place, but it is also possible to argue that the film's female characters (despite being peripheral presences) are much more ambiguously presented than Monk suggests. In one sense the men have to come to terms with an assertive female sexuality before they can think of the plan to perform as strippers. They are also comically introduced to the world of both the intrusive gaze and its implications for their sense of their own bodies. In neither case is the discovery undermined, and, arguably, the men's sense of survival at the end is inextricably linked to their assimilation of the realities of a shifting landscape of gender roles. The two female characters (Linda, played by Deidre Costello, and Mandy, played by Emily Woof) that are the focus of most criticism are both women whose material and social aspirations bring them into conflict with their husbands' lack of economic prospects and consequent crises of confidence, though by the end it appears that Mandy at least has been won round. Their viewpoint is, however, balanced to an extent by the sympathetic portrayal of Jean, by Lesley Sharp, whose patient attempts to restore her husband Dave's confidence make for some of the film's most affecting moments.

If, in the end, part of *The Full Monty*'s appeal lies in its nostalgia for a lost masculine world of industrial labour, then it must also be remembered that its narrative drive is towards the painful acceptance of change, but within the context of a renewed sense of the importance of community solidarity. In terms of what such a successful film offers to the evolution of our sense of national identity, the predominant quality is surely a sense of flux, a struggle to adapt to change and the loss of a particular kind of unambiguous male power. In this sense it is possible to see *The Full Monty* as inflected towards a particularly English, as opposed to British, experience. This is, of course, not to suggest that crises of masculine power and identity are absent from the contemporary cultures of the Celtic nations, but rather that the rise of national sensibilities in those places acted as a complicating factor which produced largely different results reflected to some extent in the films emerging during this period.

Lest the group of films to which *The Full Monty* belongs be seen too homogeneously, it is important to note briefly an example of differences within that group and the implications for this particular discussion. One particular take on a central distinction between two of the films is Claire Monk's:

> There are substantial differences between the labour politics of *Brassed Off* and *The Full Monty* that should not be effaced. *Brassed Off*'s Old Labour collectivism, for instance, is

antithetical to *The Full Monty*'s Blairite gospel of entrepreneurial self-help, labour flexibility and the sublimation of old industrial antagonisms in the interests of enterprise. (Monk 2000 c.: 277)

Whilst I would strongly question such an unambiguous reading of *The Full Monty*, it is also clear that of the two, *Brassed Off* is much more inclined to look back to pre-Thatcherite conditions of union power for its narrative inspiration and that this may have contributed to its lesser impact at the box office. The film also, it has to be admitted, is much more inclined to use its small number of female characters in ways that are either tokenistic or blatantly misogynistic. The presence of Tara Fitzgerald as the one woman (Gloria) allowed to play in the brass band, soon to die along with the coal mine that sustained it, looks suspiciously like an attempt to draw in a wider audience, especially when she forms a relationship with the equally photogenic but narratively superfluous Ewan Macgregor. The other women in the film tend to either desert their already desperate menfolk or pursue in traditional harridan-like manner to make sure they are not having too much fun. All in all, the film can feel like a cry for a return to more 'certain' times, whilst demonstrating its fatalistic sense that this will of course never happen.

Despite its limitations, though, *Brassed Off* can be seen as part of a tendency within English cinema to embrace a wider sense of regional identity and also to acknowledge the misery and sheer destructiveness wrought by the re-assertion of centralized capitalist power during the Thatcher years. Claire Monk's dismissal of this as a pure illusion because of the commercial context in which the films were made is understandable given her apparent project to find a Blairite unity in all British cinema of the late 1990s (despite the fact that *Brassed Off* appeared in cinemas a year before Labour's 1997 election victory). (Monk 2000 c.: 284) It is possible, I suppose, to read the film's ending where the band wins the national finals in London one more time as a triumph of the individual will over adversity, but it appears to be a much more likely reading to see the film as elegiac, a last throw of the dice for a powerful element in the construction of the identity of large parts of the industrial north of England.

The obvious link between the group of films represented by *Brassed Off* and *The Full Monty* and the post-devolution, New Labour era is the hugely successful *Billy Elliot*. Ironically enough *Billy Elliot* is actually set during the miners' strike in 1984 and 1985 (with a short coda that brings us to the present day), but its reading of history belongs unmistakeably to the political climate of the millennium. This is not, though, a crude New Labour revisionist reading of the strike. The worst that you could say about the film's overt political stance is that it is vague and fudges the central issue. Instead, the strike is used largely emblematically as the significant backdrop to the personal story of Billy, whose desire to become a dancer becomes intertwined with the searching questions about masculinity that are being asked in the industrial north of England as traditional forms of employment finally disappear after decades of neglect and decline.

On the whole, *Billy Elliot* was much better received by some of the critics of the mid-1990s films set in the English industrial heartlands. Claire Monk, for example, made the explicit comparison on the film's UK release: 'Daldry and screenwriter Lee Hall's film also feels a lot truer to authentic experience than *The Full Monty* or *Brassed Off*, perhaps because it's less fraudulently upbeat' (Monk 2000 b.: 40). As I have implied above, I find it difficult to share in the unambiguously upbeat reading of the earlier films and would find it equally difficult to see the total validity of this comparison. The band in *Brassed Off* is, after all, only in London for the duration of the competition at the Albert Hall. We can surely not forget so quickly that they have to return to a town with its prospects destroyed by the pit closure. Billy Elliot actually finds a more permanent kind of escape as we see him starring in *Swan Lake* by the film's end watched by his emotional father.

On the other hand, what is undeniable is *Billy Elliot*'s much more complex relationship to ideas about gender. Like the earlier films it is centrally concerned with the highly problematic way in which the relentless logic of declining heavy industry in the west has interacted with the advance of ideas about the fluidity of gender identities. However, whereas, to different extents, both *The Full Monty* and *Brassed Off* could both be said to contain a certain level of nostalgia for a fading masculinity that has so often been associated with the cinematic identity of the north of England, *Billy Elliot* appears to assert that masculine identity can only be enriched by embracing a much broader set of values in a rapidly changing world. Of course, this cannot be achieved without a fight, and Billy's symbolic rejection of his family heritage by swapping boxing for ballet is shown to be painful. It is not, though, a long struggle and even given the film's fairy-tale qualities the road to salvation via audition at the Royal Ballet School ends being a little too straight forward given the difficulties.

At one level then *Billy Elliot* represents a much fuller engagement with the idea of fluid gender identities as a component of a more generalized endorsement of the idea of self-reinvention. It toys with the audience's sense of the ossified clichés of northern industrialized life only to turn them on their head. This also goes for Billy's own sexuality as he rejects both the advances of his male friend who is experimenting with transvestism and the daughter of his ballet teacher, who offers to show him her 'fanny'. Billy is actually a fairly robust character, and the film is clearly at pains to avoid an easy correspondence between Billy's aptitude for dance and the usual clichés about gay men that so often accompany the portrayal of male dancers.

Perhaps the scenes in the film that most clearly link the film to discussion of a shifting sense of the English take place in the Royal Ballet School. Billy's father accompanies him to his audition there and his usually powerful masculine body language clearly alters as he and Billy practically tiptoe around the echoing classical architecture that is so often the cinematic signifier of imperial power. However, there is a twist to this simple collision of the two extremes of English culture, and it is one that the director, Stephen Daldry, clearly relished. In an interview around the time of the film's release, he was asked about this particular moment:

When Billy has his interview with the Royal Ballet School they [The ultra-grand panel of judges] wish his father good luck with the strike. It's an easy sentiment.

It's all that crappy liberal southern 'Oh, the miners, y'know, poor people, good luck, see you later,' meanwhile back to Hampstead Garden Suburb... It was a swipe at the liberal establishment which the dad picks up on, saying 'Fuck you lot, for your patronising sympathy.' (Lawrenson 2000: 12)

To an extent, then, *Billy Elliot* is part of a long-standing tradition of presenting English national identity in terms of class and regional conflict. The twist, of course, is that the ultra-talented dancer who will claim his place as the male lead at Covent Garden is the son of a miner, and the impact of such things being possible is potentially profound for both halves of the divided culture. Despite its historical setting and wariness of easy liberal sentiment, *Billy Elliot* does in the end appear to fully embrace its place in the newly branded Britain post-devolution. Whilst displaying flashes of traditional class anger, such as the one discussed by Daldry above, it also appears to both subscribe to the centrality of the arts in the New Labour national project and to the possibility of change being a matter of individual will and talent and certainly not of collective action of the kind that fails so badly in the film's background.

Xan Brooks in *The Guardian* likened *Billy Elliot* to Frank Capra with elements of Ken Loach et al. thrown in. This, he argues, is simply a frank acknowledgement of the true extent of Hollywood's impact on British cinema:

> Like it or not, Hollywood has shaped homegrown cinema. *Billy Elliot*, then, is a basic British story told in an American vernacular.

> Of course Luddites may argue that *Billy Elliot* is therefore not purely British. Except that Britain itself is not purely British any more (at least not in the high Tory sense of the term).

> Instead it's a land inhabited by continental-style bars and cafes, with a cuisine that's largely Asian, Mediterranean or Japanese and a décor dictated by Ikea-chic. This doesn't make the culture any less 'real' only more diverse and different. If *Billy Elliot* heralds a new strain of melting-pot cinema, it's only reflecting the wider melting-pot in the land at large. (Brooks 2000)

Though inevitably affected by journalistic clichés about the true state of Britain, Brooks' analysis has a strong ring of truth about *Billy Elliot*'s reflection of how representations of and attitudes towards England and its regional fissures had begun to evolve in the rapidly changing world since the release of *The Full Monty* in 1997. The welcome it received for its more complex treatment of gender is understandable, but, in the end, this is a film that celebrates the fluidity of sexual, regional and national identities but with little to offer as a blueprint for others to follow beyond an injunction to trust your talent and follow your dreams with determination. In this respect it reflects an England post-1997 in which questions of gender and sexual identities are seen as more fluid (for all its faults the Labour cabinet had included a larger proportion of women and, for the first time, openly gay men), but in which the possibilities of collective, social action were receding.

Perhaps the individual would-be auteur with the greatest recent claim to have set out to make deliberately English 'regional' films in a sustained way is Shane Meadows. To date, he has made three films all in settings which identify them, in Meadows own tongue-in-cheek phrase, as his 'Midlands trilogy'. There is a lot about the first two, *Twenty Four Seven* (1997) and *A Room for Romeo Brass* (1999), that link Meadows' work to the group of films discussed above, though, also a lot to distinguish too.

As has already been mentioned, Meadows work clearly belongs to the growth of a newly de-centred English cinema and its pre-occupation with the destructive forces of the 1980s. *Twenty Four Seven* in particular uses the bleak post-industrial landscapes of the East Midlands as a forceful part of the film's identity as well as the obviously dominant force that has shaped his young characters' lives. However, unlike most of the other work we have been discussing, there seems to be a desire in Meadows to use cinema as a means of finding the poetry in such landscapes that is rare in recent British cinema. The antecedents here could even be those British film-makers such as Bill Douglas or Terence Davies who have always been discussed in 'European' terms. However, it would be wrong to describe Meadows in purely art-house terms. Beyond the black-and-white images is also a fairly traditional narrative of an attempt at working-class redemption through violent sport (this time boxing) and a comic streak that would be hard to detect in Douglas or Davies.

What is perhaps particularly significant about the way that Meadows roots his films in their location is the deliberate avoidance of the 'fashionable' dimension to his native Nottingham. In fact, especially in *A Room for Romeo Brass*, it is hard to feel that we are anywhere near a city. Meadows' natural territory is not out-and-out inner-city deprivation, but the shabby, ultra-ordinariness of estates with parades of shops, but inside, which he finds a kind of magic. This is not to say that Meadows' films are sentimental about this forgotten dimension to England; in many ways this no-man's-land at the edge of the supposedly re-energized cities is a very bleak place to be, but there are also moments where the camera endows the place with a kind of beauty and which are totally at the service of his mission to give his characters' lives some significance.

In *Twenty Four Seven* and *Romeo Brass*, Meadows could be said to have made a strikingly different contribution to an English cinema in an era newly concerned with English identity. It has been common to lump Meadows work in with the likes of Loach, *Brassed Off* and *The Full Monty*, (not that these make up a very meaningful category themselves), but it seems to me that, whilst there are clearly things to link the films, Meadows operates in a regional England made altogether stranger and marginalized by both his camera and oblique, open-ended narratives. By the time he arrived at the third in the trilogy, *Once Upon a Time in the Midlands*, his apparent desperation at getting excellent reviews but little box office led him to import some of the key figures from a decade of British films to try and attract investment and exposure. To many, this had the effect both of disturbing the tragic-comic balance of his earlier work in favour of the broad comedy for which the likes of Rikki Tomlinson and Kathy Burke have become well known and, also, of blurring the strong regional identity upon which the film's conceit relied. In this respect the trajectory of Meadows' work to date takes us through the eternal trap whereby a film-maker's loss of the strong identity which made him or her an original voice is the price that gets paid for increased backing.

There is, of course, a strong tendency to equate English 'regional' cinema exclusively with parts of the north and Midlands and, in particular, with ex-industrial landscapes. In the post-devolutionary map of English cinema, it is also possible to discover the use of landscapes which make for re-appraisals of dimensions of English identity. *The War Zone* (1999), the first film to be directed by Tim Roth, deals at one level with a reversal of expectation in that it portrays a family's move from the city to the country in nightmarish terms. The Devon to which they move is not rolling green hills, but almost monochrome, its slate grey cliffs and the stone house in which the family live often shot in the wettest winter weather. Of course, such a tale of a pastoral idyll turning sour is nothing new, but Roth takes his reversal a stage further as his tale of the most brutal incestuous relationships imaginable proves to centre around the city-dwelling family and not the 'inbred' country folk of traditional British black humour.

Whilst *The War Zone* has been predominantly read in existential terms, particularly in relations to Roth's own early life and to generalized explorations of adolescent anxiety its structure does also draw attention to the urban/rural, centre/periphery oppositions which are at the heart of the family's experience. There is a real sense of a group of people in flight from something and at the same time in terrible denial and the dramatic use of the Devon location in strong contrast to the London scene that they leave behind suggests a certain representative quality.

Whilst a renewed sense of awareness of the diversity of England and English identity is key to this discussion, *The War Zone* remains a comparatively isolated example of work that uses the English west in any sustained way. Its predecessor, *Blue Juice* (1995), tended to be derided for its importing of a group of young rising stars (Catherine Zeta Jones, Ewan Macgregor, Steven Mackintosh) to play off against crudely grown local stereotypes in a story set in the Cornish surfing community. However, as Karen Lury has pointed out, the film is till part of tendency to look for an England with an 'authenticity' that transcends contemporary globalized city culture, particularly that represented by the metropolis:

> The representation of a particular community by the film is therefore designed to construct a somewhat idealised local culture as a place outwith, and literally distant from, the commercial taint and inauthenticity represented by London. (Lury 2000: 101)

Lury, in fact, goes on to make the wider point that 1990s British cinema frequently used youth cultures as a vehicle for exploring the interplay between local and globalized cultures and identities. As is the case in Blue Juice, and, to an extent *The War Zone* (narrated as it is through the eyes of a 15-year-old young man struggling to come to terms with his own identity), cultural hybridity comes to be seen as central to British youth culture in particular, but I would argue to British, and in particular English, culture in a broader sense. In *The War Zone* an old Second World War coastal defence bunker becomes the scene of one of the most brutal acts within the film, and it is tempting to read this use of a site so associated with a formerly secure national identity as part of an elaborate metaphor of denial and self-deception which embraces both personal and national narratives.

In discussing representations of national identity that involve strong modifications of the idea of dominance of the metropolis, it is too easy to ignore striking and significant re-appraisals of London itself, a number of which have appeared in the last decade. What is perhaps most significant about a number of these films is their sheer variety, though it must also be said that within the gangster genre in particular relentless tedious attempts to reproduce the influential *Lock, Stock and Two Smoking Barrels* (1998) produced a view of London men that quickly became hackneyed (if the pun can be pardoned).

Despite its Hollywood star, *Sliding Doors* (1997) has been explicitly associated with the way that popular films have negotiated a shifting sense of British national identity. In doing so, *Sliding*

Doors make specific use of London as a kind of contended space within which the competing identities of a young woman are played out and by extension so are the changing faces of London and the rest of Britain. In one sense, as David Martin-Jones has asserted, the device which *Sliding Doors* uses to this end is relatively unoriginal:

> ... despite its slightly unusual dual narrative, the way in which *Sliding Doors* constructs national identity is hardly original. It uses its two versions of the same story to offer contrasting views of national identity in 90's Britain, and asks the viewer to choose between them. (Martin-Jones 2004: 18)

However, what make *Sliding Doors* a key film in this discussion is the contrast it offers to British films that are pre-occupied with the increasing tensions within the idea of Britishness. As Martin-Jones goes on to put it:

> *Sliding Doors* strongly advocates an identity that is far more globally orientated than national. Despite emerging at the time of devolution in Britain (the establishing of separate parliaments in Scotland and Wales) the film is far less concerned with the splintering of British national identity than it is with the relationship between London and the rest of the world. *Sliding Doors,* then uses its multiple narrative structure to explore the changing face of British national identity after the development of London as a global city. In fact, by mapping the 'right' and 'wrong' ways of living in the global city the film proffers an image of a new, *transnational* identity in post-devolutionary Britain. (Martin-Jones 2004, 18)

The general point here is, I think, persuasive, and Martin-Jones goes on to support it through an analysis of the kind of London that is offered to us as a 'global city'. It is, as he points out, almost entirely devoid of the usual signifiers of British identity and, instead, we have a globalized London of bars, cafes and new offices and apartments. In addition, we also have the less 'English', more thrusting and entrepreneurial behaviour of the 'blonde' version of Paltrow's offered as a more attractive and exciting identity for us all to don as part of the denationalizing of our identities.

Given its 1997 completion date it is, however, difficult to embrace Martin-Jones explicit identification of the film with what he calls 'the selling of a Blairite vision of London' and especially his numerous references to the film's situating itself in such a way as to 'avoid the problems of post-devolutionary Britain'. (Martin-Jones 2004: 27) Although the arguments about devolution were obviously around for decades before this point, it is hard to see a film that was largely completed before the explicit New Labour commitment to devolution defining its sense of the nation in such a context. *Sliding Doors* is clearly of great interest in any discussion about British and English identity, but its vision of a blander, globalized London surely stems from an altogether more generalized promotion of a world of entrepreneurial 'international' possibility. In such a world the problematics of gender as well as national identities can be neatly resolved and the rewards of contemporary urban lifestyle are there for those prepared to work for them. A decade of New Labour has perhaps done little to dissipate this as a guiding national moral principle, but its genesis is surely further back in the national psyche.

The strongest possible contrast to the vision of London presented by *Sliding Doors* is that offered by Gary Oldman's first feature, *Nil by Mouth* (1997). Like *The War Zone*, the leading male character is played by Ray Winstone whose version of English men could reasonably be argued to be one of the defining contributions to the cinematic portrayal of masculinity in the last decade. *Nil by Mouth*, however, goes right back to the working-class London roots of both Oldman and Winstone and to visions of the capital and working-class London life that are as far away from the ideas of *Sliding Door* and the 'global city' as it is possible to imagine. The film is also a long way from traditional English, sentimental portrayals of family life of the kind mentioned in the following *Sight and Sound* review:

> On one level, Gary Oldman's *Nil by Mouth* is a literally bastardised descendant of such cosy London family dramas such as *This Happy Breed* (1944) and *Here Come the Huggetts* (1948). The extended family and the quaint grandma figure have survived from those films, but here the suburban homes and gardens have been replaced by an urban wasteland of council flats and desolate municipal space. (Tunney 1998: 62)

Nil by Mouth is though far less concerned with landscape, or indeed with the wider social space, and far more with the terrifying intensity of the small number of characters that play out the tale of domestic conflict. At an overt level it can barely be seen as a film about contemporary England at all, simply because of the concentration on one family and Gary Oldman's intense positioning of his camera seemingly in the midst of the action. However, the film's desperate study of masculinity, set as it is in London, can be read as dramatizing an episode of the end of a particular kind of easily assumed power. This is of particular interest in relation to the seemingly endless cycle of London-set gangster films that were soon to follow. Whereas the latter (to be discussed further below) often appeared most in tune with a so-called 'post-feminist' laddish vision of both men and London personified by the new generation of magazines aimed at men such as *loaded*, *Nil by Mouth* attempts an unmistakeable critique of English male culture whilst avoiding a crude reduction of the characters to ciphers. For Claire Monk, this attempt to 'humanize' the terrifyingly violent Raymond (Ray Winstone) and his associates actually undermines the film's analysis of male violence and the exercise of power:

> ... the film's concentration on Ray (who does, after all, represent Oldman's own father), coupled with the power of ray Winstone's performance, lends its critique of masculinity considerable ambivalence. Despite its seemingly critical stance on Ray and his mates, the film spends far more time with them than with Val [Ray's wife played by Kathy Burke] – suggesting an enduring fascination, more widely evident in 1990's British films, with the unreconstructed world of men. (Monk 2000 a.: 165)

There is little denying a sense of what Monk terms 'an enduring fascination' and also that much of that can look like nostalgia. However, within the parallel, extended narratives of the decline of empire and the decline of patriarchy films such as *Nil by Mouth* are important in that they both dramatize the terrible consequences of the brutal exercise of power whilst at the same time recognizing the wounded vulnerability that has also to be faced if a different future is to be brought into imaginative existence. It is not, after all, as if the central female figure in *Nil by Mouth* is in any sense denied a voice. As played by Kathy Burke, the character became for many the focus of the film's enormous power and Burke herself won the Cannes Best Actress prize for her performance. By the end of the film, there are certainly no easy, sentimental solutions, but there is a sense that the balance of power has shifted slightly towards the female figures, whose voices dominate the final scenes of the film. It is, though, hard to tell whether Oldman intends to convey a pessimistic sense of the cyclical nature of the violence between Val and Raymond or whether Ray's literal attempts to repair damage (he decorates the flat that he previously wrecked) can be taken as any sense of fragile hope.

An interesting comparator to *Nil by Mouth* as another 'outsider London' film is Michael Winterbottom's *Wonderland* (1999). Whereas *Nil by Mouth* barely acknowledges the city except for fleeting reference points (such as the men going 'up west' for a night out), in *Wonderland* the city is foregrounded to the point where it arguably becomes the point of the film. As Charlotte Brunsdon has pointed out (Brunsdon 2004: 59), the film treads an interesting line between traditional narrative uses of iconographic London (St Paul's, the Thames and so on) and a heightened impressionistic vision of London which mixes a quasi-documentary naturalism with fast-motion, time-lapse and a whole range of other devices that interweave the city as a force within the characters lives.

In some ways the narrative of *Wonderland* requires the London of *Sliding Doors* to meet the London of *Nil by Mouth*, and the result resonates as a picture of the English metropolis as well as the more generalized twenty-first-century 'city'. The very loosely constructed narrative takes place over three days of a November weekend and focuses on a south London family. The retired parents still live in the maisonette on the large sprawling estate, whereas the three daughters have left and live on the outer fringes of the 'renewed' millennial capital and its chic cafes and bars. We see their social and working lives brush up against this prosperous, fashionable world, but then return to scruffy flats and bedsits (though one sister, Molly, and partner, Eddie, seem slightly more prosperous until Eddie abandons his soulless job selling kitchens).

This is not, however, primarily a narrative about the widening gap between rich and poor that lay beneath the 'Cool Britannia rhetoric'. Rather, the film's opening scene goes straight to the heart of the film's central concern as it shows one of the three sisters, Nadia (Gina McKee), go through the agonizing small talk at the start of a completely unsuitable date arranged through a 'lonely hearts' column. The film is set just before the explosion of Internet dating services and it is likely that this desperate search for some kind of human connection would nowadays have Nadia wade through even more sheer misery and loneliness before the glimmer of hope at the film's end, but the picture painted here of her life lived through a series of desperate meetings with strangers is bleak enough. Though they are not well off, money is not the thing that is seen to blight the lives of these people so much as the sheer difficulty of maintaining healthy, open and nurturing relationships in the face of the daily grind of dull menial work, noise and the endless travel involved in large city life.

In this context what makes *Wonderland* significant is its picture of London at the very moment that the hollow truimphalism of 'Cool Britannia' was asserting the case for the capital as the heart of the new, 'modern', entrepreneurial Britain at the cutting edge of the world's youth-orientated globalized culture. At almost the same moment as resurgent capitals in Scotland and Wales staged large open-air events proclaiming the newly energized centres of devolved power, *Wonderland* gives us a London full of the hesitant, the anxious and the suspicious. One couple in the film seem to enjoy themselves, but are kept mysteriously on the edge of the action until it is revealed very late on that the man is the 'lost' brother of the three sisters. In one of the film's last scenes he is seen taking the train back to Manchester, the place were he fled from the stifling home of his parents and (we presume) found the life-enhancing exuberance of his partner, Melanie. Though by the end of the film a traditional new baby and the first flickers of new relationships beginning offer hope, these are born from the sheer human resilience of the characters who find tiny glimmers of consolation despite the obstacles of this ironically titled metropolitan 'wonderland'.

The final group of films that I want to discuss in relation to London and its place at the heart of shifting British and English identities is that given impetus by the enormous and unexpected success of *Lock, Stock and Two Smoking Barrels* (1998), although as Steve Chibnall rightly points out there is also case for suggesting that 'the whole gangster bandwagon could be said to have been set rolling by *Face* (1997)' (Chibnall 2001: 281). The sheer scale of the revival in the genre demands that any discussion such as this, which attempts to assess the way in which films have handled and contributed to ideas of English identity, takes this group of films seriously. As Chibnall goes on to say: 'In the four years between April 1997 and April 2001 at least twenty-four British underworld films were released, more than were released in the twenty years before 1997.'(2001: 282)

At one level it is clear that the gangster cycle of this period can be related to the connections that have already been made between a certain level of crisis in the idea of Englishness and broader debates around masculinity. As Chibnall and others have pointed out, these films belong at least partly to the culture of men's magazines such as *FHM* and *loaded* and, also, to the obsession with the narrative and filmic style of Quentin Tarantino and his many imitators from earlier in the 1990s. This is, of course, not to say that all these films can be discussed as an undifferentiated mass, but there is undoubtedly sufficient common ground between them to make the case that their vision of both London and English men can be seen as a significant element in the filmic representation of England in the post-1997 period.

Apart from *Lock Stock*, *Gangster No. 1* (2000), *Sexy Beast* (2000) and one or two others, the critical vitriol poured on the majority of these films has been considerable. Some of this has been overgeneralized, but the sense of jumping mindlessly on bandwagons and of climbing on board the 'new lad' gravy train has been relentless. At its worst the picture of Britain offered by many of this group of films can seem not only as limited, but at times close to sickening and dangerous despite the sub-Tarantino 'comedy' of the masculinity on display, as Danny Leigh put it:

> ... the comic lustre of the new pretenders comes off in your hands when you recall that the best-known recent example of a gaggle of white twentysomething wideboys out for a laugh – in true *Lock, Stock* style – was the gang that killed Stephen Lawrence. (2000: 23)

There is undoubtedly a nostalgia in many of the films, not only for the admirable filmic qualities of their much-referenced influences *Get Carter* (1971) and *The Long Good Friday* (1979), but also for a white, male England which is dominated by the simple moral universe of working-class

London. The most telling exception to this was *Sexy Beast*, which used the narrative trope of the old retired gunslinger being asked to do one more job to comically explore the passing of such a world rather than try to breathe new life into it. Xan Brooks compared it to late Westerns:

> *Sexy Beast* is the modern British gangster movie what *Lonely Are the Brave* (1962) was to the American Western. It is a film about the end of things, inhabited by villains past their sell-by date and touched throughout by the shadow of mortality. (2001: 50)

In what is a stylish and witty take on an old cliché, the retired gangster living with a porn star on the Costa del Sol, Glazer managed to both shake the critical establishment out of its cynical approach to British gangster pictures and also offer a vision of the end of this staple of films' approach to the idea of England. As Chibnall points out, one of the film's central characters played by Ray Winstone (in another of the film's reversals Winstone's traditional hard man has gone soft) is heard at one point to make explicit reference to what he sees as the decline of England, 'what a shit-hole, what a toilet – every cunt with a long face', and what he really refers to is the England from which he has fled, the England of grim East End hard men that has been fantasized about in so many of the recent British gangster films. *Sexy Beast* is, of course, no simple morality tale about the end of a way of life, but Gary Dove's (Winstone) haunted existence by the pool in an almost surreally deserted Spanish landscape, the giant boulder that literally crashes into his world in one of the film's truly memorable moments and his friendship and reliance on his young Spanish pool boy all suggest a struggle to transcend the earthbound clichés of his former life. When this comes back to haunt him in the shape of Don Logan (an acclaimed performance from Ben Kingsley), it is frightening but also desperate and pleading. When Gary refuses the offer of one last job, Logan screams at him: 'Do it! Do it! Do it! Yes!Yes!Yes!' in a disturbing display that leaves a sense of Logan as a metaphysical force way beyond the demands of the simple narrative. A force that perhaps signals the death throes not simply of a largely unmemorable phase of British cinema, but of a monochrome working-class England resisting the appeal of a more interesting but complex and fractured identity.

If *Sexy Beast* rescued the gangster genre from its exploitative and mindlessly imitative phase of the late 1990s, then a number of examples of the 'heritage' tradition, for so long a relatively conservative bastion of the British industry, have been seen as similarly interrogating both the filmic traditions within which they operate and also the relationship between the national past and the shifting sense of national identity in the present. To start with the most obvious example, Pamela Church Gibson reminds us of the 'eerie coincidence'(2000: 122) felt by the cast of Shekhar Kapur's *Elizabeth* (1998) as they began shooting on the same day as the funeral of Diana, Princess of Wales in August 1997. Coincidence or not, the film could not help but be inflected by the interplay between its take on one of the key icons of British national identity and the national atmosphere created by the death of another.

At one level it is surely worth at least remarking on the choice of Kapur, an experienced Bollywood director, to direct a film about one of imperial Britain's central mythic figures. Whilst much of the subversion of the traditions of British cinema is stylistic, there is also a sense of questioning around the myths of nationhood and, in particular, of efforts to hold to a unified Britain dominated by the English. Church Gibson's description of the opening of *Elizabeth* provides a telling sense of the film's distance from the mainstream heritage tradition:

The opening sequence shows us forcibly the brutality of the era – there is no chance that we will regard what is to follow as an exercise in nostalgia. A document is sealed and stamped – we track across shackles and chains, to the sound of screaming, and the camera observes from above the violent shaving of a woman's head, with strokes so harsh that her scalp is bloodied. From overhead, we watch as she and her fellow Protestants are dragged out through iron gates to be burned at the stake. (2000: 122–3)

Such scenes, along with the drastic transformation of the young Elizabeth (Cate Blanchett), demonstrate during the course of the film, as Moya Luckett puts it, 'how suffering was ultimately in the service of the grander cause of preserving national borders and establishing a national identity'. (2000: 91) Interestingly, though, Luckett's analysis does not lead her to the discovery of a new 'authenticity' in *Elizabeth*, but rather an exercise in the power of searing images over 'archival knowledge' in the making of national identity. This, she argues, is entirely in tune with the contemporary New Labour project to re-invent the nation: 'If "authentic images" replace contested facticity, then the nation might find its identity again.' (2000: 91)

In *Elizabeth*, then, we find a film that has relevance to the contesting of national identity in at least two respects. Firstly, it unpicks to a certain extent the dominant myths surrounding its subject, whilst retaining a degree of respect for Elizabeth's qualities as a woman surrounded by the viciousness of the power struggles within her court. Secondly, its operatic use of imagery and spectacle is employed in ways that are entirely consistent with the contemporary attempts to reinvent not only a sense of British national identity, but identities in the newly devolved nations that were borne amidst a plethora of newly minted icons of nationalism.

The more popular *Shakespeare in Love* (1999) is certainly far lighter in tone and less directly concerned with the national past, but its take on yet another key cultural icon was arguably still a long way removed from the mainstream heritage tradition and, therefore, from traditional projections of the nation. As Church Gibson points out (2000: 123) this is a highly self-referential film which mixes cinematic and televisual in-jokes, Shakespearean quotation and direct audience address in playful combinations that deliberately undermine any expectation that this is a film mindlessly indulging in Bardolatry. Whilst *Shakespeare in Love* is not a serious de-construction of either a period of English history or of Shakespearean mythology, it is also part of its time in the consistently playful way that it handles both the past and the creative process. In this way it is entitled to be counted as a film that runs counter to a mainstream heritage view of the national past and which, in post modern comic fashion, draws our attention to the haphazard nature of the production of stories and national myths.

From the late 1990s onwards it is possible to argue that the dominant sense in which British cinema was to reflect a reconstructing of national identity was through the small but growing group of films reflecting the experiences either of some of the country's ethnic communities or of those who have sought asylum in Britain. Whilst both of these dimensions to identity have impacted on cinema from the north of Ireland, Scotland and Wales, and they are discussed to some extent in the relevant chapters in this volume, it is fair to say that it has been England specifically that has been not only the dominant location for such films, but also the heart of the national identity that has been implicitly interrogated. There has of course been growing academic interest in the postcolonial as it relates to the newly devolved parts of the UK, (see, for example, Aaron and Williams 2005) with many stressing the specifically English nature of the imperial past (though others have questioned this) (see, for example, Jordan 2005) and it is this that underlies the way that this trend in British cinema has related much more to an idea of 'England' than to the wider UK.

It is not, of course, the intention to suggest that a tendency to include such experiences within a cinematic view of Britain began in the late 1990s. The 1980s in particular was arguably the moment when cinema most explicitly opened up questions of racial and national identity and in the two key films arsing from the collaboration between Hanif Kureshi and Stephen Frears, *My Beautiful Launderette* (1985) and *Sammy and Rosie Get Laid* (1987), this intersected with sexual identity in order to, in John Hill's words, 'exhibit a concern to problematise the very notion of social identity in the contemporary-postmodern-world' (Hill 1999: 215). Such films were commonly seen as a strong response to one of the dominant and successful trends in British cinema up to that point, namely films that dramatized the notion of Empire from a loosely liberal standpoint, whilst at the same time trading on the exotic power of location and the narrative power imperial conflict. Hanif Kureshi, in fact, made this explicit in his introduction to the published screenplay of *My Beautiful Launderette*, as Hill explains:

> *My Beautiful Lauderette*, in particular, may be read as something of a riposte to the Raj films of the early 1980s and self-consciously makes use of actors – such as Saeed Jaffrey and Roshan Seth – who appeared in both *A Passage to India* (1984) and *Gandhi* (1982). As Hanif Kureshi explains in his introduction to his script he 'was tired of seeing lavish films set in exotic locations': it seemed to him 'that anyone could make such films, providing they had an old book, a hot country, new technology, and were capable of aiming the camera at an attractive landscape in the hot country in front of which stood a star in a perfectly clean costume delivering lines from the old book.'(Hill 1999: 208–9)

A cinematic 'dialogue with inherited notions of "Englishness" and an expansion of them to include black and Asian experiences'(Hill 1999: 216) had, therefore, begun and which continues in the late 1990s and into the present decade, though changing radically, both in terms of cinematic form and in the range of ethnic experiences which it embraces.

It is worth noting how Hill is also conscious of the term 'English' rather than British, though perhaps his fundamental point is that such films raise profound questions about the 'homgeneity of national identities' and even, implicitly of the concept of national identity, something which has now progressed into contemporary debates about the 'post-nation'. Whilst not attempting to oppose the validity of such obviously profound questions raised by the various forces of globalization, this volume seeks to assert that the specific context of devolution gave the issue of the nation a resonance in Britain that cannot be so easily discounted. This is turn has met and been affected by the trends begun in the 1980s and discussed above. It is the collision of these two forces, a resurgent interest in the meaning of Englishness post-devolution and the longer-term impact on the idea of England of the ethnic diversity of the country's population, that we will now examine in terms of the ways in which it is represented in a number of key films of the last decade.

According to Karen Alexander, one of the key directors of the last decade, Gurinder Chadha, 'traces her interest in film-making back to seeing *My Beautiful Launderette*' (2000: 112) Though

Chadra's approach is generally lighter and more playful than the earlier work it too is fundamentally concerned with lives 'being lived out in the complex post-colonial hybridity of contemporary Britain' (Brunsdon 2000: 145) which, on the whole, has meant England, not just through accidents of location, but through the playful deconstruction of English icons through their interaction with newer cultural influences. So far, these have included the quintessentially English holiday resort of Blackpool (*Bhaji on the Beach* 1993), the captain of the English football team, David Beckham (*Bend It Like Beckham* 2002) and Jane Austen (*Bride and Prejudice* 2004).

Critical opinion on the importance of Chadra's contribution to a more inclusive vision of contemporary England has been divided. Both Alexander and Brunsdon are among those to recognize the significance of *Bhaji*'s attempt to give voice to the particularly marginalized female Punjabi voices that make up most of the cast, whilst Philip French's review of *Bend It Like Beckham* tends to reflect those who appeared to be annoyed at Chadra'a lack of art-house seriousness, asserting that she 'makes feel-good comedies of ethnic manners' in which 'difficult questions of race relations and the accommodation of tradition to social change are swept under the carpets on which the casts dance.'(French 2002 b.)

It is undeniable that the significance of Chadra'a work lies partly at least in its ability to take questions of identity into the multiplexes, with *Beckham* in particular proving astonishingly popular, not just in the UK but in the US and India itself. French's point would presumably be that in doing this we are presented with an impossibly optimistic vision that glosses over tensions that have reached new heights in the period since Britain's participation in the Iraq war. Certainly Chadra herself, admittedly in 2002, refused to be anything but optimistic, praising Britain for being a context in which it was possible top make a film like *Beckham* and have it viewed 'in terms of race and culture clash, but as a story about people in suburban Britain... to be suffocating in a suburb with your whole life ahead of you.'(Chadra 2002) At the time of writing, in the aftermath of what appears to be the first suicide bombings in Britain and the subsequent strenuous efforts to hold together some kind of liberal consensus, Chadra's words can appear over-optimistic, on the other hand the huge popularity of *Beckham*, its appeal to a broad age and gender range and its use of a key icon of Englishness (Beckham) suggests something with at least some significance for the idea of Englishness. It is surely as naïve to suggest that a film about a girl with a traditional Sikh father, who is inspired by the footballing prowess of David Beckham and which plays to such large audiences has no importance for the future of English identity as it would be to pretend that the film is a subtly nuanced discussion of postcolonial hybridity.

After the pleasant surprises and juxtapositions of *Beckham* and *Bhaji* (in which there is, as Brunsdon points out, the delightful spectacle of a group of women of all ages singing the Cliff Richard hit 'Summer Holiday' in Punjabi) (2000: 168), Chadra's third film that places an iconographic English institution at its core, *Bride and Prejudice*, appears to have retreated into a rather gimmicky sense of spectacle with an eye firmly on the international market. At one level, of course, the mildly subversive act of combining an idea from Austen with key Bollywood tropes has some minor significance in the history of English identity. However, the film feels a little like the idea began and ended with the punning title (an idea hilariously parodied in one newspaper piece that dreamt up other culturally hybrid Austen adaptations including

'Northanger Rabbi'!) (http://film.guardian.co.uk/features/featurepages, 2004), and there is little to suggest that Chadra set out to make anything other than an international crowd pleaser that in the West drew on just a little of the cultural capital that the Austen association would inevitably bring. Perhaps there is nothing wrong with that, and the fact that such a film is now made and financed is some tribute to the efforts of Chadra and others to wriggle out from under the 'burden of representation' just a little.

The reviews of *Beckham*, especially those that were less favourable, often made the rather unimaginative comparison with an earlier unexpected commercial success (though not on the same global scale), *East is East* (1999) (see Bradshaw 2002). One fundamental difference between *East is East* and Chadra's work is that the former uses a key moment in the national past (at least as far a national identity is concerned), the emergence of Enoch Powell as an opponent of immigration and the advance of a multicultural Britain, as a muted backdrop to the film. Its resonances for the hybridity of contemporary English identity are therefore refracted through its reading of recent history.

Significantly the film is an adaptation of a successful stage play by the actor Ayub Khan-Din, who wrote it in response to his 'frustration at being offered only clichéd Asian acting roles' (Spenser 1999 b.: 36). It can therefore be read partly as an attempt to reflect more accurately the culture from which Khan-Din came and its commercial success means that *East is East* can be seen as an important contribution to the recent cinematic construction of English identity. Much of the film's humour comes from the undercutting of expectations about the aspirations and cultural identity of the Khan family, seen here living in Salford in 1971. George (Om Puri), the patriarch, tries to raise his seven children as traditional Muslims, despite the fact that his own life is the epitome of hybrid identity having married Ella his white English wife who is anything but submissive.

To some extent the film's narrative turns on predictable attempts to arrange marriages, but it gains real vitality from the sheer diversity of ways in which the Khan children seek to resist the identities that their father attempts to impose upon them. Of course, if this were simply a story of resistance to oppressive Muslim cultural practices, it would be clichéd and offensive, but in many ways the film becomes the story of the Khan parents and their struggle to make their hybrid way of life work in the shadow of Powell and all that he precipitated. Though George Khan's fierce pride leads him to acts of cruelty and even brutality, we are left with a sense of his bewilderment and confusion rather than his patriarchal power, and, through Ella, we see a courageous effort of will to reconcile the demands of two cultures on her and her children. This is not a film that says glibly that we should all be allowed to forge our own identities, there is a real sense of struggle as the sons are revealed as gay or art students rather than the engineers and shopkeepers that Khan hoped for, and it is all the more striking for the realization that young Muslim men and women were engaged in such internecine family struggles as long ago as 1971.

More recent cinematic attempts to contribute to the complex discourse of a changing England have, I would argue, been dominated by largely principled attempts to engage sympathetically with the issues surrounding asylum seekers and refugees. However, as Roy Stafford rightly points out (2004), such films have been seen by relatively small numbers of people and in the context of the often shameful debates surrounding these issues, their contribution is overwhelmed by the plethora of images from tabloid newspapers and generic fictionalized accounts for both large and small screen. Nevertheless, it is important not to entirely discount the importance of such films. Through post-theatrical forms of distribution their audience is not inconsiderable and they represent enough of a critical mass within the total output of post-millennial British cinema to suggest a genuinely widespread interest in the implications of asylum and immigration debates for the future of the way that the English, in particular, see themselves. These, in turn, link into related debates about Europe and the perceived global threat of Islamic militancy, all of which now constitutes the central powerful influence on what has become a debate about national identity with a new urgency as politicians seek ways in which to respond to an increasingly volatile world order.

This chapter began with a critic's assertion that the purest instance of Englishness in contemporary cinema existed in the latest work from a British director with an outsider's sensibility that was the product of his Polish cultural background. Whilst this in itself may prove too neat a formulation, Pawel Pawlikowski's first successful feature after a distinguished period working in documentary, *The Last Resort* (2000), certainly offers a painfully acute vision of contemporary England that is the very antithesis of the confident resurgent 'Cool Britannia' that had been central to the political rhetoric at the turn of the century. Such a vision is of course all the more poignant for it being the background to a story of a Russian woman and her child being caught up in the nightmare of the current British immigration system. Instead of the land of economic plenty that so much popular rhetoric alleges is the motivation for asylum seekers and refugees, we are presented with a decaying English seaside resort that, in fact, possesses many of the characteristics that have become part of the way that eastern Europe so often figures in fictionalized accounts: grey tower blocks, wire fences, terrible food and a nightmarish state bureaucracy.

Perhaps the real strength of *The Last Resort* as a contribution to the cinematic discourse around English identity stems from Pawlikowski's often irritable reluctance to be seen as an 'issue-led' director. Whilst it is tempting to feel that he overstates his feelings about this kind of cinema (Gibbons 2001 a.: 2–4), it is something that clearly prevented *The Last Resort* from becoming a conventional liberal plea on behalf of asylum seekers and which instead inverted the viewpoint so that we get a bleak poetic vision of post-imperial decline that nevertheless remains capable of surprise. Instead of simply portraying his location town 'Stonehaven' (a barely disguised Margate) as a hellhole, Pawlikowski and his DP, Ryszard Lenczewski, give us a landscape of almost abstract shapes so that the overall impact is of bewilderment and alienation on both sides of the asylum fence. Wholly predictably the act of shooting the film brought down the wrath of the local Tory MP who had almost certainly not seen the film and equally certainly would not be persuaded by its grim poetry. Nor would he have been comforted by the paradox that Stonehaven is as much the abandoned 'victim' of the film as the beautiful Russian woman and her young son:

Images of prison colonies and life without hope have been reversed. If you can't be computer-enhanced, talked up by spin doctors, you don't exist. New Labour, following on from Thatcher's brutalist realpoliitik, has decreed that certain zones are never to be mentioned. Margate is a sanctioned nowhere, a dumping ground for immigrants, runaways and inner-city scroungers. (Sinclair 2001: 18)

As long ago as 1953, Margate was the subject of what Philip French called 'a documentary of Larkinesque misanthropy' (French 2001), namely Lindsay Anderson's *O Dreamland*, but *The Last Resort* is altogether more complex as it plays with images of Margate as both part of an Eastern European–style totalitarian future and at the same time full of a strange kind of beauty as well as unlikely sources of kindness and humanity. Paddy Considine's role as Alfie who runs the amusement arcade is an extension of this playfulness with the audience's expectations. His kindness to Tanya and Artiom (Dina Korzun and Artiom Strelnikhov), the Russian asylum seeker and her son, runs counter to the usual narrative expectations that surround his occupation. Whilst Stonehaven is undoubtedly an extremely bleak vision of the promised land of Western Europe, Pawlikowski's detestation of easy issues refuses to let the audience settle entirely. For England, though, the potency of the use of Margate cannot be entirely denied; a place that thrived on working-class day trippers and holidaymakers is now, in the so-called classless society, a symbol both of decline and of the hollowness of the re-branding of Britain. The quintessentially English seaside resort now a real prison camp, a blackly comic twist on the humour of the *Carry On* films and the real-life Butlins and Pontins and a potent symbol of the hidden underbelly of an England bitter and resentful of its new role in the world.

Although, as Roy Stafford (2004) has discussed at length, Michael Winterbottom's work has frequently engaged in striking and original ways with the contemporary issues surrounding asylum seekers and refugees, the films have tended not use them to explore England itself. Instead the concentration is on the asylum seekers themselves and, in *In This World* (2002) and *Welcome to Sarajevo* (1997), the places from where refugees are fleeing war and oppression. In both Stephen Frears' *Dirty Pretty Things* (2002) and Jez Butterworth's *Birthday Girl* (2002), contemporary England forms the backdrop to very different stories about people seeking to live in Britain in ways that bring them into conflict with the immigration authorities and in both cases the nature of English society becomes an important element of what the films have to say.

Of course, the films could not be more different. Whereas Frears' film is a bleak look at the lives of those living in the black economy of the inner city and being forced into the darkest recesses of the ways that human flesh is traded, both sexually and medically, Butterworth's is altogether lighter, though not without its dark moments as suburban England becomes entangled with small-time Russian criminals. *Dirty Pretty Things* can, in many ways, be read as a bleak corrective to any complacency there might be about a contemporary multicultural London. All the characters are either working illegally or exploiting those that do, and the vision of London is of a place whose economy thrives on the backs of those that it explicitly excludes. Okwe (Chiwetel Ejifor), one of the films leading characters, is a doctor in his native Nigeria; forced to flee the country he performs the ugliest tasks in a London hotel. At one point in the film, he allows his sense of who he really is here in England to become explicit, saying to a business associate of his boss: 'We are the people you don't see. We drive your cabs. We clean your rooms. We suck your cocks.'

The London of *Dirty Pretty Things* is not so much a place where English/British identity is seen as the product of centuries of different kinds of immigration, but one where so much is hidden under the veneer of politic re-invention and re-branding. The film graphically demonstrates how the 'service' industries that are so often trumpeted as the hallmark of a post-industrial Britain depend so heavily on immigrant labour that remains cheap because so many of the workers live in fear of arrest and deportation. However, such a description distorts the film which is fundamentally a thriller, heavy on plot, and it is perhaps by virtue of this that its contribution to a vision of contemporary Britain is significant. Philip French's review of the film put it into the context of the release in the same year of films by Ken Loach and Mike Leigh, speculating how they may have treated the story that is told in *Dirty Pretty Things*, (2002 a.) The fact that this is a film written by a popular television writer (Steven Knight) and can be patronized as a piece of popular TV drama in *Sight and Sound* (Sinclair 2002: 32–4) is arguably the true significance of its contribution to the cinematic construction of contemporary national identity. In *Dirty Pretty Things*, there is a sense of some of the uneasiness that surrounds the ways that we are facing both our colonial past and our globalized future entering popular genre in ways that go beyond token characters.

Birthday Girl is a strange project if only for the fact of persuading Nicole Kidman to play an exotic Russian woman who disrupts the sit-com English suburban existence of John (Ben Chaplin). The film met with mixed reviews and its take on English middle-class existence tends to take jokes that work well in the context of a sketch show such as *Little Britain* and attempt to transfer them to a feature length narrative where they undermine the surface realism of the rest of the film. What is interesting about the film perhaps is its reformulation of a relatively old cinematic joke about staid suburban England in the era of Internet brides, the rise of organized crime in Eastern Europe and middle England's demonization of asylum seekers.

The film seems at its most comfortable when crudely satirizing the mores of contemporary England through the inhabitants of St Albans (the director's home town) and, in particular, John, who has ordered 'Nadia' (Kidman) on the Internet. Much of the time this satire feels altogether too easy playing off the exoticism of Kidman and her two Russian 'cousins' (Vincent Cassel and Mathieu Kassovitz) against a backdrop of new housing estates and Chaplin's twin fastidiousness and interest in soft porn. The jokes are often too easy though sometimes more interesting when touching on the problems of language ('Nadia' pretends not to know any English for much of the film), but the fact that a decidedly average British film should touch on contemporary xenophobic fears is what makes *Birthday Girl* interesting here. We are taken to the heart of the kind of an England that fears 'swamping' by Eastern European 'economic migrants' most and then the film shows us one of the upstanding citizens bringing one of them into his home and playing bondage games with her. Furthermore, after it all blows up in his face, his solution is not to return to his Barratt home existence, but to go with Nadia back to Russia with a suitcase full of stolen money. A well-worn narrative path, of course, but given some new life by its application to a Britain with new-found ways of expressing its anxieties at any hint of a loss of control (at least in public).

Many of the films discussed in this chapter work implicitly or explicitly through explorations of anxiety about the contemporary nature of what it means to be English (inevitably, at times, mixed up with British). Some times, as in the films of Gurinder Chadra, for instance, such feelings are relegated to the background and instead we have populist celebrations of new possibilities presented by changes to what it means to be English. The dominant note, however, is much more likely to be doubt and anxiety as the accumulated forces of devolution, European Union expansion and new kinds of immigration have combined to push age-old debates about what it means to be English further into the contemporary cultural arena. Perhaps, appropriately, I would like to close the chapter with a final film that is also about anxiety and loss, but which only has passing reference to a changing contemporary world and, instead, concentrates firmly on the past and an England that it acknowledges has gone forever.

Directed, in a way that is in perfect ironic tune with the film's thematic concerns, by an Australian (Fred Schepisi), *Last Orders* (2002) is an adaptation of Graham Swift's novel of the same name which takes us on another journey to Margate as the epitome of a particular kind of England. Appearing as it did within the same year as *The Last Resort*, it is inevitable that the two have been seen as representative of something larger than themselves with both appearing to use the decaying seaside resort as a metaphor that is at least partly about the identity of England. While such comparisons could be too easy, fastening upon the word 'Last' in each title to conjure up to turn the films into simple essays on national decline, there is undoubtedly more than co-incidence in the release of two intelligent films so close together, made in Britain, but by 'outsider' directors.

The variety of 'Englishness' explored in *Last Orders* is perfectly epitomized by its cast with the older generation of working-class Londoners being played by Michael Caine, David Hemmings and Tom Courtenay with Caine's son, the new generation represented by Ray Winstone. Winstone is, of course, best known for a series of high-octane performances, usually portraying men capable of huge rages and terrifying violence; here he is in a supporting role to an older version of the class from where his characters usually originate, what Philip French called 'a working class generation who grew up in the war, believed in honour, duty and patriotism, lived quietly and had a stoical attitude to life.'(2002 a.) In fact, in the same review, French makes explicit comparison between the world of *Last Orders* and a number of the other versions of contemporary Englishness (especially those surrounding London) including those that often featured a performance by Ray Winstone, describing the world of the film as:

... about the end of a working-class generation who grew up during the Depression, served their country in the war, believed in honour, duty and patriotism, lived quietly and had a stoical attitude to life.

It's a world far removed from Albert Square and recent mockney gangster pictures. They took on the obligations of work and marriage, though they're closer to their friends at the Coach and Horses than to their wives. (2002 a.)

Lest it be thought that the film is simple nostalgia for a vanishing English culture it is important to point out that much of the film's energy goes in to revealing a quietly poignant truth that underlay the cheery working-class lives. Jack (Caine) and Amy (Helen Mirren), the couple central to the film (the narrative revolves around the scattering of Jack's ashes by his closest friends into the sea at Margate), are revealed to have had a severely disabled daughter who Jack would never acknowledge, which in turn led to Amy conducting a highly restrained and guilt ridden affair with one of Jack's closest friends. None of this, of course, is allowed to fully surface, it remains contained within the social conventions of the world that all the characters inhabit and no one ever refers to it in any direct way, but it successfully undercuts the idea of this vanished England being tough but idyllic in its attitude to friends and family. The parallel sense of lives stunted and repressed is too strong to allow any unambiguous wallowing in nostalgia for this world that is slowly vanishing.

Perhaps the film's key scenes in the context of this discussion are among the least typical of its overall tone because they take place in relation to very public events. On their journey to Margate, the four men (three friends, plus Jack's son, Vincent) stop at two places that make explicit reference to British history, namely the Royal Navy Memorial in Chatham and Canterbury Cathedral. In neither place is there an unambiguous reverence for the days of Empire and British military history, but there is a sense of the four working-class men looking for a connection with a past in which there was a greater sense of national certainty. For some of them this came in the Second World War and the sense of right that came from fighting a war fought against a background of national unity and at one point explicit mention is made of the British withdrawal from Aden, a traditional marker for the end of Empire. In these two scenes, we seem to see confusion and a barely acknowledged sense of abandonment by a changing world. One is reminded of a much earlier landmark drama that reflected on the tectonic shifts in British national identity that were taking place in the 1950s, John Osborne's *Look Back in Anger* in which a very different figure, Colonel Redfearn, a retired officer who spent much of his life within the certainty of colonial rule, and has now become in the words of Jimmy Porter, the central character, 'an old plant left over from the Edwardian Wilderness that can't understand why the sun isn't shining anymore'(Osborne 1976: 66–7). The gap is enormous in terms of class, and there is a huge difference in the rights of the respective characters to our sympathies; but what unites them is the sense of loss and confusion that comes from the radical changes taking place in the construction of national identity and, in turn, their personal identities and those of the people they surround themselves with.

In some ways, *Last Orders* can undoubtedly be read, partially at least, as a reactionary text, and there is little in the way of analysis of the causes of the changing world that the men are experiencing. It does, however, connect to what I have argued to be a series of concerns that have formed an important part of British cinema over the last decade and it does so from the point of view of a deeply unfashionable section of contemporary society, namely ageing, white working-class men from the East End of London. If it feels like a pessimistic tale, I would argue for a slightly modified point of view in so much as we see not so much the end of a desirable world as the end of the veneer of certainty, not simply about national identity but, of course, about the interconnected areas of gender and class. This is what in the end makes all the cinematic tales of an uncertain and rapidly changing England add up to a narrative that can only be welcomed in that it chronicles a developing awareness of the multiple possibilities contained within the idea of Englishness and Britishness. This is, of course, not to be complacent. At a time when debates about national identity have taken on a fresh urgency in the UK after the 2005 London bombings, it is important that the collective cinematic story is cautious as well as aware of hope and possibility, and, through the likes of *The Last Resort* and *Dirty Pretty Things*, such a caution has been properly sounded. However, the overall picture is not simply of the end of something, but of fluidity, of new inflections of identity opening up and of nationalism being only one dimension within the complexity of the way we choose to live. If English identity is more than ever in a state of radical flux it is to be hoped that cinema can remain in touch with the sheer diversity of the possibilities that this opens up as well as the dangers of a resort to a nationalist essentialism in the face of what are perceived to be threats to an older way of life.

3

BEYOND 'PRIESTS, PIGS AND POVERTY': IRELAND AND CINEMA

It is worth stating at the start of this chapter that any attempt to assess the way that dramatic fictions have both responded to and contributed to the changing nature of Britain in the last two decades must include at least some discussion of films from the Republic of Ireland as well as from the north. Whilst this is true of theatre to some extent, in the case of film and television, the combination of the way that the two media circulate across the two countries and the nature of the past and present relationship between Britain and both parts of Ireland make films produced in the Republic of particular relevance to the changing place of Irishness in the larger paradigm of 'Britain'.

For much of the 1990s, at least, it is possible to argue that in a significant number of ways the Republic of Ireland fostered a film culture that was in advance of that in the UK. This was founded upon relatively vigorous government support in the form of tax incentives which gave rise not only to an enormous rise in indigenous production, but also to a massive increase in Ireland's use as a base for overseas productions. Academic work on cinema in Ireland has been correspondingly extensive, much of it excellent, and I am indebted in this chapter to work by those such as Martin McLoone, John Hill, Kevin Rockett and Ruth Barton, who have all written from different perspectives on aspects of national cinema in Ireland.

In Ruth Barton's recent book, *Irish National Cinema*, she quotes Michael Higgins, the Irish Culture Minister, on the rationale behind his government's fiscal support for an Irish film industry. For Higgins the central question is this:

> ... whether we become the consumer of images in a passive culture or whether we will be allowed to be the makers of images in an active culture, in a democratic society. (Barton 2004: 3)

Of course, the central issue behind Higgins question is that of the global dominance of American-produced cinematic images and it is one that has been asked in different ways by governments across the world during the last century. However, what is far more significant is that the kinds of responses made by governments have differed widely. Even in the context under discussion here, we see elsewhere in this volume the different views of the film industry taken by the new devolved authorities in Scotland and Wales, whilst the various attempts at protectionism in the area of moving-image production by successive French governments have had mixed success in stemming the dominance of US films in France. The Irish response was avowedly positive, seeking not to keep out the immensely popular products of Hollywood and beyond, but rather to encourage a cinema that would produce images of Ireland that could be more genuinely representative of the reality of the country today.

Such an aspiration has clear relevance to our discussion here as the expansion of the Irish film industry that took place in the 1990s runs roughly parallel to both the Peace Process in Northern Ireland and the changing status of Ireland within Europe linked to the rise of the Celtic Tiger economy. In other words, a number of key factors came together during the last decade of the twentieth century that all contributed to a fundamental shift in the way that people in Britain would view Ireland in a generalized sense and, more specifically, how Ireland (or any part of it) is seen as part of a wider sense of 'Britain'. This chapter will attempt to examine how films from both the Republic of Ireland and from Northern Ireland reflect and contribute to these changes and to the resultant changed sense of Britain.

As intimated above, by far the largest numbers of films produced in Ireland since the start of the Peace Process have originated from the revitalized industry in the Republic, though since the late 1990s a more modest, but significant, number of films have originated from the north mainly through a combination of broadcasting initiatives and the impact of the National Lottery. In both cases, however, there is a strong case for agreeing with Martin McLoone's judgement that:

> ... contemporary Irish cinema is beginning to emerge as a cinema of national questioning, one that seeks to reimagine the nation in excitingly different and profoundly challenging ways. (1999: 28)

Whilst it is arguable that not all of that national questioning is of direct relevance to an understanding of a changing British national identity, there are clear instances in which the two are intimately related and inevitably bound up with questions of postcolonial identity in ways that tend to be more explicit than in either Scotland or Wales. As Barton puts it:

> ... the strategy of the periphery 'writing back' to the centre, discussed by Salman Rushdie in terms of the re-fashioning of the English language by post-colonial writers has given Irish producers the impetus to grasp the language of dominant cinema, tailor it to reflect a local idiom (through the appropriation of genres such as the gangster film, the road movie and the historical epic) and direct their product back at the home territories of that dominant cinema. Irish film and television have conventionally attempted to write back to two centres – Britain and Hollywood. (2004: 9)

However, as Barton goes on to suggest, it would be a mistake to understand this sense of 'writing back' as a unified obsession with identity, particularly in relation to Britain. Whilst many of the key films produced in Ireland during this period are implicitly or explicitly concerned with the interlocking national identities bound up in the unresolved issues in the north, there are also those that seek to reimagine the nation by attempting to get away from identity politics altogether. There are also those which unashamedly trade on older discredited identities in the interests of capturing a particular sector of what their producers imagine to be 'the market'. As Hugh Linehan puts it:

> Despite rumours to the contrary, stage Irishness is alive and kicking. Films such as *The Matchmaker* (1997), and, most recently *Waking Ned Devine* (1997), play on the sort of awful whimsy that sets Irish teeth on edge. (1999: 46)

Such images form a relatively small proportion of those produced in Ireland in the 1990s, but they were often popular, particularly in the United States where the determination to retain a nostalgic view of Irish culture is its strongest. Typical in this respect was *Circle of Friends* (1995), which, in Lance Pettitt's description, 'opens with a long-shot of the green rural surrounds of Knockglen (filmed in Kilkenny) and Irish pipe music'. (2000: 265) Superficially, the film suggests a society in a state of transition as traditional family values are briefly threatened through the 'freedoms' accorded to a group of young women away from home at college. However, as Ruth Barton says of the central character, Benny, played by Minnie Driver, 'if you look closely, it turns out that her real triumph is not ousting the embezzling clerk who had been running down the family business but it is getting a boyfriend despite being fat'. (1999: 44) Indeed, as Barton says elsewhere the film's ending 'is particularly disappointing, given that in the original story (Maeve Binchy 1990), Benny's triumph is to turn her back on marriage and embrace a career.' (2004: 152)

For many commentators, then, *Circle of Friends* belonged to a group of films characterized by a relatively conservative 'heritage' sensibility and which might be said to include *The Run of the Country* (Peter Yates 1995), *Hear My Song* (Peter Chelsom 1991), *The Secret of Roan Inish* (John Sayles 1995) and *The Closer You Get* (Aileen Ritchie 2000), as well as the examples mentioned by Linehan above. Not all of these are Irish in terms of their dominant cast, crew and financial support, but all can be seen as part of a popular phenomenon that ran counter to the more interesting trends in the representation of Ireland during the last two decades:

> The alternative response to the social crises of the last decades has been to reinvent the past as a period of halcyon innocence. A cycle of films dating from the early Nineties has presented audiences with a view of Ireland which is deeply nostalgic, rooted in pastoral values, and organized around a strong sense of community. Many of them are set in the past, others depict an Ireland of today which has little or no relationship with modernity. (Barton 1999: 44)

Much more significant, however, has been a confident trend towards representations of Ireland that either attempt to avoid questions of identity altogether or which consciously foreground a departure from the traditional representational tropes described above. Such 'positive' images of the culture are not, unsurprisingly, without their critics. Some, such as Hugh Linehan, have been particularly scathing about what is seen as the replacement of one set of national cultural orthodoxies with another:

The old, much-reviled conformism of Irish society has been replaced by a new and more pernicious variety, its parameters defined by smug liberal platitudes and mass-media cynicism. Whether the face of this new, smug Ireland will find its way onto the cinema screen is a question that remains to be answered. (1999: 49)

Whether one agrees with the pejorative thrust of such comments or not, there seems little question that a number of key films have attempted to find a setting in various versions of a self-consciously 'contemporary' Ireland that have contributed to a distancing of the concept of Irishness from either the rural nostalgia discussed above or the urban violence that has tended to pre-dominate in the consciousness of the UK mainland. A representative film in this regard is *About Adam* (Gerard Stembridge 2001). Stembridge's film is set in a contemporary, prosperous, Dublin, an Irish screen landscape that was welcomed by at least one reviewer:

It's good to see prosperous, modern Dubliners on-screen behaving like the denizens of Notting Hill, just about as far as you can get from the priests, pigs, and poverty that stereotype so many Irish films. (Perry 2001)

However, as Barton points out (2004: 112), at least one part of the UK critical establishment disliked the film precisely for what it saw as the film's lack of a strong sense of place: Geoffrey Macnab suggesting

There's a sense that the film-makers were so keen to appeal to an international audience they have strained out everything that might have made *About Adam* distinctive. Like the recent Kevin Spacey thriller *Ordinary Decent Criminal* (which Stembridge scripted), this is a film without a clear sense of local identity. (2001: 38)

For the film's director, Gerard Stembridge, this misses the point entirely. For him the film is very much about a political moment in Ireland, but not in a way that is readily recognized by those seeking the familiar signifiers of Irishness. This is a film that unashamedly depicts an affluent, pleasure-seeking middle class that is representative of a particular strand of contemporary Dublin life. For Stembridge this in itself makes it a political film:

One of the things that interests me is that it would have an entirely different emphasis in Ireland than elsewhere; here it has more to say about issues like guilt, the secular society and the liberal agenda. Rather than depicting a Government view of society I would sooner bring it to the Labour Party Conference and say, 'Here is the liberal agenda on film. Here are people who are no longer priest-ridden, here are people who have no guilt.' (Quoted in Barton 2004: 111)

Some of the products of recent low-budget digital initiatives have arguably taken Stembridge's liberal agenda and run with it: *Goldfish Memory* (Liz Gill 2003) was referred to rather dismissively by *Sight and Sound* as '*Love Actually*, Irish-style' going on to say that 'There is an IKEA feel about *Goldfish Memory*, it is a blonde wood bookcase of a movie, functional but uninspiring'. (Westwell 2004: 52) It is tempting to read into such comments a resentful colonialism surfacing as a desire for an Ireland as an angst-ridden culture beset with both public and private conflict. The reviewer goes on to bemoan the fact that the film's lesbian and gay relationships are presented as too trouble-free in what he imagines to be a still-restrictive culture:

> Apart from one cursory 'coming out' scene early on, little attempt is made to show how sexual preferences generate friction if they go against the grain of socially determined norms; but then the film's soft Dublin is predictably free of homophobia. (Westwell 2004: 52)

Whilst not wishing to make great claims for a modest feel-good film such comments are, in a sense, highly revelatory about the importance of this strand of contemporary Irish film-making. Clearly, a 'soft Dublin' would be only part of any real sense of this highly diverse city, let alone of the country as a whole, but it has surely become a significant part and one which young film-makers should be allowed to access. It is easy to forget how unthinkable such a light-hearted representation of shifting, fluid sexual identities would have been in Ireland even one generation ago and such films make a slight, but significant, contribution to the avowed mission for Ireland to be able to tell stories about itself free of the preconceptions of the past. In turn, such images make a fundamental difference to a sense of Britishness that has relied on a particular sense of Ireland. As the *Sight and Sound* review suggests, it is clear that Britain still struggles to come to terms with an Ireland that defines itself less and less in narrow postcolonial terms, and films such as *Goldfish Memory*, along with others such as *When Brendan Met Trudy* (Kieron Walsh 2000) are part of a process in which the relationship between the two cultures is being redefined.

By contrast it is also important to briefly discuss a trend in films about Ireland that run counter to the comparative freedom and optimism found in *Goldfish Memory*. These are films that, according to Barton have 'chosen to scrutinise the underside of the Celtic Tiger' (2004: 186) and include *Disco Pigs* (Elizabeth Sheridan 2000) and *On the Edge* (John Carney 2001). Both films concern a dysfunctional teenage existence, but do not get into the traditional territory of poverty and class conflict but rather choose to link the experience of Irish teenage life with those of a wider international culture. In a sense this is paradoxical as *Disco Pigs* in particular is based on the specifics of growing up in Cork, on the margins of the contemporary Irish 'centre', though the film version of Enda Walsh's original stage play tends to de-emphasize this in favour of a more individualized shrinking from the adult world in general. Though these films are far from the comforts of any 'soft Dublin', they are linked to *Goldfish Memory* and the like through their lack of connection with the traditional preoccupations of Irishness and, therefore, though they are far from glib about the sustainability of the new Irish mythologies of prosperity and designer living in Dublin, they become an important element in the cultural confidence to broaden the range of stories that can be told about Ireland. Such a concern is made quite explicit by John Carney:

> 90% of stories should be able to be told anywhere, unless specifically historical or something. What's bad about a lot of stories, especially Irish films, is that they're overtly stuck on three or four preoccupations and everything else is avoided like the plague for some reason. (Quoted in Barton 2004: 111)

If one sign of a fundamentally changing national identity is for a culture to become confident enough not to endlessly gaze inward at itself, then the films discussed so far are part of the contribution of Irish cinema to such a confidence. However, it would be a huge distortion to suggest that films from Ireland have contributed to a changing sense of Britain only through assertions of the Republic's new status as a modern European nation with a booming economy. Since the Peace Process began a significant number of films from both sides of the Irish border have continued to reflect the political tensions that remain in Ireland, though, it will be argued in ways that are far more diverse than would have been likely a generation ago.

Of the films that involved direct representation of the struggle over the status of Ireland during this period it was a historical epic that attained by far the highest profile both in Ireland and internationally. Released at such a point in the Peace Process that it could not fail to resonate controversially with the contemporary situation, *Michael Collins* (Neil Jordan 1996), for all its trappings of Hollywood stars and conventions of sweeping bio-pic melodrama, can be seen as part of a highly significant shift in the popular representation of Anglo-Irish conflict. Seen in this way, it also a landmark film in any discussion of the representation of a new sense of Britishness.

The film's opening captions refer directly to the power of the British Empire in the early twentieth century and to the achievement of those in Ireland responsible for taming that power. At the end of the twentieth century the way that events around the life of Michael Collins are depicted clearly reflect another stage in the break-up of old ideas of a powerful monolithic British state. Jordan himself clearly saw the making of the film as carrying a great deal of responsibility: addressing his remarks to students on an education website he said:

> I have never lost more sleep over the making of a film than I have over *Michael Collins*... but I'll never make a more important one. In the life of one person you can tell the events that formed the north and south of Ireland as they are today. (1996)

Jordan's sense of the film's importance clearly reflects his realization of the film's contemporary relevance, borne out by the IRA ending their ceasefire with the Canary Wharf bombing very close to the film's UK release. Although it received a decidedly mixed critical response, especially in the context of Jordan's reputation, *Michael Collins* became a hugely popular film in Ireland, according to Martin McLoone, 'second only to *Titanic* in the all-time box-office list' (2000: 217) adding to the sense that the film's contemporary importance had a very broad base in the country as a whole.

This box office popularity was not, however, an indication of a national consensus about the true significance of *Michael Collins*. Both of the excellent recent attempts to provide an overview of Irish national cinema have drawn attention to the way that the film drew criticism from a very broad political spectrum with claims being made both for its innate conservatism as

> ... a validation of the worst aspects of Irish nationalism and its violent republican past (and present), an atavistic celebration of an Ireland thankfully now long gone, radically transformed from its inward-looking nationalism by acquiring a modern, secular European identity. (McLoone 2000: 218)

– but also for its crucial importance as a key text of the post-Peace Process era. A film that dared to face, for the first time within the conventions of a popular genre, some of the problematics of the violent creation of independent Ireland, which in turn could act as a reminder to those responsible for contemporary negotiations about Northern Ireland.

The film's use of genre conventions, particularly those associated with the gangster film (a key sequence involving the assassination of twelve British undercover operatives, intercut with contrasting scenes including Collins lying with Kitty Kiernan holding a rose, discussing the role of love in his thinking, recalls an epic sequence at the end of *The Godfather* in which Michael Corleone's men clinically wipe out all the leaders of the rival mafia families) are not without difficulty.

As Barton says, 'Jordan's film is a "closed" discourse. History is presented as "knowable"...' and through such elements as casting and the interpretation of the central characters we are given a clear sense that the film's sympathies are entirely with Michael Collins. Interestingly, though, the film's critical and political reception suggests that it has become anything but 'closed' and instead has acted as a catalyst for debate that might ultimately be its important contribution to a re-imagination not only of Ireland, but of Britain too. In the end it is arguably an important signifier of radical change that the film was made and widely distributed, though it does more than that. For Barton, though, *Michael Collins*

> ... fails in its project of bridging the past and the present, of effectively suggesting that the situation in Northern Ireland should be resolved through negotiation rather than paramilitary tactics. It may end with the admonition that Collins died as he was trying 'to take the gun out of Irish politics' but, given that it has so effectively celebrated its hero as a strategist and as the father of guerrilla warfare, there is little sense that progress may be made through a new policy of negotiation and conciliation. (Barton 2004: 144)

Such a view is understandable, given the visual romance that the film attaches to Collins earlier exploits, but there may well be those that see in the film a trajectory from 'freedom fighter' to peacemaker that is not entirely remote from that of the 1990s key icon in this respect, Nelson Mandela. For such a reading to be possible, the Peace Process had to be in place and it is therefore the film's great misfortune that it was made as the process gathered momentum only for its release to coincide with the collapse of the ceasefire and a subsequent period of terrible violence in Northern Ireland.

If *Michael Collins* was still able to arouse controversy despite the distance of history, then, at a time of great political sensitivity, it was doubly difficult for film-makers wishing to engage directly with the contemporary reality of Northern Ireland. This was true whichever side of the border the film originated. As was discussed above, for many the most significant political act that a film-maker could engage in was to work with a 'new' Ireland, particularly that associated with metropolitan Dublin and its status as a 'European' city and to avoid being trapped by association with violent political and military struggle. However, there are strong examples of films that continue to engage more directly with the evolving politics of the north, on a variety of levels, and, clearly, these responses to a rapidly changing situation are of vital importance to any sense of film's response to a changing Britain.

Jim Sheridan's *In the Name of the Father* (1993) and Neil Jordan's *The Crying Game* (1992) are not only two of the highest profile films ever to emerge from Ireland, they are also in a sense benchmarks of pre-Peace Process cinema that sought to engage directly with the politics of Northern Ireland, the military conflict in the north and the relationship between the UK and both parts of Ireland. They of course do this in radically different ways with Sheridan's film providing an interpretation of a key incident in the recent history of Anglo-Irish relations – the trial, imprisonment and ultimate acquittal of the Guildford Four – whilst Jordan offers a far more elliptical vision that is concerned with identity politics in ways that intertwine the nation with complex ideas of gender and sexuality.

Whilst both are sensitive and complex examples of popular cinema when judged by the standards of crude representations of Irish 'terrorists' such as those in Philip Noyce's *The Patriot Game* (1992), they both feature Irish republican characters that, to varying extents, illustrate the two films' antipathy to the crudely violent nature of the contemporary IRA. *The Crying Game*, of course, also contains a remarkable and complex portrayal of a member of the IRA in Fergus, played by Stephen Rea, but it has been the ruthless character of Jude (Miranda Richardson) that for many expressed Jordan's view of the conduct of the conflict by the paramilitary organizations.

In Sheridan's generally uncompromising attack on the British legal establishment and the politicians that used it for its own narrow ends, there is still room for a relatively brief portrayal of what many have seen as another crude creation of a psychopathic terrorist in the character of McAndrew played by Don Baker. For a brief period in the narrative, McAndrew appears to offer the wrongly imprisoned Gerry Conlon (Daniel Day-Lewis) a way to channel his seething sense of injustice at his wrongful imprisonment as one of those convicted of the bomb attack on an army barracks in Guildford. McAndrew, though, totally undermines Conlon's faith in him and his methods through a vicious flame-thrower attack on the one prison warder that has been set up as sympathetic earlier in the film. The film's depiction of Conlon's rejection of McAndrew and his subsequent embrace of his dead father's passive, non-violent stance are at the film's moral centre.

Perhaps too conveniently, the appearance of *The Crying Game* and *In the Name of the Father* within a year of each other, and right at the start of the period of a radical change in relations between the UK and Irish governments and more significantly between the UK government and those able to speak for the Republican movement in the north, can be seen as marking the beginning of a new phase of representation of the conflict over Irish nationalism. What they accurately signal, perhaps, is not so much a marked shift in the political position of mainstream cinema about Ireland, but as the beginnings of a decade where political change would open up the possibility of a diversity of positions becoming 'acceptable' (to a limited extent) and for the 'Troubles' to be seen as part of the complex texture of life in Ireland rather than its single defining narrative.

This said, one of the key creative figures behind *In the Name of the Father*, screenwriter Terry George, would go on to write and direct one of the decade's most direct pieces of commercial cinema in terms of its treatment of recent Irish history. *Some Mother's Son* (1996) focuses on the hunger strikes of the 1980s and the Thatcher government's uncompromising stance when dealing with the negotiations that surrounded the protest. As George has subsequently asserted, by 1996 the film was able to resonate in ways that went beyond a simple reminder of the ferocity of the struggle to arrive at the political position of the mid-1990s:

The end of this film is both analogous to and almost a mirror image of what's happening at the moment... the attempts to resolve the hunger strikes fell down over the interpretation of certain words... We need to fight out this battle of ideas in the arts: in films, theatre, books, literature, debate and take it off the street... (Quoted in McLoone 2000: 76)

At one level *Some Mother's Son* is important in this context simply by having been made in any kind of commercial context. As McLoone has argued (2000: 74), this would have been inconceivable only a decade before and its release can be seen as a highly significant indicator of a changing popular sense of Ireland in the broader British context. This is not necessarily to make great cinematic claims for the film. Most reviewers saw it as relatively conventional and unadventurous in these terms. It is, though, undeniably important as another reflection of what was happening to the idea of 'Britain' with the use of footage of Margaret Thatcher's first election victory at the start of the film, acting as a reminder of the imperial rhetoric that had enjoyed such a chilling revival during the early 1980s.

Sheridan's own, *The Boxer* (1997), is arguably even more of its time in its handling of the contemporary rhetoric of compromise that dominated the politics of the decade to varying degrees. It deals with the changed political landscape of Northern Ireland by focusing on its impact on someone who has served fourteen years in prison and who needs to restart his life in a place that is attempting to move away from everything that gave his time inside any meaning. The film is an uneasy mixture of melodramatic love story and contemporary political commentary, and McLoone's judgement of a key scene in which members of both the IRA and loyalist paramilitary groups sing 'Danny Boy' together at a boxing match as a 'crass impossibility' (2000: 78) is reflective of the overall critical consensus and, as McLoone says, of the most extreme kind of wishful thinking. If the film's making is obviously reflective of a changing Ireland, then, on the whole, its frame of reference remains within the traditional paradigms that have characterized the dramatization of the military conflict in the north with, in particular, there being a lack of fresh insight into the Protestant community that lurks in the film's shadows.

Marc Evans' *Resurrection Man* (1998) does bring the loyalist paramilitary community centre stage, but in a way that has generally been seen as crude and regressive in its treatment of the Protestant community. Ruth Barton in particular discusses the film as 'offensive' (2004: 163) on a number of fronts, though there is a sense in which Evans' film has been burdened by its release at such a time of political sensitivity. Barton and others seem to equate this knowing genre piece about a member of the notorious Shankill Butchers with a view of the Protestant community at large. This is, perhaps, understandable given the historical moment, but, especially given Evans' subsequent concentration on the horror genre, this seems a film preoccupied with post-Tarantino style as much as anything. There is little sense of involvement in a wider political struggle, and it is possible to argue that Evans' film attempts to legitimize the idea of Belfast as a place with a filmic existence outside the confines of political violence. Of course, this is ironic given the central character's concentration on the murder of Catholics, but his reference point is James Cagney rather than the red hand of Ulster and the film seems set in a grim postmodern landscape rather than the Belfast of checkpoints and armoured cars.

Thaddeus O'Sullivan's *Ordinary Decent Criminal* could in a sense be said to be a mirror image of *Resurrection Man* in that it is overtly focused on a major 'ordinary' criminal, whilst also possessing profound resonances for the politics of Ireland. Mired in controversy from the start, *Ordinary Decent Criminal* suffered from the release some three years earlier of *The General* (1997), John Boorman's take on the Dublin criminal Martin Cahill. Whilst *Ordinary Decent Criminal* calls its central character Lynch, it is fairly clear that Cahill is the inspiration here too. However, whilst *The General* is a more sombre, conventional bio-pic, shot in documentary black and white, *Ordinary Decent Criminal* gets away from a realist aesthetic and makes most of its stylistic references to the caper movie.

For Emer Rockett, *Ordinary Decent Criminal* is most important for its 'liberation' of Dublin in particular, and Ireland in general from the narrowness of definition imposed upon it by the twin burdens of, on the one hand, the conflict in the north and, on the other, the continual efforts to appeal to the world via a rural idyll. Referring to one of the film's key comic chase sequences, Rockett suggests that the film 'undercuts the dominant tourist (and film) image of the tranquil countryside, the log fires, the Irish music and the pint of Guinness, with images of a noisy congested Dublin'(2005: 240), whilst later in the film the character of Lynch (Kevin Spacey) makes explicit reference to a key focal point of the newly branded Ireland when he says to his gang 'We're number one, not the guards, not the IRA, not anyone else. The whole country is in awe of us, because of a little divine intervention – we're bigger than "Riverdance".'(Quoted in Rockett 2005: 247)

Rockett's analysis of the way that the film comments on the rapidly changing contemporary power relations within Irish society relies on the film's extensive use of the 'colonial' architecture of central Dublin:

> The Four Courts (actually the Customs House), the police station, the building outside which he leaves the police informant art expert, the National Gallery of Ireland (government buildings), the social welfare office, the Judge's house (once a Big House), and the bank of the opening scene as well as the one in the climactic scene at College Green (once the eighteenth century Irish Houses of Parliament), visually encapsulates the symbolic nature of his [Lynch's] crimes. That the Irish State should be represented as an ersatz coloniser is suggestive, and inevitably hints at the ambiguous relationship of Ireland to Britain (and, at the cultural level America)... (2005: 243)

For Rockett and others, then, *Ordinary Decent Criminal* is a key film amongst several that began to redefine the nature of Irish representation through a kind of playfulness with old debates about identity and the country's relationship to Britain. The film's adventurous approach to genre and film form, in general, as well as its implicit admiration for its lawless central character, can be read as indicative of a contemporary desire to be rid of guilt and obligation which have found expression in a range of films already discussed. The widespread circulation of such representations can in turn be said to be part of a shifting symbolic relationship between Britain and Ireland, one that I would argue furthers a sense of a wholly separate identity for Ireland, both North and South.

That Thaddeus O'Sullivan chose to work with an iconography that is essentially disruptive of traditional views of Ireland comes as no surprise to those that saw his first major breakthrough as a director, *December Bride* (1989). Here the landscape is entirely rural, but far from exploiting its picturesque qualities, O'Sullivan's film relies on a series of reversals of traditional representations. To begin with the film centres on a scandalous three-cornered relationship between a young woman, Sarah (Saskia Reeves), and two men who she originally keeps house for. The film is set in a strict Presbyterian community in an area of traditional rural beauty and, as Martin McLoone has pointed out, O'Sullivan's frequent use of a pounding Lambeg drum within such a landscape can itself be read as disruption of the norms of Irish representation:

... the insertion of Orange drums and a devout Presbyterian community into the Irish landscape is a reminder that the industrial workers of Belfast are only part of the Protestant story and that the romantic nationalism of Catholic Ireland is only part of the story of the Irish landscape. (1999: 30)

Just as December Bride is an example from a number of reconsiderations of the myth of idyllic rural Ireland so dominant in both the UK and the US, there has, of course, also been a series of films that have attempted, often in fairly gentle ways, to offer a vision of post-Peace Process Belfast that is attempting to redefine itself. Michael Winterbottom's With or Without You (2000) relegates its involvement with a 'Troubles' agenda very firmly to the sidelines with the central character, Vincent (Christopher Ecclestone), having left his promising RUC career for a job as a glazier in his father-in-law's small firm. This central metaphor of movement from participant in conflict to one who mops up after it is over is generally treated lightly, and the film is a not altogether satisfying comic mix of infertility and infidelity. Its value for those desperate for a post-Troubles cinema seems to lie in its setting and art direction in particular, with extensive use being made of Belfast's Waterfront Hall, which for many is symbolic of the city's aspiration to accompany Dublin to the promised land of recognition as a city fit for the European weekend-break crowd. Tellingly, despite Winterbottom's growing reputation and the presence of two rising British stars (Ecclestone and Dervla Kirwan), the film failed to secure any kind of distribution and became part of a raft of failed ventures that contributed to the decline of FilmFour – a Belfast without the frisson of helicopter searchlights and city centre checkpoints proving difficult to sell apparently.

In a similar vein, though slightly more successful, was Divorcing Jack (1998), and it is tempting to associate the film's comparative success (though it still fell far short of the expectations of its various backers) with its eventual de-bunking of the idea of Belfast as a hip, post-Troubles city. The film is the first feature-length adaptation of a novel by the phenomenally popular Colin Bateman and, though largely operating through the black humour for which Bateman is famous, it is essentially a highly cynical view of post-Peace Process Northern Ireland. It is also, for all its black humour, an essentially conservative film in that oldest of traditions that displays the perils of adultery with the hero relieved to be safely home with his forgiving and long-suffering wife as the credits roll.

The film's early scenes include one shot at the same Belfast Waterfront Hall that features so heavily in With or Without You, but whereas Winterbottom's film largely remains in this new Belfast of glass, steel and pavement cafes, Divorcing Jack only uses the concert hall and the loft-style apartments to lull its audience into a false sense of security. Barely half an hour into the film and the European art-house style romance between the Belfast satirical journalist Dan (David Thewlis) and the student he meets on a park bench (Laura Fraser) has been brutally interrupted by Margaret's very bloody murder. The film is set on the day of the (fictional) elections for a new Northern Ireland 'government' and the front runner in the race to be the country's first 'prime minister' is the candidate that claims to rise above the past and to transcend sectarian divisions. Naturally, by the end of the film, he is seen as the most brutally cynical of all the many candidates we get to meet.

The huge popularity of the Bateman novel and the reasonably positive reception of the film, especially in Northern Ireland, suggest that *Divorcing Jack* captured the post-Peace Process zeitgeist more successfully than the glossier vision of *With or Without You*. However, it would be a mistake to overrate the film's political acumen which amounts to little more than the long-held British mainland view that all the political violence in Ireland can be laid at the door of criminal gangs on both sides of the sectarian divide, all of whom are as bad as each other. This is reinforced in *Divorcing Jack* through the often very funny, though politically unsophisticated, representation of the paramilitary hoods through the classic iconography of the gangster movie.

According to Brian McIlroy, Colin Bateman saw his original novel as a 'unionist thriller' (1999: 56) and it is in these terms that McIlroy praises *Divorcing Jack* as one of the few films to address the problem of a lack of Protestant voices in dramatic fictions about the politics of the north. However, the film barely mentions that the leading character, Dan Starkey, comes from a unionist background and, instead, as McIlroy himself says, 'occupies that intellectual middle-class centre ground, a man who wishes the warring factions would destroy themselves rather than the innocent people around them'. (1999: 60) Whilst such a position is an entirely understandable emotional response by someone who has lived through the Troubles, it hardly represents any kind of intellectual position, let alone a new secular Protestant one that has been given voice by the Peace Process.

As John Hill has recently pointed out, the removal from the Starkey character of the novel's attribution of an overt unionist sensibility left the film devoid of any moral centre, something which led the producers to insert at the end an entirely incongruous speech on behalf of 'the individual'. (2005: 232) As Hill says, this tacked-on device is entirely undermined by the main strength of the film which is Starkey's dark, cynical world-view, which would scoff at such easy liberal sentiment.

However, it is still possible to argue for the representative importance of *Divorcing Jack* through its sheer irreverence for both political and filmic certainties, the two things being ultimately intertwined in the films impact. The *Sight and Sound* review of the film (Kemp 1998: 42) understandably makes much of the entrance of Lee Cooper (Rachel Griffiths), a gun-toting nun who turns out to be a strip-o-gram by night and nurse by day and it is at the level of such playfulness with filmic clichés that *Divorcing Jack* ultimately works best. In the end, though, there is little denying its fundamentally reactionary stance, particularly through its ending in which, as has already been suggested above, the 'hero' Starkey returns to his wife and their so-called 'magic settee' (on which they frequently make love). As Hill suggests, Starkey's chaotic straying into the world of sectarian politics and violence is started by his temptation into adultery, and the film's ending restores equilibrium only through a simplistic denunciation of all the political actors in the north:

In a sense this concluding coda reinforces the conservative nature of the film's outlook. Starkey's involvement in the world of 'chaos' has been precipitated by the appeal of marital infidelity. His escape from 'chaos', and return to normality is signalled by his return to the marital home and reconciliation with his wife. In this way the film is pressing home the dangers of straying from the security of home and marriage but also counterpointing this private, domestic universe to the threatening world of public disorder beyond the home. It has been a common feature of 'troubles' movies to set up a conflict between the 'private' spheres of romance, home and domesticity and the 'public' world of politics and violence. In this way, for all its postmodern twists, *Divorcing Jack* conforms to a longstanding tradition of representing the Northern Irish conflicts. (2005: 234–5)

The most obvious signifiers of a film culture responding to the rapid changes of the role of Ireland in any notion of Britain are, then, films that offer us images of a place of change, a society alive with possibilities that transcend the traditional narratives of either violent conflict or rural whimsy. Perhaps harder to assess, but equally significant, are films typified by the unexpectedly successful (in terms of distribution) *Magedelene Sisters* (2003), which could just as easily be discussed in the chapter on Scotland because of the origins of its director, Peter Mullan, and a significant proportion of its funding which came from Scottish Screen. However, funding also came from the Irish Film Board, and, more importantly, the film makes a striking contribution to the confrontation of old certainties that has characterized a great deal of the cinema that this chapter has discussed. What makes *Magedelene Sisters* different from most of the cinema from either side of the Irish border that has been discussed so far is that its contribution to a new sense of Ireland is its relentless honesty about a dimension of Irish history that runs directly counter to the predominant myths of rural Ireland that have tended to dominate its cinematic history.

One of the smaller of the many visual shocks available in Mullan's film is the glimpse we get of the photograph of John F. Kennedy that sits on the desk of the sadistic nun that runs the Magedelene laundry that is the setting of the film. In fact, we have already been told in a caption that the date is 1964, but, nevertheless, it still feels impossible to credit that such scenes of Victorian hard labour and brutality were taking place in the decade of The Rolling Stones, Jane Fonda and Jean-Luc Godard. Kennedy's photograph, glimpsed only very briefly two or three times during the film, serves to remind us of the terrible isolation of the women from any sense of a wider world and, in turn, to emphasize the extent of the grip of the Catholic Church on large swathes of the Irish population such a short time ago.

Although *Magedelene Sisters* is a relatively straightforward treatment of a story that is becoming more and more familiar as Ireland continues its journey away from Catholic dominance, its refusal to shy away from the physical and mental horrors of the Magedelene laundries has a great deal of raw power. In scene after scene, young women who have committed no crime are subjected to beatings, sexual abuse, spartan living conditions and the mental torment of separation from families and any kind of normal social contact. There are a number of scenes in which Mullan employs iconography which sparks comparisons to even darker episodes in European history. A clear example is a scene where a group of the younger women are forced to strip naked and are then subjected to mocking abuse from a senior nun who delights in passing obscene comment on their bodies. Such sadistic manipulation of power and the display of the twisted internal values generated by this distorted, closed society cannot help but transport us to filmic representation of the more brutal atrocities that have haunted Europe since 1945, especially as the final credits tell us that 30,000 women passed through the laundries.

Reaction to the film from the Catholic Church in Italy was reportedly strong, but in Ireland the audiences were enormous, and the Church remarkably silent (See Mullan 2004). In some ways this is not surprising given the plethora of sex-related scandals that have beset the Church in Ireland and the UK in recent years. On the other hand, the widespread distribution of the film in Ireland, the UK and the US amounts to a significant contribution to a shift in the way that cinema is able to deal with Irish history, not simply in terms of the oppressive theocracy, but also in broader gender terms. Clearly there is a risk of adding to negative stereotypical notions of a Catholic Ireland, but outweighing this is the sense of a mature culture able to face its past in the context of a mature present that includes a complex variety of representations within its visual culture.

Magedelene Sisters can be read then as part of the significant contribution made by contemporary cinema to the cultural redefinition of Britishness through its willingness to face the trauma of a recent history that goes beyond ideas of nationalism and the relationship with Britain. It is part of a generation of Irish films that demonstrates a plural Ireland: one that contains cities with glass-and-steel homages to contemporary culture, smart coffee houses and all the paraphernalia of European tourist destinations, but also many unresolved tensions, many of which still need to be understood by reference to history, however painful that may be. If there is optimism, it is to be found in a tentative new honesty and relative freedom from the old taboos, whether this be through the dark comedy of the *Divorcing Jack* or the unrestrained anger and brutal realism of *Magedelene Sisters*.

If a single historical moment can be said to have been central to the populist imagining of the Troubles it surely occurred on 30th January 1972 when a civil rights march ended in tragedy when members of the parachute regiment shot dead thirteen civilians and wounded many others in the Bogside area of Derry. That the 30th anniversary of the event should have been marked by the making of two British films about the tragedy is, in many ways, one of the most significant shifts in the way that the mainstream media have come to represent Ireland in the last decade. Whilst, on the one hand, both *Sunday* (2002) made solely for Channel 4 and *Bloody Sunday: A Day in History* (2002) return to the iconography of armed conflict and urban deprivation in their representation of the country, they do so in order to radically re-appraise (at least in terms of the mainstream British media) an event in recent history that has always been amongst the most sensitive of all for both sides of the armed conflict in the north.

Whilst *Sunday*, scripted by leading television writer Jimmy McGovern, was made exclusively for television, *Bloody Sunday* was given a theatrical release whilst also being given a British television airing close to the date of the anniversary of the event itself. In a sense it is the idea of the two films being made itself that represents the their true significance in this context, (though it is fair to say that the latter, directed by Paul Greengrass, achieved widespread success on the international festival circuit). After two decades in which the British government and most of the British media remained in virtual denial about the events and their role in escalating the armed conflict, the mainstream television showing of two films that demonstrated clearly that unarmed civilians had been shot by British soldiers was of the highest importance as part of a process of re-imagining the north of Ireland.

This is not, of course, to say that there is no difference between the two films. It is widely accepted that *Sunday* suggests a responsibility for the shootings that goes much more directly to the heart of government, whilst Greengrass's film sees the culture of the Parachute regiment and the official sanctioning of a more generally aggressive style of soldiering in the province as more likely to have been behind the events. Some reviewers have seen *Bloody Sunday* as part of an international tradition of representing the kind of conflict seen in the north of Ireland which arguably gives the film a particularly postcolonial resonance:

> Its analogues are not handsomely calibrated, patriotic combat movies like *Saving Private Ryan* and *Black Hawk Down*, or even the Troubles films of Loach (*Hidden Agenda*) and Leigh (*Four Days in July*), but scrupulously unglamorous and anti-rhetorical historical re-creations like Gillo Pontecorvo *Battle of Algiers* and Costa-Gavras' *Z*. (Fuller 2002)

Cinematically *Bloody Sunday* asserts its credibility by draining all the qualities of conventional drama from the shootings themselves and throughout the film by drawing heavily on the documentary aesthetics familiar to Greengrass from his early career. *Sunday* on the other hand is much closer to character-led television drama as McGovern creates a fictional landscape rooted in the testimony of people close to the events themselves. Whereas Greengrass's focus is on local politicians, civic leaders and army commanders, McGovern mainly follows who, in one sense or another, would become the victims of the conflict. In their different ways, both films make contributions to a newly liberated sense of the origins of the armed conflict in Ireland and take such insights to sizeable audiences. Whilst filmic re-appraisals of the conflict were gradually becoming more and more commonplace, the actual events of Bloody Sunday were so symbolically important as to make the release of two films so close together of a significance much greater than any new light than either was able to shed on the events themselves.

Continuing this spirit of honesty into more recent Irish cinema, though, with the focus not on external colonizing forces, but rather on disruptions to the contemporary image of Ireland as a tolerant, European social democracy, is the quasi-documentary feature *Pavee Lackeen* (2005). The film scrutinizes the life of Winnie, a 10-year-old Irish traveller girl and her family who are barely surviving as they live in a battered trailer on wasteland on the edge of Dublin without water or basic sanitation. *Pavee Lackeen* has little or no narrative progression except that it appears to show the duplicity of the local authority as it seeks to avoid its responsibility to house Winnie and her family.

The ultra harsh conditions in which the travellers live, the illiteracy of Winnie's mother, Rose, and the casual marginalization of the travellers are all put on display by the unrelenting gaze of the documentary style without sentimentality. Furthermore, what is never explicit but clearly present throughout the film is the relationship of such a community to contemporary Ireland's (Dublin especially) 'brand' or sense of itself. Ultra conscious of its modernity in the era of the Celtic Tiger, the principal images of contemporary Ireland have tended to eschew anything approaching the kind of life lived by Winnie and her family. That *Pavee Lackeen* has been released to considerable acclaim across Europe is for many a welcome corrective to the sometimes relentless re-branding of Ireland/Dublin that has gone on for the best part of a decade. By drawing on the world of the traveller that has so often been at the core of a British racist attitude to the Irish with its reference to 'tinkers' and the like, *Pavee Lackeen* opens up the fault lines within contemporary Irish society, rather than using reference points from outside. That this is possible within contemporary Irish film culture suggests a postcolonial honesty and freedom that has at least some space amongst what has seemed to some an increasingly market-orientated environment. This does not of course make such a small token any kind of panacea. As Fiachra Gibbons makes clear, what has sometimes been referred to as Ireland's apartheid is very deeply entrenched indeed:

> They get it in the neck from everyone, north and south, official and revolutionary. Rosie had to fight for a year in the courts to get Winnie a place in the local primary school. No one wants the trouble. Discrimination is so deep that the worst abuse is justifiable. Ireland is currently divided over the trial of a Mayo farmer who battered a traveller he found on his property with a plank, then shot him in the hip and hand, before reloading to finish off the fleeing man. Pádraig Nally was cleared of murder but jailed for six years for manslaughter, yet his many supporters are still protesting that the sentence was too harsh. (Gibbons 2006)

Gibbons goes on to further implicate paramilitary elements in the persecution of travellers and assert *Pavee Lackeen*'s right to be considered among the few truly honest Irish films of recent times. In the context of a discussion of the way that cinema has contributed to a re-consideration of Britain, *Pavee Lackeen* is undoubtedly of some significance. Even down to its title, which means 'traveller girl' in an Irish Gaelic dialect common amongst travellers, the film attempts to re-capture the language and imagery of contemporary Irish culture from those who would impose upon it a new orthodoxy based upon its economic value. As Gibbons says later in the same piece it is truly astonishing that the pre-twentieth-century life of Winnie and her family should be taking place 'in the wealthiest postal district of the third richest city on earth' (Gibbons, 2006). What would once have been almost as shocking is that such a film should be made in Ireland and be praised for its honesty, that this is now even slightly less the case is an important contribution to a different kind of national redefinition, and one that asserts a new sense of separation from an older colonized identity.

At the time of writing, actual political devolution in the north of Ireland is once again an aspiration rather than a reality. On the other hand, as the increase in cheap flights and weekend breaks testify, there has been a fundamental shift in the way that Belfast, in particular, and Irishness, in general, function in the popular imagination. Some of this amounts to little more than the replacement of one set of reductive urban paramilitary stereotypes with an equally grotesque tourist board vision of cities crammed with European-style cafes and villages modelled on *Ballykissangel*. As we have seen, the best of recent cinema from both the north and south of Ireland has proved capable of an interrogation of such images from a variety of perspectives whilst also asserting and clearly demonstrating the capacity of the film-maker working in Ireland to break free from the burden of national representation.

Whilst the last decade in Ireland has undoubtedly witnessed a number of brave and powerful engagements with competing narratives of the armed conflict and the turbulent history of relations with Britain, perhaps equally significant in terms have been films that have problematized the simple equation of oppression and colonialism. Films that have examined a 'priest-ridden' past, contemporary racism and a desire to join an international cultural elite all, in different ways, are part of an assertion of an increasingly diverse and confident culture. A culture with cinema playing its part in ensuring that the country becomes, as Michael Higgins was quoted as saying at the start of this chapter, a 'maker' of imagers rather than simply a consumer.

'We Can't Even Pick a Decent Country to be Colonised By': Scotland and Cinema

Of the four countries under discussion, it is, perhaps, in Scotland that it is possible to find the clearest manifestations of a post-devolutionary sensibility in cinema. As Duncan Petrie has said, 'One of the most interesting and significant developments in British film making in the 1990's was the emergence of a distinctive cinema in Scotland.' (2001: 55) Furthermore this emergence, as Petrie goes on to say, was one of the most effective and striking challenges to conventional ways of describing 'British' cinema and of providing a riposte to the idea that it 'could somehow still be considered a culturally homogeneous or unified entity'. (2001: 55)

As has been the case to greater or lesser extents for the other British 'nations', this chapter cannot be entirely confined by the actual moment of political devolution. Instead it will take the growth of a devolutionary momentum in Scotland and the response to that by film-makers as its central focus which will necessitate the inclusion of work from throughout the 1990s. Whilst beginning at any precise moment is something of a distortion, there is something of a consensus that during the 1990s Scottish film began to revive again in a number of ways after the lull that followed the short-lived 1980s 'boom' focused mainly on the early films of Bill Forsyth.

For Petrie, who has been the most active of those who have documented the recent renaissance in Scottish cinema, this boom has clear foundations in a number of strategic decisions made by those in a position to secure investment in Scottish film production. These include the expansion of the Scottish Film Production Fund, the introduction by the City Council of the Glasgow Film Fund and the establishment of Scottish Screen which now administers both Lottery funds and the Film Production Fund itself (Petrie 2000: 173–80). In British terms this represented a genuinely concerted effort to establish a production base in Scotland that was clearly linked to a wider devolutionary impulse. It resulted not only in an increase in the number of 'Scottish' films, but also in the attraction to Scotland of a number of productions utilizing Scottish talent such as the series made by London-based Parallax Films and directed by Ken Loach. As Petrie says, 'All of this has helped to establish Glasgow as the most cinematically high-profile British city outside London in recent years'. (2000: 56)

However, Petrie's strong argument for the existence of a fragile, but distinctive, 'devolved' Scottish cinema has not been based solely on the scale of the production base, but rather on what he sees as a distinctive aesthetic, far more capable of absorbing influences from both American independents and European art cinema. This, he argues, is what has protected a 'devolved' Scottish cinema from the dominant commercial wisdom of contemporary mainstream 'British' cinema based mainly in London, with its obsession with emulating high-profile genre box office successes such as *Lock Stock and Two Smoking Barrels* (Guy Ritchie 1998) or *Notting Hill* (Roger Michell 1999). Such an analysis is based largely upon, on the one hand, the street-smart *Shallow Grave* (Danny Boyle 1994) and *Trainspotting* (Danny Boyle 1996) and, on the other, on the more oblique detachment of *Ratcatcher* (Lynne Ramsay 1999) or *Orphans* (Peter Mullan 1997). Whether such an analysis is sustainable across the broader landscape of recent Scottish cinema and moreover whether it has held up as Scottish cultural devolution has tried to develop since 1998 will be the questions that inform the bulk of this chapter.

The 1990s before devolution

There is little doubt that the two films made in the mid-1990s by the team of Andrew Macdonald, John Hodge and Danny Boyle were central to the revival not only of a Scottish film culture, but were also hugely significant for UK film as a whole. First, *Shallow Grave* and, later, *Trainspotting* have tended to take on a significance which when added to the release of *Rob Roy* (Michael Caton-Jones 1995) and *Braveheart* (Mel Gibson 1996) during the same period in the middle of the decade elevated cinema to the forefront of the frenetic scramble for a new Scottish aesthetic prior to the creation of a new political landscape. In reality, of course, these are very different films with different origins and different agendas, but the historical moment of their release and the coming together of a critical mass of 'new' cinematic images of Scotland produced a sense of something altogether more concerted.

It is obviously not even true that Scottish cinema in the 1990s began with this group of films, and it is certainly worth briefly considering the kind of work that emerged from the earlier part of the decade and the contribution it began to make to a Scotland anticipating real change after such a period of sustained disenfranchisement under successive Tory governments. To begin with it is fair to say that Scottish cinema in the period immediately preceding the mid-decade revival has received very little coverage. Typical of such a tendency is the work of Ian Sellars whose two features, *Venus Peter* (1989) and *Prague* (1992), were seen as Scottish art cinema in the tradition of Bill Douglas (with whom Sellars worked on Douglas's trilogy), but who does not even warrant a mention in either Robert Murphy's *British Cinema of the 90's* or the same critic's *The British Cinema Book*. Apart from Petrie's *Screening Scotland*, the decade appeared to begin for most writers on Scottish film around 1995 and 1996. What this misses, perhaps, is the start of a tendency towards a particular kind of distinctive sensibility that later got so much attention when it surfaced again in the films of Lynne Ramsay and Peter Mullan.

Prague is perhaps instructive as an example both of what was admirable about what a number of film-makers were attempting at the turn of the decade, but also of the kind of controversies that were engendered within such a tight funding regime. To take the latter point first, *Prague* received funding of around £130,000 from the Scottish Film Fund, which at the time represented a considerable portion of the total budget and this in turn enabled the company to attract a range of European co-funding. Colin McArthur has strongly argued that such funding was hugely disproportionate and, furthermore, to support his case, McArthur argues that the film had far too little to do with Scotland to be funded to this extent. (1993: 30–2) McArthur's argument has, of course, got wide implications for much of the material in this volume, but to take the limited example of *Prague* alone it is possible to argue as Petrie has done (1996: 100) that *Prague* is a distinctive film for Scotland precisely because it seeks to take its story which begins in Scotland and link it to a wider European identity. In telling the story of its central character's (Alan Cumming) search for a piece of film that will help to complete the story of his grandparent's struggles as European Jews under the Nazis, *Prague* is arguably reflective of a widespread pre-devolutionary feeling that Scotland should associate itself more and more with Europe, as it were 'beyond' Britain. Unfortunately, the film became an early example of a production widely associated with the derogatory term 'Europudding', though largely one suspects for relatively superficial reasons such as the pan-European cast which boasted significant performers such as Sandrine Bonnaire and Bruno Ganz.

Petrie makes the convincing argument that Sellars' work, alongside that of those such as Margaret Tait who have sought to work in what might loosely be described as a European art-house tradition, is a vital dimension to the emergence of a new Scottish cinematic sensibility because it connects Scotland to a wider European tradition. In Sellar's case this extends to the subject matter of his film as well as the aesthetic traditions within which he works. As Petrie puts it, 'In his own quiet and tangential way, Sellar uses the quest [of the central character] to implicate Scotland in European history, and this, in turn, raises important questions about the nature of contemporary European identity.'(1996: 100)

Whilst the work of Sellar and Tait could reasonably be said to be most representative of the work that emerged from Scotland in the early 1990s, it would be false to suggest that it lacked entirely the more populist impulses that emerged in the middle of the decade and which will be discussed below. Stefan Schwartz's *Soft Top, Hard Shoulder* (1992) is a case in point with its clear connections to the earlier Scottish mini-boom of the early 1980s and the work of Bill Forsyth. The film is in fact quite explicitly connected to one of Forsyth's most critically and commercially successful films, *Local Hero* (1983), by the casting of Peter Capaldi in the lead role and through Capaldi's own screenplay with its references to minor details in Forsyth's film. *Soft Top, Hard Shoulder*, in a sense, provides a link both backwards to Forsyth and the Ealingesque 'quirkiness' in the humour and also forwards to the more hard-edged engagement with genre represented by *Trainspotting* and *Shallow Grave*. Like Forsyth's work, *Soft Top, Hard Shoulder* manages to contain a mild ambivalence about Scotland's appeal as a country whilst mostly avoiding the more obvious territory for those interested in national identity. This is a road movie in which the journey back home is undertaken unwillingly, though by the end there is the discovery of at least a more honest relationship with the idea of home and family.

It is, of course, the middle of the 1990s that has come to represent the really significant turning point in respect of a revival in the fortunes of Scottish cinema with the release not only of the two independent features involving the Producer/Director/ Writer team of Macdonald, Boyle and Hodge, but of the two historical epics *Rob Roy* and *Braveheart*.

Whilst the last of these clearly has little to do with Scottish cinema in any indigenous sense, the timing of its release and subsequent usage in various forms of political advertising makes it an important object of discussion in the context of the relationship of cinema to a changing British political landscape. Made by an Australian who had taken root in the United States, *Braveheart*'s importance to this chapter lies not so much in its relationship to contemporary Scottish cinema as in its illustration of the importance of cinema *per se* to the contemporary idea of Britain. The penetration of the imagery of *Braveheart* into one of the key moments in recent Scottish political history has been well documented and is well summarized by Sally Morgan:

> In the period leading up to the 1997 national referenda on devolution in both Scotland and Wales (which would result in the establishment of a Scottish Parliament and a Welsh Assembly) the media in the United Kingdom, and particularly in Scotland, was full of references to *Braveheart*. The Edinburgh-based newspaper *The Scotsman* (5 September 1997) warned the country to be 'Ready for a Braveheart frenzy' and, on the morning after the vote, the *Aberdeen Press and Journal* (12 September 1997) recorded that: 'The vote to give Scotland its first parliament in 300 years came on the 700th anniversary of "Braveheart" William Wallace's victory over the English at the Battle of Stirling Bridge.' Alex Salmond, the leader of the Scottish National Party (SNP), on hearing of the overwhelming 'yes' vote for the devolution of power to a new Scottish Parliament, announced on national UK television that Scotland looked forward to this self-determination with a 'Brave heart', causing a cheer of recognition to arise in the crowd around him. So caught up in this imagery was the SNP that, in the run up to the referendum they had distributed posters bearing an image of Gibson as Wallace along with the words: 'Today it's not just "Bravehearts" who choose independence – its also "Wise Heads" – and they use the ballot box.' (1999: 376–7)

Morgan's article goes on to make the point that in fact Mel Gibson's Wallace has little to do with Scottish history and is rather part of 'another phase of America's envisaging of herself'(1999: 390), with the central figure representing the archetype of a romanticized free-born postcolonial spirit. However, as she also concludes, what is remarkable is not the film itself, but its wholesale appropriation by certain elements with Scottish nationalist politics in order 'to fill a space created by the crumbling of "British" identity after the demise of the Empire and the consequent resurgence of the notion of a separate, self-determining Scotland.' (1999: 390)

The attention accorded to *Braveheart* can then be seen as a case study not of cinema's response to a changing Britain, but of a powerful recognition by politicians of the power of cinema in the creation of Anderson's 'imagined community'. Whilst *Rob Roy* (Michael Caton-Jones 1995) appeared on the surface to possess the potential to be similarly exploited it was never accorded anything like the same attention, though the proximity of the two film's respective release dates certainly caused them to be classed together in ways that were usually superficial. *Rob Roy* certainly has greater claims to being Scottish through its production and direction team, though in reality it is financed by United Artists with a Hollywood (albeit part-British) cast list. *Rob Roy's* main difference from *Braveheart* lies not in its inherent Scottishness, but more in the way that (comparatively) it resists the reductive uses to which *Braveheart* was put in the contemporary domestic political context. This is the result of the far more complex portrayal of divisions within the Scotland inhabited by Rob Roy Macgregor (Liam Neeson) rather than the simplistic Scotland/England divide posited by *Braveheart*. That said, *Rob Roy* is at heart a genre picture with its roots firmly in the western genre in which its screenwriter, Scotsman Alan Sharp, had originally made his name. In this sense the film does possess at least a passing relationship to questions of colonialism, but it recognizes too that colonial oppression has often drawn heavily on various forms of internal collaboration in return for personal advancement and it is this that made it less accessible to those that used *Braveheart* both as internal propaganda in the run up to the devolution referendum and also, in America, as fuel for what Joyce Macmillan called 'diaspora dreaming'. (Cited in Morgan 1999 : 378)

The year that *Rob Roy* was released saw the first commercial success connected to an investment by the new Glasgow Film Fund in the shape of *Shallow Grave*. Although their investment was small – £150,000 out of a total budget of £1m – the example it set was to become a truly significant catalyst for a whole raft of similar scale projects over the coming years. The funding pattern of *Shallow Grave*, with the bulk of its finance coming from a broadcaster (in this case Channel 4) and the Glasgow Film Fund topping up to ensure the viability of theatrical release, was to be copied by a number of small-scale Scottish successes which will be discussed later in the chapter and, moreover, its relentless energy and revelling in the callous black humour would spawn countless pale imitations in Britain over the next decade.

For a film that contains the line 'This could have been any city – they're all the same', *Shallow Grave* was recognized quickly by many reviewers as distinctively Scottish with Philip Kemp in *Sight and Sound* asserting that 'To claim *Shallow Grave* as a British film would be misleading. It's very much a Scottish film in its dry, razor-edged humour and its knack of cutting to the narrative quick...' (Kemp 1995: 58) While it may be difficult to sustain the reasoning behind Kemp's analysis, it is easy enough to agree with its central assertion. At every opportunity the film's art direction foregrounds both the distinctive architecture of Edinburgh's Georgian New Town and the distinctive characteristics of the newly affluent young professionals that inhabit its spacious converted flats. The raw energy of the film's opening sequence, as a camera mounted on a speeding car races through the streets of Edinburgh to a track by Leftfield, announces the film's intentions clearly enough and is sustained visually in the vivid colours and sparse furnishing of the flat that is to be the location for so much of the film. There is little doubt that this is Edinburgh, but it is a long way from the tourist board images of the castle or Arthur's seat. Moya Luckett sees this stylization of the Scottish city as part of a clear and deliberate attempt to break with older versions of Scottishness and construct a 'playful attitude towards Scottish iconography and cultural traditions'. (2000: 92)

As Luckett goes on to say this is brought most sharply into focus by a bizarre scene in which the three central characters, Alex (Ewan Macgregor), Juliet (Kerry Fox) and David (Christopher Ecclestone), attend a charity ball at which most of the guests wear tartan. Curiously, Luckett reads the fact that even the iconoclastic Alex wears tartan and enthusiastically joins in with the Scottish dancing as evidence of how 'modern Scots respect their culture and tradition but are not defined or limited by it' (2000: 92), whereas the dominant cynicism of the film's dialogue would suggest rather that Alex is merely engaging in playful parody, adopting an exaggerated version of Scottishness for his and his friends' amusement.

As Luckett later suggests this is a film that deals in the surfaces that are the mainstay of its characters lives. It is above all a film about image-consciousness and the essentially superficial nature of so much modish contemporary living defined by Sunday colour supplement style pages. This is not to suggest, however, that it is any sense po-faced. On the contrary there is a sense of revelling in the wit that underpins the cruelty and cynicism of the central characters' moral universe, most memorably in an extended sequence where the three interview for a new flatmate humiliating a succession of hapless candidates as they fire questions at them in the manner of an interrogation. As a portrait of a Scotland cranking up to formalize its independence it is a startlingly brutal vision of the affluent professional young who have abandoned politics and best understand the world through the relentless pursuit of wealth and status.

In filmic terms, however, *Shallow Grave* was to demonstrate to a generation of film-makers that it was possible to work in a British context whilst escaping the normally accepted confines of British cinema. As countless reviews made the obvious comparisons with Tarantino and the Coen brothers, the film's Scottishness took on a different meaning and set a tone for a decade of Scottish film that came to be known for its highly developed sense of cine-literacy with reference to both North America and Europe. In the case of *Shallow Grave*, the balance is clearly in favour of North America, but it is the burgeoning American independent scene that is the key reference point, not Hollywood, and it is this alignment of a Scottish cinema with an international art-house sensibility that makes it significant in the context of a Britain that was about to institutionalize its changing cultural shape.

In an interview that coincided with the result of *Shallow Grave*'s release, its director, Danny Boyle, appeared anxious to distance the film from the work of those such as Ken Loach with what he saw as a tendency to preach to audiences. He chose instead to emphasize the film-maker's responsibility to entertain and provide the narrative drive that the audience seeks (Bennett 1995: 34–6). To find a view of a changing Scotland or a changing Britain in the film, one has to resist such directorial protestations and read the obsession with style and surface as a double-edged judgement on a culture, which, while memorably casting off the constraints of a puritanical mistrust of visual opulence, can also breed the steely cruelty exhibited by the flatmates in *Shallow Grave*. In Boyle's next film, the state of the (Scottish) nation becomes a much more explicit concern, albeit still in the context of a film with its eye firmly on the audience that had flocked to the films of Tarantino and his imitators. In one of *Trainspotting*'s key scenes for those who would emphasize its state-of-the-nation qualities, the characters make a rare journey out from the urban landscape that dominates the film and sit looking at the rolling hills:

TOMMY: Doesn't it make you proud to be Scottish?

RENTON: I hate being Scottish. We're the lowest of the fucking low, the scum of the earth, the most wretched, servile, miserable, pathetic trash that was ever shat into civilization. Some people hate the English, but I don't. They're just wankers. We, on the other hand, are colonized by wankers. We can't even pick a decent culture to be colonized by. We are ruled by effete arseholes. It's a shite state of affairs and all the fresh air in the world will not make any fucking difference.

(Cited at http://www.generationterrorists.com/quotes/trainspotting.html)

What defines *Trainspotting*'s attitude to Scottish national identity then is a playful disgust at its central driving force, namely, the desire to be anything except English coupled with the usual, dated versions of Scottish representation. Even the film's setting is part of a central resistance to a clichéd sense of Scotland as it focuses its attention on squalid urban locations not in Glasgow, but in Edinburgh, usually the focus of tourist fantasies. The Edinburgh we see in *Trainspotting* is in many ways the flip side of the relentless chic style of *Shallow Grave* and, taken together, they form an acute vision of mid-1990s Scotland that has little to do with social realism and everything to do with situating Scottish film-making in the vanguard of international independent cinema that was breaking through to a mainstream audience. As Duncan Pertrie puts it:

The neo-expressionist aesthetic of *Trainspotting* draws on a number of inspirations including the paintings of Francis Bacon and Stanley Kubrick's 1971 film *A Clockwork Orange*, transcending the naturalistic limitations of low-key television dramas such as Peter McDougall's *Shoot for the Sun*. The film sets out to subvert expectation both at the level of representation of the experience of pleasure/pain at the heart of the junkie subculture and the depiction of contemporary urban Scotland. (Petrie 2000: 195)

In the decade since *Trainspotting* such subversion in relation to contemporary urban life has become more commonplace so it is harder to remember that the film's nihilism and refusal of an easy moral centre had rarely been seen before in British cinema (and it is much more hard-edged in the novel) and that previous representations of Scottish working-class life may well have shown it as difficult and full of hardship, but with some sense of a purpose or pride. *Trainspotting* on the other hand is full of loathing, particularly for the false pieties that try to construct a sense of belonging to a place so rotten at the core. Andrew O'Hagan quotes a passage spoken by Mark Renton in Irvine Welsh's original novel, which was omitted from the film but still keenly expressed in much of what the characters say and do:

"Ah've never felt British, because ah'm not. It's ugly and artificial. Ah've never really felt Scottish either, though. Scotland the brave, ma arse; Scotland the shitein cunt. We'd throttle the life out of each other fir the privelege ay rimmin some English aristocrat's piles." (Cited in O'Hagan 1996: 8)

O'Hagan goes on to argue that such a searingly honest vision of contemporary Scotland was, ironically, much more likely to engender a genuinely broad-based attitude in favour of some measure of independence than all the pantomime nationalism of *Braveheart*.

This kingdom is in trouble at the extremities. If there are to moves in such places towards self-government... then such moves are unlikely to be hurried on their way by the wits of Mel

Gibson. *Trainspotting* is set in a Scotland that has hitherto been without existence for filmgoers. It features places that are little known outside of themselves. It is to the like of *Trainspotting* that people will go for a sense of what life is like there, for a sense of what has gone wrong... *Trainspotting*, of course, will carry little of this by itself, and neither would it want to... The makers of *Trainspotting* and the novelist with whom it originated, won't be looking for much more than a few laughs. And they'll get their laughs. But it is laughter in the murk – once the giggling stops, people may start to examine the murk. (1996: 8)

Whether this was borne out is finally hard to determine. We know that the 1998 referendum was a resounding success and, as discussed above, that *Braveheart* featured heavily in the advertising campaign for a 'Yes' vote. It would be a brave politician that would use *Trainspotting* as part of their unique selling point. Of course none of this means that the film made no contribution to the growing sense of desire for a new Scotland, but its contribution is much more likely to be through, first, its daring in refusing the obvious way to make a 1990s film about drugs and, secondly, through making that daring a runaway international success. In achieving both of these things the film became one of the key cultural texts announcing a new Scottish independence of spirit well in advance of political change, whilst at a practical level its financial success provided the confidence that led to investment in the huge increase in Scottish production during the decade to come. A film whose anti-hero affected to despise the idea of 'Scotland' arguably became a key symbolic part of that idea turning into a political reality two years later.

As has already been indicated, the impact of the worldwide success of *Trainspotting* and, to some extent, *Shallow Grave* on Scottish cinema over the subsequent decade has been enormous, providing confidence to investors, policy-makers and the artists themselves that Scotland could be a significant centre for film-making, at least on a European scale. The two films also became hugely influential on British film-makers more generally and films that are often associated with this kind of work, such as *Twin Town* (Kevin Allen 1997), are discussed elsewhere in this volume. In short, the impact of these two films was to create an air of fashionability about contemporary Scottish culture that was undoubtedly mobilized in the political campaigns to come. The next section will now look specifically at cinema in the period after 1997, when devolution was back on the agenda and, subsequently, a political reality that could be engaged with by artists of all kinds.

Scottish cinema after devolution

Whilst there is little doubting the powerful influence of *Shallow Grave* and *Trainspotting* on the development of Scottish cinema in a generalized sense, it is equally interesting that what has followed in their wake in Scotland has been highly diverse rather than consisting of successions of would-be imitations. Whilst these two films encouraged the expansion of funding and confidence in the new devolved culture, film-makers themselves have taken significantly different paths. To oversimplify just a little, the post-devolution era has been characterized principally by two dominant strands with very different relationships to any idea of Scottishness: on the one hand there has been a Glasgow-set series of films by Ken Loach and his collaborators with a strong emphasis on the social-realist concerns that have always been Loach's territory, though with uniquely Scottish inflections at times, and on the other there has been the revival of what Duncan Petrie and others have discussed as the Scottish European art-house film (see Petrie

2001), most prominently in the work of Peter Mullan and Lynne Ramsey. Both strains of film-making have made strong contributions to the sense of a devolved cinema in Scotland and, conversely, both owe much to the funding structures that have themselves been refined and strengthened through the process of political devolution.

Loach's first 'Glasgow' film was, in fact, *Carla's Song* in 1996 which predates the moment of devolution, but ironically is the one in the 'series' that deals most directly with issues of colonialism, albeit the variety that uses guns and Contras secretly funded by a superpower rather than that sitting in an unrepresentative Westminster parliament. Though the film makes no direct attempt to draw real parallels between the situation in Nicaragua where much of the film is set and contemporary Glasgow where the story starts, there is a clear sense of an exploration of varieties of oppression and powerlessness. The central character, George (Robert Carlyle), is a Glasgow bus driver whose journey to Latin America is precipitated by his keen instinctive sense of injustice as he defends Carla (Oyanka Cabezas) when she is challenged by a zealous ticket inspector. That she is a very beautiful young woman with whom he falls in love was seen by some critics as undermining of the film's narration of political discovery, and most were not convinced by the uneasy combination of serious analysis and romantic adventure. (Smith 1997: 38)

In screenwriter Paul Laverty's introduction to the published screenplay of *Carla's Song* he talks movingly of his experiences of Nicaragua as a human rights lawyer during the long years of war and bitterly of the machinations of the Reagan and Bush governments in opposition to the legitimately elected Sandanista government. In particular he talks of the huge increase of urban begging and visible signs of poverty that he witnessed on a visit after the Sandinistas have been removed from power (Laverty 1997: 3). Though the film never attempts to force parallels (and it would be likely that Laverty's intimate knowledge of the torture and human rights abuses perpetrated by the American-backed Contras would make him resistant to any easy equation with the situation in the UK), there are surely links to a Scotland so bitterly resentful of the devastation of two decades of Tory rule and which was soon to result in the wiping out of any Tory representation at Westminster at the 1997 election. One of the key visible legacies of that era in Britain has been the re-emergence of street begging, and Laverty's words surely hint at a sense of the two society's disenfranchisement by different varieties of the far right in global politics.

It is, however, the fact of Loach being attracted to Glasgow by the funding available that was to prove more significant than *Carla's Song* itself for the future of an independent Scottish cinema over the coming decade. It extended the fund's influence to a director of truly international stature and enhanced the status of Scotland as a cultural environment that was seriously interested in cinema and could help put the funding in place to make films for an international audience. However, Loach and his collaborators' contribution to this sense of promise was only beginning with *Carla's Song* and was increased hugely by the much more positive critical reception given to *My Name is Joe* in 1998. This second Glasgow project directed by Loach was much more deeply 'Scottish' in every sense as its funding depended not only on the Glasgow Film Fund, but also the Scottish Arts Council National Lottery Fund, added to this was the much more exclusively Scottish setting and narrative and, of course, a central performance from Peter Mullan, destined to become one of the key figures in Scottish cinema over the next decade.

In terms of a changing Britain, *My Name is Joe* is clearly a film that looks back rather than forward, not necessarily in a negative sense, but as part of what Loach has clearly seen as his overdue debt to a society that had been ravaged by Thatcherism. In an interview not long after the release of *My Name is Joe*, Loach describes the principal motivation behind the films he made in the 1990s, an incredibly prolific period for him after the long silences of the 1980s:

> As Britain emerged from the spell that Thatcher had put on it, I and perhaps some other film-makers felt very dissatisfied with ourselves. We felt we hadn't put on the screen the appalling cost in human misery that aggressive Thatcherite politics had brought on everybody. We should have made films in the early eighties that really showed what was happening, but I know that I didn't. I think the last few years have been an attempt to remedy that. (Fuller 1998: 111)

For Loach, *My Name is Joe* is linked to *Riff-Raff* (1991), *Raining Stones* (1993) and *Ladybird, Ladybird* (1994) as portraits of a devastated British working class, though now the focus has shifted to Scotland and the new twist in the tale is that the landslide election of a Labour government has done little to change anything. For many, *My Name is Joe* was Loach's bleakest film to date with even long-time admirers such as John Hill suggesting that 'the sense of pessimism dominates completely' and that there is 'something remorseless about the way the narrative imposes its deterministic grip'. (Hill 1998: 21) It is tempting to ascribe this deepening of Loach's despair to the lack of radicalism within the New Labour government, with its strong Scottish element adding a further ironic twist of the knife in the context of *My Name is Joe*. There is certainly no evidence in the film either that the prospect of devolution and a measure of Scottish self-determination has impacted on Loach's Marxist analysis. On the whole Glasgow becomes another all too convincing backdrop to the narrative of alienation and despair that is woven through all Loach's 1990s films, though this time, as Hill suggests 'The film has no character who can offer a more politicised perspective...' (1998: 21).

For Loach the principal rationale behind using Scotland generally and Glasgow in particular for *My Name is Joe* (apart, of course, from the availability of funding in Scotland) seems to revolve around its reputation as a centre for substance abuse of every variety. In another interview in the same year as the film was made, Loach discussed Glasgow in ways that, at times, got close to an uncharacteristically stereotypical vision of the place:

> Scotland is a very hard-drinking country and Glasgow is a very hard-drinking city. Organizations like Alcoholics Anonymous are very effective, though. AA was the model for the opening scene in the film. Peter [Mullan], Paul [Laverty], and I went along to their meetings. But, of course, they are Alcoholics Anonymous, so they couldn't supply alcoholics for the film [laughs]. But you don't have much problem finding people who have had problems with drink in Glasgow. (Ryan and Porton 1998)

The film itself is obviously totally sympathetic to both the problems of alcoholism that beset the central character Joe Kavanagh and those of heroin addiction that are destroying the young couple that Joe tries to help, seeing them largely as the inevitable consequences of the hopelessness visited upon communities by poverty and unemployment. However, the vision of an 'emerging' Scotland that it presents is clearly diametrically opposed not only to tourist board clichés, but also those images of dynamic, progressive cities embracing a bright 'European' future beloved by some politicians making the case for a 'new' Scotland. There is little cappuccino or sushi in Loach's vision of Glasgow, though for some there is the endurance of something much more important, what Petrie calls 'a Glasgow where the last vestiges of community life manage to cling on in the form of small quiet interactions between friends, colleagues and lovers' (2000: 203), though for many the sheer hopelessness of the film's ending has the power to overwhelm these vestiges of optimism.

If *My Name is Joe* was arguably made a little too close to both the moment of devolution and the election of New Labour to be seen as genuinely reflective of a changed Scotland, then Loach's next 'Glasgow' film; *Sweet Sixteen* (2002) is unavoidably set in a world that was supposed to show at least some dim signs of change. Instead, we see an urban landscape where the grim reality of the drug-related economy has an even stronger grip on day-to-day existence and its victims are even less likely to find any means of escape. Like so much of Loach's work, *Sweet Sixteen* had its best reception in Europe where, for example, Paul Laverty won the principal screenwriting award at Cannes for the screenplay, whilst here many drew attention to the unremitting gloom of Loach's vision. However, there was also the opinion, voiced strongly by Ryan Gilbey in the context of an optimistic *Sight and Sound* feature on British cinema, that Loach and others were providing an essential antidote to the 'feel good' imitators of the likes of *Billy Elliot* or *The Full Monty*:

> ... Sweet Sixteen would seem uncompromising in any year, but context undoubtedly makes their achievements look even more significant. The most pressing concern is that the Miramaxation of what was formerly known as independent cinema has nurtured a desperation in film-makers to be placatory. New directors are bred to see the value in the coveted bums-on-seats, but not in less measured responses – throwing tomatoes at the screen, say, or stomping out of the cinema in a blind rage. In other words, cinema has become a safe place, and British cinema something of a franchise where certain names can engender in audiences those same feelings of comfort that a fast-food junkie experiences on glimpsing that big yellow 'M'. (Gilbey 2002: 17)

Ironically, then, in relation to the tourist board vision of Scotland, *Sweet Sixteen* succeeds in contributing to the idea of Scotland as a home to independent thought and vision precisely by running counter to a glossy vision of an emergent post-devolutionary Scottish culture. Loach's films suggest the cultural confidence to fund films that unflinchingly portray the post-industrial misery of urban Scotland and, what is more, a misery that it suggests is class-based, unlikely to be remedied by any parliament likely to occupy the expensive new building being erected at Holyrood.

Like so many of Loach's films, *Sweet Sixteen* was dogged by the tedious issue of 'unintelligible' accents. As always Loach used local actors, many completely inexperienced, and encouraged the use of their own natural voices. This time though he and his collaborators attempted a slight variation on the use of subtitles, at least in the rest of the UK, by including in the opening titles the announcement that the film's first fifteen minutes would be subtitled, but 'after that you're on your own like Liam [the film's main character] – nae problem'. It is a rare glimpse of humour in one of the bleakest Loach films to date, but it is also a gesture of defiance that marks out the film's territory from the start and it encourages us to see the film in a post-devolutionary context, even if Loach's politics appear to set little store by the ability of devolution to change much of the misery in the lives he portrays.

Loach's final Glasgow story at the time of writing is *Ae Fond Kiss* (2004), which many have seen as the closest he has got to romantic melodrama. It is also the closest that Loach has come to putting the politics of a broader identity, rather than class, at the heart of his narrative with the central protagonists being respectively a Roman Catholic woman (Roisin, played by Eva Birthistle) and a Muslim man (Casim, played by Atta Yaqub). They start a love affair and, inevitably, their backgrounds conspire to pull them apart in time-honoured fashion. In terms of Loach's work, what is perhaps even more remarkable is the contemporary Glasgow that the two characters inhabit: both are from a young upwardly mobile middle class that inhabits trendy bars, clubs and IKEA furnished flats and uses the cheap flight revolution to take breaks at short notice in the warmer parts of Europe. In a number of ways *Ae Fond Kiss* seems to be Loach's assertion that even the comfortable, liberal middle classes are not immune from the politics of ethnic and religious identity in an increasingly polarized and paranoid world.

Both Loach and Paul Laverty (the screenwriter) have been quite explicit about the film's genesis in the global atmosphere generated by 9/11 and, in particular, the implications of that for particular kinds of British (and Scottish) identity. Asked in an interview for the BBC's website where the idea of the film came from, Laverty replied:

> I suppose it was really coloured by September 11th. I was actually in the States when that incident took place. It was amazing just seeing the propaganda and how it was covered. Right in the middle of it I got an e-mail from a friend who's Asian Scottish. She told me of the experience of her nieces, how they were scared, frightened and touched by it. I just thought it was fascinating to see how young adolescents in Glasgow, simply because they were Muslim, are somehow targets for something happening in the States... And my friend said something to me that really struck home. She said, 'No matter how long I live here, I'll always feel like a stranger.' (Foley 2004)

However, the film is far from being a straightforward analysis of the problematic nature of contemporary black or Muslim identity and, for many, the balance of sympathy will be for the way that Roisin, white and Catholic, is treated by Casim's family. In the end, though, the film attempts to be not so much 'balanced' in a traditional liberal sense as reflective of what one review of the film referred to as the 'Balkanisation of culture and politics'(Bradshaw 2004 b.) in the middle of which Casim and Roisin are caught. In a sense Loach's choice to have his characters (especially Roisin) inhabit the bright airy living spaces that are part of contemporary Glasgow emphasizes the bitter irony of the survival of much darker instincts that surface so easily as the film's narrative unfolds. Perhaps the darkest of all comes not from the orthodoxy of Casim's family, but from the Catholic parish priest (Gerard Kelly) whose interview with Roisin in the smoky gloom of his study informs her that sexual relationships with 'any Tom, Dick or Mohammed' will prevent her from working in the Catholic secondary school where her work is so valued and popular.

As most reviewers tended to remark, *Ae Fond Kiss* is cautiously optimistic for its two central characters individual fates, as it ends with both of them defying the prejudices of their two communities by continuing their relationship. In Casim's case, though, we are left in no doubt of the massive impact on his family: his oldest sister, Rukshana (Ghizala Avan), will have to call off her own marriage because of the 'dishonour', and his much stronger younger sister Tahara (Shabana Baksh) will face even more intense pressure to give up her plans to study away from home when she goes to university. It is actually Tahara's actions in loudly asserting the full complexity of her identity in a classroom debate that is the initial catalyst for the film's central narrative: her remarks provoke anger and hostility outside the school gates, Casim intervenes and ends up chasing his sister's tormentors into the music room where Roisin is working. However, it is perhaps Tahara's words that provide the underpinning for the film's implicit plea for the recognition of the fluidity and rich complexity of contemporary Scottish identity: 'I'm a Glaswegian Pakistani woman teenager who supports Glasgow Rangers in a Catholic school'. Although Tahara's brother's life may recover from the trauma of the family rift, the film leaves one uneasy about the consequences of the politics of certain kinds of British identity in the post-9/11 world for the many Tahara's living in all parts of Britain today. *Ae Fond Kiss* certainly seeks to help us understand the fears that underpin Casim's father's (Ahmad Khan) entrenched attitude to his marrying an outsider, but it is also a darker warning about the dangers of ignoring how profoundly the nature of identity in a British multicultural society has changed and that we all try to ignore this at our peril.

Loach's unofficial 'trilogy' on contemporary Scotland ranges much more widely than most of his critics give him credit for and, taken together, the films form an uneasy portrayal of an evolving sense, within a broad social-realist framework, of what post-devolution Scotland is coming to mean. The work of both Lynne Ramsay and Peter Mullan has, so far, been much less directly concerned with any sense of contemporary Scottish reality, but equally it is no less relevant to the emergence of a changing Scottish identity. To begin with Ramsey's relatively small output to date, the most common reference point for critics has been the work of Bill Douglas with, for example, Duncan Petrie asserting that '*Ratcatcher* (1999) provided Scottish cinema with its most obvious homage to its most revered cine-poet.' (2004: 167). As has already been mentioned, Ramsey's work can also be related to a mid-point between *Ratcatcher* and Douglas through the work of those such as Ian Sellars and Margaret Tait in the late 1980s and early 1990s who could be seen as keeping alive a strain of European-inflected Scottish art-house cinema and in Petrie's view contributing the primary distinctive features of a 'devolved' Scottish cinema. (2001)

A quick glance at the time and place in which *Ratcatcher* is set would immediately lead to the conclusion that Ramsey's work was situating itself in precisely the tradition exemplified by Loach. It is set during a Glasgow dustman's strike in the early 1970s in an area where people aspire to get out of the crumbling tenements in which they live and to the new towns being built with a glimpse of the countryside. The poverty is unremitting and it is accompanied by domestic violence and exploitative and abusive sexual behaviour. However, after only a few frames, it is obvious that a different kind of sensibility is at work and that whilst Ramsey remains interested in telling the stories of the variously dispossessed characters she will choose to do it more through asking to look again, and in different ways, at the details of these lives rather than by foregrounding the root causes of the economic and social injustice that has made their world.

Although there is a tendency to automatically prefix the term 'art house' with 'European' the film-maker that Ramsey alluded to most often in the publicity that followed the release of *Ratcatcher* was, ironically, American:

'I wanted to make a film that was driven by emotion and images rather than narrative,' says the director, who was inspired to go into film-making after watching Maya Deren's avant-garde classic *Meshes of the Afternoon* (1943). Seen through the eyes of its 12-year-old protagonist, *Ratcatcher* shares that film's poetic subjectivity and its atmosphere of surreal, slightly sinister reverie. (Spencer 1999 a.: 17)

Ramsey's first feature is then firmly associated with the difficult, experimental and oblique traditions of art cinema whether it be North American or European. Yet *Ratcatcher* is essentially a simple, childlike fable interrupted at times by brutality and pain and it is perhaps the combination of what Petrie even refers to as 'understated naturalism' (2000: 216) with a photographer's obsessive dwelling on small details (Ramsey's original training was in still photography) that makes the film so distinctive and its contribution to contemporary Scottish film culture so complex.

This contribution can be seen on a number of different levels, not least of which is the emergence of a significant female voice in film that, in *Ratcatcher*, is interested in dealing with the traditional Scottish masculine experience in subtle ways. It is something of a pattern across post-devolutionary culture that there has been a belated emergence of a higher proportion of female artists who are central to a re-appraisal of the central images of the new nation, and Ramsey's work can be seen partly in that tradition. Her central character, James Gillespie (William Eadie), struggles to make sense of his role in the traditional Scottish working-class male world of his father and, as is so often the case, football becomes the battleground where the son's sense of difference emerges. In other hands this can become something of a clumsy metaphor (see, for example, the use of boxing in *Billy Elliot*), but Ramsey's shooting style and its insistent dwelling on detail away from the centre of the narrative make it simply a contribution to the disorientation and struggle for an identity that dominate James's short life rather than the single defining fact of his existence. *Ratcatcher* contains all the ingredients of a traditional essay on male-dominated Scottish urban deprivation, but chooses to look on it obliquely and totally eschew explicit moral and political judgements. In this sense, *Ratcatcher* has little to do with the 'new' Scotland emerging in the late 1990s. On the other hand, Ramsey asserts a new freedom to examine some of the central pillars of the representation of her culture and manages to create a sense of real ambivalence about what she sees. In an interview following the release of her second feature, *Morvern Callar* (2002) Ramsey was asked about the origins of *Ratcatcher*.

I remember the dustmen's strike in the 1970's, and it was quite weird because there were football pitches filled up to the goalposts with rubbish, it was really quite medieval. It was also the time when punk rock was starting and the Labour government was coming to an end, so there was a depression and an excitement in the air. When I did the research I though that it was much worse than I remembered.

So it started off with a place of deterioration with something new happening with a boy caught up in a very macho environment – he's quite sensitive, but he's not supposed to show it. It felt like a beautiful backdrop for that. (Andrew 2002)

Though set in the bleakest of urban landscapes and ending with the suicide of the hero, Ramsey's film still manages to find hope through the impulse of her central character to dream beyond his surroundings and through the startling images that she makes of the details of the lives that are also not sentimentalized. In the remarks above she talks about the end of something, but also of an excitement in the air and in the promise of such a startlingly original first feature from a young woman director, commissioned boldly by Andrea Calderwood at BBC Scotland, there is, perhaps, also a hint of the spirit of the excitement of the period surrounding devolution.

Ramsey's second feature *Morvern Callar*'s similarity to *Ratcatcher* lies principally in its mix of bold cinematic language with an essentially simple narrative that has an untimely death at its core, and for which the leading protagonists carry around some measure of guilt. Its critical reception was generally very favourable, with many critics not only admiring its seriousness, but also being seduced by its eclectic assurance around some key features of the contemporary cultural landscape. Linda Ruth Williams, for example, referred to it as 'perhaps the bravest, and certainly the coolest, film of the year', whilst unambiguously celebrating both its vibrant celebration of female pleasure and its eerie creation of the Scottish 'world' which the central character, Morvern (Samantha Morton), is so desperate to escape.

Morvern Callar is chiefly of importance in this context because of its extension of the idea of Scotland as the chief outpost of serious, demanding, independent cinema which in turn can be connected to the broader desire to foster cultural independence post-devolution. It does, however, through the very desolation of its vision of life in the film's Scottish sections, speak of a different kind of cultural confidence that begins to transcend the rhetoric of politicians and the tourist board. To begin with, Ramsey has actually talked of toning down the distinctive 'local' feel of Alan Warner's original novel, 'There were bits in the book that I was less interested in, like the crazy Oban culture, which I felt was quite parochial. I wanted to make it more generic.' (Andrew 2002)

Here, there is a sense of attempting to capture something which, whilst recognizably set in Scotland, is part of young female experience, at least in Western European terms. The film, of course, builds on this sense of a search for something beyond the confines of national identity with Morvern's use of the money she gets through her bizarre passing off of the novel her dead boyfriend has written as her own. The publisher's advance liberates her and enables her to escape to Spain and into a hedonistic embrace of club culture. Like *Human Traffic* (1999) did in the context of Wales, *Morvern Callar* uses the club scene as a way of connecting contemporary Scottish youth culture to a wider world mercifully free of the traditional trappings and concerns of national identity. In *Human Traffic* the characters' escape from the orthodoxies of life in contemporary Wales is virtual – the weekend becomes their territory and means of escape from the drudgery of service industry jobs and into the liberation of clubs and the drugs that give them meaning. In *Morvern Callar* the leading character has to escape the country altogether and make her connection with a wider Europe through the club scene that transcended national boundaries. In this respect Ramsey's second feature harks back to Ian Sellars's *Prague* which was discussed earlier (in fact, Ramsey was a student at the National Film and Television School where Sellar's was a tutor) and continues a strong tradition of film-makers whose sense of national identity is oblique, uneasy and based upon a desire to transcend the national and connect to a Europe that is less bound up with parochial British concerns about their internal borders.

Apart from Ramsey, arguably, the other most significant director to emerge from Scotland in the post-devolutionary period is Peter Mullan. Mullan's career as both actor and director is woven in and out of so much of late twentieth- and early twenty-first-century Scottish screen culture that it is tempting to see him as the single most significant figure in Scottish film during this period. Mullan's career also fascinatingly spans what could be called the different strains of film-making in Scotland with, on the one hand, his award-winning performance in *My Name is Joe* and, on the other, his much more oblique and 'European' feature directorial debut *Orphans* (1999). Duncan Petrie, in particular, has situated Mullan's work at the heart of what he has argued is a 'devolved' Scottish cinema, one based firmly upon a distancing of itself from 'British' social realism and, instead, seeking inspiration in bolder European forms:

> In a conscious attempt to distance *Orphans* from a social-realist esthetic, Mullan draws on an eclectic range of primarily European stylistic references, including the contemplative stillness of Bill Douglas or Terence Davies, the surrealism of Bunuel, the carnivalesque energy of Fellini, and the magic realism of Emir Kusturica. This stylistic richness is supplemented by a range of non-cinematic textual references running from Shakespeare to the New Testament to the scatological humour of Billy Connolly. (Petrie 2001: 56)

As was the case in the work of Lynne Ramsey there is sense, through the obvious debt to Bill Douglas, of picking up the threads of an ambitious Scottish art cinema that had flickered into life in the 1980s and early 1990s and injecting a new-found sense of confidence. Also, like Ramsey's work, *Orphans* chooses territory that has traditionally been the preserve of realist fictions, as a working-class family gathers to mourn the loss of a parent and the adult male children variously exhibit symptoms associated with a crisis of masculinity. It is tempting then to see *Orphans* as an attempt to take on an older Scottish cultural landscape and weave the narrative around its attempt to re-make itself, with a profound questioning of a tough masculine identity at the heart of that attempt. As one reviewer put it at the time:

> *Orphans'* quietly assured surrealist slant places it in a Scottish tradition diametrically opposed to the hard-boiled realism of such writers as William McIlvaney and Peter McDougall. Indeed that tradition's insistently masculine bias – and the lasting stereotype of the Glasgow hardman it has perpetuated – is slyly subverted throughout *Orphans*. (Lawrenson 1999: 54)

Both Mullan's best-known work as an actor (in *My Name is Joe*) and the details of his own early life tie in fascinatingly with this pursuit of a more fluid male identity, continually pursued by the reality of the demands of daily life as a working-class man in Glasgow. In interviews Mullan has displayed understandable irritation with media presentations of his own past as dominated by violence:

> There's a big thing when people do profiles and stuff. Like when they give you a big gong at Cannes... and this guy jumped up in a kilt and got his prize from Scorsese. That was how I remembered it. When I got back home, BBC Scotland had done this unbelievable voiceover – this wee Highland guy [puts on camp Highland accent] Peter Mullan, a member of one of Glasgow's most notorious gangs and once arrested for attempted murder, here he is

rubbing shoulders with the stars... I went to university when I was 17, but I spent one year in the gangs when I was 14. (Hattenstone 2003 b.)

Orphans is then at least partly about a Scotland that is concerned with a multi-dimensional questioning of male-dominated cultural past. This is, of course, not to suggest that issues of masculinity have not also been prominent in other work from the UK in the last decade, but rather that the dominance of the 'hardman' in representations of Scottish culture has previously been so dominant as to make its relevance to a changing Scotland particularly pointed.

Interestingly Mullan's own view of the film's success is that it was comparatively ignored or rejected by English audiences whereas it was much more successful in both Scotland and Ireland as well as in Western Europe (Hattenstone 2003 b.). Some of this revolved around old questions of accents and subtitles, but there is also a sense of a particularly English resistance to a Scottish vision that refused to conform to the angst-ridden norms surrounding the representation of Scottish working-class life. Mullan remains bitter about Film Four's reluctance to distribute the film, seeing it as the result of a metropolitan superficiality and pursuit only of the fashionable, 'They just felt it wasn't *Trainspotting*. They wanted a film that was going to make them rich, something hip and cool, and I was determined not to go down that road.' (Hattenstone: 2003 b.). Whether or not Mullan's assessment of motives is right, the film's wider UK distribution was undeniably poor compared to its critical reception and the potential to trade on Mullan's success at Cannes as an actor.

Orphans can then be seen as film that, in significant ways, is a strong example of a post-devolutionary Scottish film that appealed beyond England to a wider international audience. However, it is only fair to point out, before leaving *Orphans* entirely, that Mullan's own view of the film relates much more strongly to class identity rather than nationalism, though in the following statement there is the implication that it is class inflected by a specific national context:

> *Orphans* was about the death of socialism in Scotland as we understood it. And it was trying to suggest, to those of us on the left, that we may have to re-examine what it is that we actually believed in. It's like these children in Orphans – where all their beliefs were wrapped up in their mother and so had lost everything. (Hattenstone 2002)

Perversely, then, we can hold up a film that is so strongly about loss as a personification of a post-devolutionary period that in so many ways is about huge political and cultural gains. However, the ending of *Orphans* gives us to understand that the loss of the mother may be a catalyst for a radical re-appraisal of the lives that she dominated and there may even be a cautious kind of hope. Clearly it is a mistake to attempt a rather reductive symbolic reading of the film against the specific political circumstance of devolution, but in its portrayal of characters who are confused by change and loss and who at times thrash around illogically in response to the challenges they now face, the film has clear resonances for the period in which it was made.

Mullan's second feature, *The Magdalene Sisters*, is discussed elsewhere in this volume, under the chapter that discusses cinema and Ireland and here it is simply worth reiterating that it is a film that draws attention to the slightly unsatisfactory nature of some of the divisions that this book has been forced to use. Clearly on many levels *The Magdalene Sisters* can properly be called a 'Scottish' film – it is directed by Mullan with some of its funding coming from Scottish sources (though also some from Ireland) and its story of a society emerging from the grip of religious orthodoxy has clear relevance to a Scottish society in a state of transition. However, both the use of Irish finance and the explicitly Irish settings and context made Mullan's film of principal relevance to an Irish culture demonstrating its willingness to break old taboos, particularly in terms of state-endorsed religious oppression; hence, its principal inclusion in the chapter on Ireland.

Since both Mullan and Ramsey came to prominence in the late 1990s it would be reasonable to suggest that no individual in Scotland has managed to establish themselves in quite the same way, though the critical mass of film production in Scotland has remained proportionately quite considerable in comparison to other parts of the UK. There are, of course, many who would scoff at the notion of a Scottish film 'industry' (as indeed many do at the notion of a British industry) and in most senses they are right. However, because of the sheer diversity of the work, the relatively strong institutional support and the prevalent sense of a willingness to take at least some aesthetic risks it would be only fair to describe Scottish film culture in the early years of the new millennium as alive and active in a way that has in part to do with the political and cultural context. Here there is only space to discuss a small proportion of the work, though what is selected can justifiably be seen as representative of the dominant strains of the broader film culture.

So far the films of May Miles Thomas have attracted a reasonable range of festival attention and fringe critical comment, though very little in the way of either distribution or mainstream reviews. Their primary significance probably lies in Miles-Thomas's enthusiastic adoption of digital video as a suitable medium for feature-length fiction which, though by no means unique, has been some way ahead of most work in the UK context. Both *One Life Stand* (2000) and *Solid Air* (2003) were made by Elemental Films (run my Miles Thomas and her husband, Owen Thomas) using high-definition digital video, and the company's own literature makes it clear that it sees one of its primary functions as being at the cutting edge of technological change within a British film industry context:

> Formed in 1995, Elemental believes the advance of digital technologies as the means of acquisition, post-production and content delivery is the future of film-making. We also recognise that technology cannot replace the basic craft and individual talents and skills necessary to produce high quality work. Our methods are based on the use of new technologies whilst retaining the best aspects of conventional production; it is a paradigm for the cinema of the new century. (http://www.elementalfilms.co.uk)

This sense of a mission to change thinking about the whole craft of film-making in a low-budget context has been further enhanced by Miles-Thomas being the recipient of an award from the National Endowment for Science, Technology and the Arts. Despite the difficulties of both *One Life Stand* and *Solid Air* in achieving any kind of distribution there has then been some recognition of the pioneering nature of Miles-Thomas's work which, when added to the different achievements of the likes of Ramsay and Mullan, gives credence to the idea of an independent Scottish visual culture which has taken on a more traditionally European willingness to take risks.

Paradoxically, in terms of content, Miles-Thomas work does hark back to Bill Douglas in much the same way as *Ratcatcher* does. However, as Duncan Petrie has said, the constraints of the digital technology produce an aesthetic that has an immediacy that distances Miles-Thomas work from the more obviously European art-house feel of either Ramsey or Mullan, '... it remains more immediate and naturalistic than Ramsey's more overt use of pictorialism and the possibilities of long lenses and shallow focus to concentrate the eye and the mind on specific details' (2001: 57).

It would be a distortion, however, to leave the impression that Scottish cinema in the decade since devolution has been entirely about defining itself as the natural UK home of the low-budget art-house movie. There has also been a number of attempts either to break free from the art-house ghetto through the securing of bigger budgets and the attachment of established stars or alternatively to fully engage with popular genre, sometimes through an attempt at a distinctive Scottish take on the established formula. The most successful recent attempt at the former has probably been *Young Adam* (2003), directed by David Mackenzie whose previous feature, *The Last Great Wilderness* (like Miles-Thomas's work shot on digital video), was an attempt at a Scottish Highland road movie which attracted praise for its neat reversals of the conventions of the contemporary Gothic. Having established his credentials, Mackenzie was able to attract Ewan Macgregor to play the lead in *Young Adam*, a major factor in securing a budget of around £4m. This is not say that *Young Adam* is not firmly part of an art-house tradition, it has inevitably been compared to Ramsay as well as to Terence Davies (Bradshaw 2003), but the casting of Macgregor inevitably elevates the attention it received, as well as its filmic ambition to a different level.

One consequence of *Young Adam*'s success has been to raise the awareness of contemporary audiences with Alexander Trocchi, the author of the 1954 novel on which the film is faithfully based. The significance of this is arguably the re-connection of a distinctively Scottish culture with the broader international counter-culture and the consequent broadening of the possibilities of contemporary Scottishness. As the *Sight and Sound* feature on the film makes clear (Gilbey 2003: 16), Trocchi's life and work made him a 'Beat icon' and brought him contact and friendship with the likes of William Burroughs, Leonard Cohen and Terry Southern. Mackenzie's film brings such a sensibility to the attention of a contemporary audience and what is more shows it at work on the bleak canals of what Mackenzie himself refers to as 'moody, broody, industrial Scotland' (Gilbey 2003: 19). Other reviews have drawn attention to the implicitly existential nature of the emotional journey undertaken by the central male figure though Philip French for one sees the world as more that of Zola and his sometime adaptor Renoir. (French 2003) Either way, Mackenzie's film can be seen as significant for Scottish cinema through its attempt to connect its undoubted strength as a home for innovative art-house production with a broader audience, mainly through the casting of Macgregor.

Probably the closest that contemporary Scottish film culture has come to producing a significant body of work that operates in or around the territory of popular genre has been through the 'romantic comedies' of David Kane. Unsurprisingly, it is Duncan Petrie, the most eloquent voice arguing for the distinctive nature of Scottish cinema since devolution, that sees Kane's take on the genre as decidedly Scottish. Talking of Kane's first feature film, *This Year's Love* (1999), Petrie says:

... the accent of the film is distinctively Caledonian, retaining a hard-edged comic sensibility that is darker, more acerbic and ultimately more socially-concerned than most of the British romantic comedies to which it has been compared. Moreover, the distinctly 'Scottish' perspective of *This Year's Love* serves to reconfigure class conflict along devolutionary lines with the familiar – if essentially problematic – association between Scottishness and the virtues of proletarian culture contrasted against the values of a bourgeois and Anglo centric British culture. (2004: 108)

It is, of course, the romantic comedy as conceived of by Richard Curtis in *Four Weddings and a Funeral* (1994) et al. that has been the box office staple of the broader British film industry during the last decade and which is the point of comparison for Petrie here. Whilst the setting of *This Year's Love* is London rather then Glasgow, a number of its characters are Scottish and much of the humour, as Petrie suggests, has more of an acerbic edge that anything that Curtis attempts. This is at least partly a film about Scots in exile and there is at least a hint of their bringing a much needed critical edge to the world of middle-class Camden Town drifters that they inhabit.

Unfortunately, Kane's next film, *Born Romantic* (2000), rather confirms the suspicions of anyone who might feel that Petrie's view of *This Year's Love* is both too generous and too anxious to discover the spirit of devolution in even the most gentle of commercial offerings. The repeat of the formula of observing a number of couples orientated around a single London location suggests an attempt to trade on the previous success and, worse still, the success of Curtis's films. Whilst some reviews praised Kane's ability to photograph London in distinctive ways (Turner 2001: 40–41), most saw the future of this kind of work on television following in the footsteps of the phenomenally successful ITV series *Cold Feet* (Bradshaw 2000).

Before bringing this discussion of the cinematic response to a changed Scotland to a close it is worth at least attempting to summarize some apparent trends and significant events that are emerging at the time of writing. Firstly, as is the case in other parts of the UK, the last five years has seen the emergence of a significant critical mass of female directors working in Scotland. This phenomenon is arguably building upon the success of the likes of Lynne Ramsay, and, to a lesser extent, of Coky Giedroyc whose *Stella Does Tricks* (1997) was one of the first Scottish films to put uniquely female experience at the heart of its narrative structure. The last two years has seen the debut features of Alison Peebles, Eleanor Yule and Shona Auerbach with writer Andrea Gibb contributing the screenplay to both Peebles's *Afterlife* (2004) and Auerbach's *Dear Frankie* (2004). Giedroyc's 1997 debut can be seen as the most explicitly connected to questions of national as well as sexual identity and was therefore seen as a key British film of the late 1990s. Charlotte Brunsdon's summary of 'Women in Film', for example, places it at the heart of an evolving female cinematic vision, which she, in turn, links to a changing British nation by highlighting the powerful comparisons that the film makes between its two principal locations in London and Glasgow:

London is tightly framed in medium and medium long street shots – always showing more than the figures on which the frame is focused, but never stretching to give a sense of space or distance. It is a city of seedy hotels and cafes, flats and a dusty inner city street park... Glasgow, in appropriate contrast for a city visited in the film mainly in memory and fantasy, is more spacious and is revealed more often in twilight long shots... Glasgow in these longer spacey shots which include a park and a cemetery, is still a place where things might have been going to be all right. (Brunsdon 2000: 170)

Stella Does Tricks was, of course, made and released just as the political landscape of Britain was about to change, and in more recent work by women this comparatively overt use of the 'otherness' of a Scotland on the point of securing some measure of self-determination is much less evident. In fact, there is strong sense of diversity among the more recent films made by Scottish women and this is particularly evident in the way that they envisage contemporary Scotland. All the films, to a greater or lesser extent, explore Scottish landscapes that lie outside either the traditionally urban (and usually impoverished) or the *Brigadoon*-like retreat to the misty hills. Instead, the significant locations are often those usually marginalized by cinema such as Eleanor Yule's gothic take on a Lanarkshire left behind by de-industrialization and where her blind central figure's main task is to dump useless machinery into a seemingly bottomless pit. Peebles's *Afterlife* is also concerned with a different kind of 'marginality' through her story of an ambitious young journalist's dilemmas over the care of his sister who has Down's syndrome. Critics tended to see the film as slightly formulaic in its presentation of stark moral choices, but equally praised its avoidance of sentimentality, largely through its use of traditional notions of Scottish 'reserve'. (Lawrenson 2004: 53)

Finally it is worth recording what could prove to be the most significant trend of all, not only for Scotland, but for all film cultures rooted in small nations. That is the emergence of Scotland as a particularly significant centre for films that have attempted to use digital technology as a means to increasing feature film output on micro budgets. The work of May Miles-Thomas has already been discussed above and some of the work of the newer generation women directors has also employed high-definition video, but, perhaps, the most widely distributed example to come out of Scotland so far was Richard Jobson's *16 Years of Alcohol* (2003). What both Miles-Thomas and Jobson's work testify to is a new combination of cine-literate filmic ambition coupled with a desire for the freedom and independence that low-budget digital shooting can bring. Ironically, for his feature debut, Jobson chose to bring this fresh sensibility to bear on that most traditional of Scottish literary and cinematic archetypes, the hard man trying to escape the gangs and the alcohol of his early years. What was different of course was that the film completely eschewed social realism and invested heavily in testing the perceived limits of what HD had been capable of doing. It was this genuine leap into what cinema could achieve visually without the support of large budgets that set ·*16 Years of Alcohol* apart for most critics, with many implying that Jobson had made the kind of breakthrough that could revolutionize thinking about the visual possibilities of digital video:

In the main, his intoxication with dramatic effect is contagious. The film takes visual and rhetorical risks motivated by a real sense of adventure. It was shot on High Definition digital video, apparently for £420,000, and its sheer textural richness marks something of a breakthrough for British low-budget film-making. Not only does the HD format look as textured as film, but John Rhodes's widescreen photography is strikingly composed, atmospheric and sculpted in practically every scene... (Romney 2004)

As a result Jobson's work, like so much to appear from Scotland in the last decade, became associated less with a traditionally British aesthetic and more with Europe and beyond, something which Jobson himself has acknowledged in interviews frequently naming Wong Kar-wai in particular, but also the likes of Kieslowski, Tarkovsky and Terence Malik. (Archibald 2003)

It is perhaps to this last point that we have to return again and again when we look back on the impact that a changing Britain has had on Scottish cinema. As we have seen there have, of course, been a number of shifts of emphasis, some more tangible than others, but what remains constant is the burgeoning of a desire to look beyond the hegemony of 'Britain' and towards Europe (and in some cases other world cinemas) that can be traced much further back into Scottish cultural history. What Jobson, Miles-Thomas and their contemporaries are embarked upon is an important journey into the emerging digital technologies that may liberate others toward the pursuit of challenging, and ambitious cinema that can emerge from nations with limited resources.

5

'A Beautiful Mistake': Wales and Cinema

In terms of the establishment of a genuinely separate and distinctive national screen culture, Wales's situation within the UK is unique, principally because of the remarkable story of S4C (Sianel Pedwar Cymru). Often cited as one of the few times that Margaret Thatcher's Conservative government capitulated to popular pressure, the establishment of the fourth television channel in Wales as a principally Welsh language service has had far reaching social and economic effects, and has frequently been, from its earliest days, a source of conflict and division as well as great pride within Wales itself.

What made the setting up of S4C in 1982 so newsworthy outside Wales was that its separation from the main UK fourth channel had been the result of a long campaign by Welsh language activists, culminating in a hunger strike by the then Plaid Cymru leader, Gywnfor Evans. Given the Thatcher government's subsequent attitude to hunger strikers in other contexts, the decision to accede to the activists' demands gave the channel significance far beyond Wales. However, such a beginning in conflict and drama was to set a tone for S4C throughout its existence with some Welsh-language campaigners seeing it as a ghetto for the language, whilst English speakers have continued to draw attention to its privileged status as the most heavily subsidized television station in the world in relation to its audience, arguing that it largely caters for a minority elite.

As the digital age gathers momentum, S4C faces a fresh set of challenges with its entire Welsh base able to access not only Channel 4 but hundreds of other channels via a variety of delivery systems. In turn, of course, S4C will increasingly be able to access the Welsh diaspora, particularly as delivery via the Internet becomes more viable.

In this context, though, the contribution of S4C to Welsh film culture is what is significant and in this sphere as much as any other S4C has proved highly controversial. Such controversy really stems from the situation in which the wider British film industry found itself during the

1980s with Channel 4 becoming its major means of substantial support. Many have argued that, as a result of the separate existence of S4C, English-language Welsh film-makers were largely ignored during this period. As a result they have lagged behind their counterparts in the rest of the UK during a period when British film struggled financially but developed something of a record for innovation and small-budget international success. Such a situation resulted in a certain amount of bitterness and resentment with Karl Francis, one of the leading Welsh film-makers of recent times, threatening to instigate a private prosecution against Channel 4 under the Race Relations Act because of the way its film production arm had ignored proposals from Wales. The feeling was that London's attitude was that Wales had been 'given' S4C and that they should be satisfied with that. The problem, of course, is that S4C's remit was very different from Channel 4's, lacking the dimension to its film commissioning policy that is described by John Hill below:

> ... it has to an extent 'subsidised' film production insofar as the relatively high percentage of the Channel's overall budget (6.2 per cent between 1982 and 1992) devoted to Film on Four has not been matched by the number of programme hours or audience ratings which it has provided. As Isaacs [Jeremy, Channel 4's first chief executive] explained in the early days of Film on Four, he regarded such films as having a 'socio-cultural provenance and purpose' which went beyond their financial returns or contributions to the ratings. (1996: 161)

The fact that S4C's budget was both much smaller and focused on the promotion of the Welsh language rather than on innovation and cultural diversity resulted, in may people's view, in the stagnation of film culture in Wales during the very period when other parts of the UK were experiencing at least modest growth.

Of course, such a polarized view is only partly true and the positive contribution of S4C to Welsh language feature film production and to the general development of a moving-image culture in Wales will be discussed below. However, it is hard to deny entirely the argument that the generally low level of film production in Wales at the moment of devolution was in part due to the way that the creation of S4C had been viewed beyond Wales.

In terms of work in the Welsh language (or sometimes bilingual production) S4C got off to what many felt was a poor start, with Dave Berry asserting that 'S4C's opening feature films betrayed a fatal lack of confidence and ambition.'(1994: 322). Such lack of boldness and confidence set the tone of much of the early output of S4C, though they themselves were taken aback by the sudden simultaneous appearance in London's West End of two Welsh language feature films, Karl Francis's *Boy Soldier* (1986) and Stephen Bayly's *Coming Up Roses* (1986). S4C had budgeted only for a 16mm shoot and both films had to be blown up to 35mm for their London run.

Both *Coming Up Roses* and *Boy Soldier* are films that deal in radically different ways with the question of national identity in which Wales had become more complex than ever after the spectacular failure to gain a 'Yes' vote in the 1979 devolution referendum. However whilst Bayly's film has most frequently been seen as gentle satire in the Ealing tradition, Francis's film is a savage attack on the behaviour of the British army in Northern Ireland and makes fascinating use of the moral dilemma facing its central character who arrives at the point where his Welsh identity cannot deal with being part of a colonial army of occupation in a fellow Celtic country. Francis himself has made such an interpretation and its connection to broad issues around Wales's 'postcolonial' status quite explicit, stating 'The Welsh soldier in the British Army may feel like the Ghurka or the Maori soldier for example – an outsider.' (Berry 1994: 393)

On the whole, though, S4C's contribution to the development of a contemporary film culture in Wales has not been anywhere near as sustained as the 'moment' of 1986 briefly suggested. With one or two exceptions its investment in feature film production has tended to concentrate on films set in the past, often with literary sources and, ironically, in the period since devolution itself, its contribution to feature film production and its relationship to the new nation has tended to be small.

Two of the films financed by S4C during the 1990s, however, were, interestingly, nominated for Academy Awards in the Best Foreign Language Production category and whilst neither eventually won the 'Oscar' it is clear that their nominations were significant enough for a small film culture such as the one in Wales. Both *Hedd Wyn* (1992) and *Solomon and Gaenor* (1998) are explicitly concerned with questions of identity and both also work within the broad category of 'heritage cinema' that was so prominent in the UK during this period. Arguably, though, both work hard to avoid some of the worst excesses of what Alan Parker has called the 'Laura Ashley school of film making' (http://www.channel4.com/film/reviews/film.jsp?id=106460) and to use the past to make reference to the contemporary situation in Wales. Both can in different ways therefore be read as essentially hybrid versions of a form that is often characterized as conservative and can be seen as contributing to what some have seen as a postcolonial discourse in Welsh dramatic fiction that gained particular momentum during the 1990s.

Hedd Wyn and *Solomon and Gaenor* make a useful pairing in this context because of the obvious crude oppositions that they represent: North vs South Wales, urban vs rural and the Eisteffod-based literary heritage versus the more overtly popular, class-based culture of the southern industrial valleys. They are also set within the same period, so that together they offer us a potentially very interesting take on early twentieth-century Wales that is geographically and culturally inclusive.

To take Solomon and Gaenor first it is abundantly clear that its primary impulse is far from the conservatism that many have found within the heritage tradition. Whilst the film is not a profound analysis of the complexities of early twentieth-century industrial relations, it is rare enough to find a British film that includes such things at all within its motivational framework, and *Solomon* deserves praise for that alone. It is abundantly clear that the brutality in the second half of the film, as the uneasy relations between the indigenous Welsh and the Jewish families erupts into violence, is the product of a community dominated by an utterly ruthless coal industry. Central to this is the character of Crad, Gaenor's brother, described by one reviewer as 'a brooding hulk of a man, visibly torn up by his repressed rage as a worker subject to the whims of distant bosses, searching for scapegoats among the closest strangers'. Crad's graphically filmed beating up of Solomon and enthusiastic leadership of the gang of looters that turn on the Jewish shopkeepers successfully echoes through current anxieties about ethnic conflict across Europe.

Hedd Wyn's departure from the conservative tendencies of 'heritage' film lies in its treatment not merely of the First World War from a pacifist perspective, but also in its depiction of the imperial army's demands on Wales. In this respect it situates itself right at the heart of the debates about Wales's postcolonial nature. In the latter third of the film we are shown the brutalizing results of the British army's scorn for the Welsh (particularly with respect to the language) alongside its insatiable demand for cannon fodder from the rural poor. In a key scene, a government official calls at the Evans' farm to determine the number of men living there that are eligible to fight; Elis Evans' (the central character) mother attempts to hide behind her non comprehension of the language, but is exposed by the naivety of her young daughter proudly displaying her prowess in the foreign tongue (English). The fact that the moment leads indirectly to the pacifist Elis going to his death makes it a powerfully symbolic one, full of the ironies and cruelty surrounding the politics of the status of the Welsh language as well the quasi-colonial status of Wales itself. It is arguable that the film tends to weaken this powerful section through its depiction of every English character as either a racist bully or upper-class chinless wonder, though there is also strength in the way that sections of the Welsh chapel establishment are seen to collude with the oppression and press-ganging.

In radically different ways, it is through their respective uses of language and the possibilities of making cinema in a bilingual culture that *Hedd Wyn* and *Solomon and Gaenor* most clearly express themselves as part of a Wales seeking to establish a separate cultural identity.

In the case of *Solomon and Gaenor*, the film has a complex history in relation to its use of language. It was actually shot 'back to back' in two different versions: one for Welsh-language audiences, the other for English. However, it is not as straightforward as this as even in the 'English' version some Welsh is used, and in both versions there is some Yiddish. In a world where exhibitors regard subtitles as the kiss of commercial death this was clearly some risk and it is one justified by much more than a desire for straightforward authenticity. The use of language, I would argue, is a key feature in the film's claims to be fundamentally about culture and cultural change rather than its superficial narrative interest in two star-crossed lovers (the characters that give the film its title) outside time and history.

In the 'English' version, ironically, the role of language in the two cultures is more apparent as it becomes something they retreat into either in the comfort of being surrounded entirely by their own or as a defence against intruders. In other words, it is clearer how fundamental it is to identity. However, for Welsh audiences, and those with an interest in Wales, perhaps the real significance will be that the location of the film is not just anywhere in Wales, but in the valleys, long considered the English-speaking heartland. For all bar historians the use of the Welsh language in this location is a valuable corrective in itself and it was a brave aesthetic decision by the film-makers to use it. Beyond this, though, the easy and skilful bilingualism of the community becomes fundamental to the filmic representation of their identity.

The same also applies, of course, to the Jewish community, though their isolation, even from their own class, tends to heighten the use of the language as more of a defensive strategy to retreat into and take refuge in. It is, perhaps, more through the use of Yiddish that the film is honest enough to depict the other dimension to minority languages, though it is present in the Welsh scenes too: that is language operating as a barrier to understanding and being used as a tool to exclude others and to manipulate power. *Solomon and Gaenor* therefore shows us language as a means of arousing hostility and suspicion in the majority population in ways that are uncomfortably close to home today, but also the minority language as a means of creating an elite and inner circle of power in certain contexts.

We have already touched briefly on the role that the politics of the Welsh language plays in *Hedd Wynn*, but I would like to return to it again briefly in order to contrast the approach with that of *Solomon*. Unlike the latter there is only one version of *Hedd Wynn* shot entirely in Welsh, apart from a small number of scenes involving English characters, mainly army personnel. There is, of course, nothing at all to quarrel with here, particularly on naturalistic grounds. Interestingly, though, it tends to reduce the Welsh language to a fairly straightforward liberal 'issue', whereas *Solomon* works linguistic conflict into the spectators own experience of the film as a deliberate aesthetic strategy. In this respect, its embracing of a formal hybridity is clearly more radical than *Hedd Wynn*'s and it is tempting to attribute this to its completion further on in the decade when devolution for Wales was secure and the embrace of a distinctive cultural identity had gathered more momentum.

We can see then that both *Hedd Wynn* and *Solomon and Gaenor* perform the important function of attempting a cinematic re-reading of the national past, reinvigorated by the political present. Both films are full of the tensions involved in simply understanding Wales as any kind of 'colony' with newly devolved powers, but taken together they also play out some of the most powerful forms of oppression perpetrated both by imperialist governments and remote controllers of labour and capital. In attempting these things and in receiving wide international circulation through their respective Academy Award nominations, both *Hedd Wyn* and *Solomon and Gaenor* deserve to be seen as part of the powerful cultural response to the devolutionary impulse that dominated the last decade of the twentieth century in Wales.

Beyond these two high-profile successes (both of which, to differing extents, have struggled to find distribution deals to match the publicity offered by the Academy Award nominations), S4C has tended to provide openings to talented Welsh directors, but on rather spasmodic basis and without the marketing infrastructure to enable Welsh-language cinema to flourish in the same way that, say, Danish or Finnish cinema has managed to do. Ceri Sherlock, Endaf Emlyn and Steve Gough all made powerful contributions to the international festival circuit, though none has managed a sustained theatrical output as a result.

Of the three it is Sherlock's films that offered the most sustained interest in questions of identity. *Branwen* (1994) followed Karl Francis on the path of attempting to explore the relationship between the Welsh sense of separation from the rest of the UK and the armed Republican struggle in Northern Ireland. The film also makes explicit connection with a Welsh mythological past through its use of central figure, Branwen, from the *Mabinogion* collection of folk tales. In neither case is the connection a laboured one and, instead, Sherlock is able to offer a powerful, sometimes disturbing, reflection on both national and gender identities.

Emlyn's work, especially *Un Nos Ola Leuad* (*One Full Moon*) (1992), can be seen as important in this context chiefly for their substantial contribution to the credibility of there being a theatrical audience for cinema in the Welsh language, something which, to date, has not been built upon.

Emlyn's work is also notable for its variety and concern for what are usually seen as European art-house virtues in terms of their use of cinematic language. After *One Full Moon* Emlyn's other significant success was *Gadael Lenin* (*Leaving Lenin*) (1993), which was altogether more rooted in a comic contemporary realist frame. Unlike Sherlock's, Emlyn's film seems much less obviously relevant to the changing sense of Wales's relationship to the rest of the UK except perhaps in their assertion of a Welsh right to belong to a European cinematic tradition that is generally distinct from the British mainstream.

More recently S4C's increasingly spasmodic investment in cinema has produced two highly contrasting films from Marc Evans, one of the few Welsh directors to have established himself and sustained a career (most often in the English language) during the last decade. The first of these, *Beautiful Mistake* (2000), is a highly original piece of work based around the idea of bringing John Cale back to his native Wales and getting him to collaborate with a number of musicians working in contemporary Wales and film the results at Cardiff's Coal Exchange. The music is also intercut with location footage of Cardiff. This is, above all, a light-touch, playful approach to identity woven through a film with a real concern for the music that is its main subject. Cale is clearly a source of continuing fascination for Marc Evans as he also used his work on the *House of America* (1997) soundtrack and in this appearance he becomes a fascinating embodiment of the hybridity and freewheeling nature of the possibilities inherent in a new Welsh identity. One of the Velvet Underground was a Welshman and here he returns to play alongside James Dean Bradfield (of the Manic Street Preachers) and Cerys Matthews amongst many others.

Essentially Evans's film plays with the facile concept of 'Cool Cymru', a variant on 'Cool Brittania' and based mainly around the emergence of bands such as the Manic Street Preachers, the Stereophonics and the Super Furry Animals, and disrupts it through the laid-back setting in which Cale plays with the much younger musicians. Most of the work is acoustic and filmed in the empty Coal Exchange and is the antithesis of the fake fashionability of a newly 'cool' Wales. Instead, Evans delights in the sheer strangeness of the interplay between Cale and the younger musicians as they open up new musical possibilities, whilst at the same time performing new possibilities for identity as the country itself emerges from old rigidities. The images of the musicians are in turn intercut with images of contemporary Cardiff that are at least questioning of the tourist board vision of 'Europe's newest capital city' and, instead, suggest a much more ambivalent and thoughtful view of an energetic place, though one that is still struggling with the problems that regeneration schemes try and leave behind.

The title of Evans's film acts as a warning that would haunt this film as well as so many others struggling to secure any kind of distribution in Wales and beyond. The 'beautiful mistake' of the title refers to the way that emergent Welsh artistic talent gets there by 'mistake': the new wave of bands, the film-makers, the poets and novelists have emerged not through a coherent effort and systematic support but by mistake. In turn, the lack of an infrastructure would mean that a film that contained rare and beautiful sessions with some of Europe's leading rock musicians would fail to get not only a theatrical release but any kind of release on DVD. To many, this beggars belief and it typifies a problem that can be seen as at the heart of the difficulties faced by indigenous film-makers in Wales.

Evans's most recent work in the Welsh language in partnership with S4C has fared slightly better in terms of distribution, partly because it has been marketed heavily as an educational resource and partly because its combination of young Welsh stars (Ioan Gruffydd, Rhys Ifans, Matthew Rhys) and Welsh literary heritage has given it a following amongst the Welsh diaspora. *Dal: Yma Nawr* (Still: Here/Now) (2004) is really a series of short films (some made by guest directors under Evans's overall guidance) that respond to verses from the Welsh bardic tradition, one of the oldest in Europe. What makes the film constantly surprising is the sheer variety of imagery and rhythmic response to the poetry. The locations range from the hip bars of contemporary Cardiff Bay to recreated medieval battlefields whilst the poetry itself ranges from Gwyneth Lewis (whose lines are built into the architecture of the Wales Millennium Centre in Cardiff Bay) to the ancient Gruffydd Ab yr Ynad Goch.

For someone such as Evans who is forging a strong mainstream career out of skilful takes on the horror genre to attempt a film such as *Dal: Yma Nawr* is in one sense a strong cultural statement. It is not so much any kind of assertion of nationalist pride as another experiment in hybridity which enacts the freedom in ways to be Welsh that a new cultural confidence has brought. It is also clearly an attempt to forge a kind of continuity in the face of those who would suggest that only now is there anything 'cool' about being Welsh. Often through powerful imagery and music the Welsh bardic tradition is connected to contemporary images of a Wales embracing a new freedom to construct a range of identities that refuse the imposed and inflexible ones of the past.

A final example of the way that Welsh language cinema has attempted to find space in the new Wales is *Diwrnod Hollol Mindblowing Heddiw* (A Totally Mindblowing Day Today) (2000). Directed by Euros Lyn, the film is powerfully influenced by the Danish Dogma group, though the director admits to interpreting the groups' 'rules' very liberally. It has elements of road movie about it and is an interesting, unsystematic exploration of competing identities within contemporary Wales as the central characters journey to Cardiff and back from their fictitious offshore island home off the North Wales coast. It is witty and lyrical and turns the imperatives of small budgets and resultant hand-held improvisation to good effect. The commercial result was, sadly, a complete disappearance. This is light touch art cinema, with a relatively simple narrative structure and strong points of identification both visually and on the soundtrack. It is, however, in Welsh and made on a very low budget and the two factors appear to have combined to have alienated potential distributors completely. As a non-Welsh speaker, I felt only that language is again used intelligently as part of the film's playful attitude to identity, but it seems that once again, unlike somewhere like Denmark from where it drew inspiration, there is not yet the will to make the marketing and distribution work in imaginative ways.

The story of film in Wales made in the English language in the last two decades is one of uneven and highly erratic development. In 1997 it seemed that the year that saw the election of New Labour and the establishment of the constitutional path to devolution was also the year that would see a Welsh film culture established that could begin to perform a similar function to that in Scotland. Within the space of a few months three very different feature films were released that all made significant contributions to the idea of a Welsh film culture: *Twin Town* (Director Kevin Allen), *House of America* (Director Marc Evans) and *Darklands* (Director Julian Richards) all used Welsh settings and distinctively Welsh concerns, even if their funding arrangements involved the usual contemporary complications that make the notion of national cinema a highly contested one in the twenty-first century.

Perhaps most importantly the aforementioned three films all, in their very different ways, presented a Wales to the world that is as far from male voice choirs and rugby as *Shallow Grave* and *Trainspotting* were from the 'Tartanry and Kailyard' of the once dominant filmic representations of Scotland (see a number of the essays in McArthur, 1982) (something which Philip French discussed in relation to the later and equally significant *Human Traffic* (1999) which is discussed below). Yet all contained implicit or explicit engagement with the 'orientalized' vision of Welshness that they sought to cast off (like *Trainspotting* to a limited extent – as in the speech where Ewan MacGregor sits on a heathery hilltop and berates his fellow countrymen for their endless obsession with defining themselves in relation to the English).

Twin Town, the nearest of the three to making an impact on a wider UK popular culture landscape, does this in the most irreverent way to the extent that it brought down the almost inevitable (but still hugely comic) wrath of the tourist board and Swansea civic authorities. The film's biggest handicap, perhaps, stems from what undoubtedly got it made in the first place; its connections with the *Trainspotting* team of Andrew Macdonald and Danny Boyle as producers. This resulted in a large number of unfavourable comparisons in the national press and even condemnation from *Sight and Sound* whose reviewer opened with snide sideswipes at what he calls the picture's '*eagerness to be to South Wales what* Trainspotting *was to urban Scotland*' and goes on to an extremely odd piece of moralizing from a magazine of this nature:

> It seems to take pleasure in its leading character's lack of any redeeming features, and from the dog's decapitation through the death of the twins' whole family to the concluding clutch of 'comic' murders, in themselves enough to drive the most diehard defender of free speech kicking and screaming into the censorship lobby a streak of sadism as wide as the M4 runs through the entire narrative. (Thompson 1997: 53)

Those concerned with tourism and the image of the City of Swansea had more specific, material concerns than the high-minded Mr Thompson (above), of course. They were worried that all their efforts to attract people to a Wales they had worked so hard to construct (as a land of sheep, choirs and Celtic twilight) were being undermined and would have preferred Mel Gibson as Owain Glendower no doubt.

Perhaps *Twin Town* was a little stuck in the wake of *Trainspotting* and it is undoubtedly not overly concerned with new Welsh filmic discourses. But that is in a sense the point; it has an elusive confidence to either ignore the obvious ways to 'be Welsh' or to laugh at them from within. Its reported reception with Welsh audiences suggests that for younger people at least it is a welcome phenomenon, though, as Nigel Morris has pointed out, the reaction of sections of the Welsh establishment suggests the need for quite a substantial quantity of irreverence yet:

> The film itself was attacked by clergy – whose warnings of copycat poodle beheadings surpassed the satire on screen – perpetuating a century of mistrust epitomised by the poem 'Beware of the Cinema' by Reverend Thomas David Evans. (1998: 27)

On the other hand, *Twin Town*'s detractors were not entirely confined to the easily parodied self-appointed guardians of the nation's dignity. Dave Berry whose *Wales and Cinema: The First Hundred Years* has done more for Welsh cinematic culture than any other single artefact is quoted by Julia Hallam as suggesting that the film demeans Wales because of its view that 'traditions such as community loyalty, decency and camaraderie, a shared love of culture, music and rugby are all redundant in an avaricious world' (Berry 1997 a.). For Berry the film still looks at Wales from the outside and trades in the stereotypes, whereas there is also a strong case for arguing that the film is an important advance on the road to the end of the country's association with such iconography altogether.

Clearly the film is not unaware of its aggression towards an older view of Wales, as Julia Hallam points out by quoting the lines from the film that became part of its marketing campaign: 'Rugby. Tom Jones. Male voice choirs. Shirley Bassey. Snowdonia. Prince of Wales. Daffodils. Sheep shaggers. Coal. Now if that's your idea of Welsh culture, you can't blame us for trying to liven the place up can you?' (Hallam 2000: 268), and for Daryl Perrins and others this is a sign that, far from being an exercise in cheap self- loathing, *Twin Town* can be read as in terms of cultural maturity:

Perhaps then we have grown in confidence enough to stop laughing, as we did according to Kim Howells in 1980 ' at an externally manufactured image of ourselves...' In short we may be beginning to learn, to paraphrase Caradoc Evans, not to hate ourselves, but to like each other well enough to criticise our own behaviour. (2000: 164)

Whatever one's final view of the cultural sensibility of *Twin Town* is then at the very least it managed to make Wales visible on the 'British' cinematic map in the late 1990s and to provide it with its own brand of post-industrial iconography to set alongside not only *Trainspotting* but also *The Full Monty* and *Brassed Off*. Importantly, this was an iconography capable of taking the film outside the art-house ghetto to provide the first film from Wales to make its way (albeit relatively modestly) into the multiplexes. Despite the hand wringing of those that fretted about the damage to the image of the emergent nation, it is likely that this did more for the cultural confidence of those left underwhelmed by the official face of devolution than most of the officially sanctioned icons of the era of the National Assembly for Wales.

Julian Richards's debut feature, *Darklands*, is the nearest to a genre piece of the three films released in 1997, but ironically is therefore the one to have received least widespread distribution. Its treatment of traditional Welsh icons is potentially the most subversive and irreverent of the three, though, as Dave Berry has said, the tone of the piece should make us wary of drawing too many strong political conclusions. (Berry 1997 b.)

Drawing heavily and openly on Robin Hardy's cult British horror piece, *The Wicker Man* (1973), Richards' film attempts the very difficult job of combining the devastated industrial landscapes of South Wales (the crucial scenes shot on location in Port Talbot) with a particular take on paganism, druids and a brand of Welsh Nationalism that is seen to be openly linked to fascist ideas. The central character is a journalist investigating a number of instances of animal sacrifices which lead him to a local nationalist businessman. This then develops into a sometimes fascinating, but also improbable, plot involving forced impregnation, human sacrifice and the linking of ancient fertility rituals with attempts at modern urban renewal. The villain is, of course, the neo-Nazi nationalist businessman.

Richards has certainly frequently associated himself with those lamenting the lack of opportunities for monoglot English speakers in the Welsh film and television industries, and although, perhaps, a little tongue in cheek, in his first feature he was brave enough to take risks while working within an always prickly local political culture.

'My film's not primarily political,' Richards says now. 'But the Devolution vote proved that Wales remains a deeply divided country and part of my agenda was to say that, in Wales, English language culture has a right to exist equally'. (Berry 1997 b.)

As an English-language film-maker struggling to establish a career in his native South Wales the centrality of language to the age-old internal divisions that underlay the emergence of a post-devolutionary Wales had a strongly personal dimension. For Richards the problem is clear, though clearly for many his view is a reductive oversimplification of the problem:

The opportunities in Wales have to a degree been monopolised, especially in media, by the Welsh speakers, who believe that the only way to preserve Welsh culture is through its language, and the only way to do that was to have a Welsh language television station. What that resulted in was something like £60 million being spent on S4C, a Welsh language television station that serviced two hundred thousand people in an over all population of two and a half million. But those who don't speak the Welsh language, who are in the majority and in the south, found themselves in no-mans-land. (http://www.prolificfilms. freeserve.co.uk/Questions.htm)

Perhaps, not surprisingly, *Darklands* fared little better at the hands of the UK critical establishment than did *Twin Town*. In the context of this discussion it was particularly strange to see *Sight and Sound* criticize Richards for his attacks on a particular kind of Welsh identity, when from the safe distance of London the Welsh industry is virtually always ignored altogether:

... *Darklands* remains boringly on the side of the (English-speaking) status quo, offering little insight into Celtic, pagan or even Welsh nationalist beliefs, let alone inviting us to flirt with sharing them. (Monk 1997: 37)

Considering the amount of attention paid to Welsh moving-image culture (at this point in time at least) it is tempting to ask quite how the reviewer would know enough about the subtleties of the divisions to which she refers to put her in a position to pass informed comment. There would certainly be many in Wales itself that would see power relations around the issue of language as very different to that implied in Claire Monk's review.

Darklands remains an essentially minority-interest cult film but, in 1997 especially, its appearance both as a genre piece and as a film with strong views on nationalism seemed an optimistic addition to the small Welsh cinematic canon. It displayed both political and aesthetic independence and suggested a broadening of the scope of what was possible in a developing local culture. That it now seems more of a curiosity than a trailblazer is not so much the fault of the film, but a signal of the failure, so far, at least, to create an infrastructure to make and distribute feature films in Wales.

House of America, whilst probably faring the best of the three 1997 films in terms of overall critical perception, still incurred the displeasure of the *Sight and Sound* reviewer assigned to it. What seems to link its review with those of the other two (very different) films is a kind of displeasure at the way a Welsh film has taken on its own heritage and tried to develop an ironic discourse around it. *House of America* it seems to me was criticized mostly for avoiding the mainstream social-realist British film tradition and instead substituting a range of linguistic and visual pyrotechnics more commonly associated with American or European independent cinema of the last decade. This in turn made it hard for reviewers to see it as a credible film 'detailing the frustrations of being stranded in a one-street town in South Wales with no jobs, no money and no hope.' (Spencer 1997: 45) In other words, it was being criticized for failing to be, as Ed Thomas (the writer) has put it, a 'British miserabilist' film (Blandford 2000: 68), something which, in fact, it sets out scrupulously to avoid.

Like *Twin Town* (but with even less reason), *House of America* also suffered comparisons with *Trainspotting*. In almost every way the two films are different, though their release in the mid-1990s could clearly be said to be connected by the phenomenon of film culture suddenly coming from everywhere that was not the metropolitan centre. There was also the connection that both films had to independent music, though, again, *House of America* signalled its greater distance from anything approaching contemporary social realism in Wales by foregrounding the involvement of John Cale, the Welshman from Haverfordwest, who ended up in The Velvet Underground with Lou Reed (Director Marc Evans's enduring relationship with Cale is also discussed earlier in the chapter).

Beginning life as a stage play by Edward Thomas, *House of America* is an exploration of the relationship between the contemporary Welsh imagination and the American culture which, in Thomas's formulation, is, or at least was, its most powerful stimulus. However, this is no simple condemnation of homogenized globalized culture, but rather a powerful and poetic celebration of the power of myth that shows us both how it liberates lives and has the capacity to destroy.

House of America is set in a kind of de-industrialized landscape, but some of the very long period which it took to get the film off the ground was taken up by Thomas and Marc Evans's attempts to get various executives to understand that the film was not a British social-realist piece about poverty and unemployment in the South Wales valleys. Using the French cinematography team that had worked on *La Haine* (1995), Evans used a range of devices, including a bleach by-pass process, in order to emphasize the strangeness of the landscape surrounding the opencast mine at the centre of the story and to further distance the film from any association with a realist aesthetic.

The reason for these and a multitude of other strenuous attempts to distance *House of America* from what is commonly seen as the mainstream British social-realist tradition can be traced, at least in part, to Thomas and Evans's keen sense of the Welsh, rather than British, context in which they were making the film. As Evans put it, 'Social-realism, or "miserabilism" as we called it, was the enemy. We didn't feel that we were working in the context of "British film" at all, but in a void, our own Welsh void.' (2002: 292).

The idea of a void is, however, slightly misleading out of context. Though the film was released in 1997, in reality its ideas are older, though clearly they evolved many times during the period since they first saw the light of day in a stage version in 1989. They come, in other words, not so much from a Wales anticipating devolution with some of the new confidence that Thomas and Evans would become so much a part of, but from an older Wales, something that Evans admits with typical honesty:

> In some ways *House of America* and *Twin Town* were not the first of a new generation of films but the last of the old. Although Ed was remarkably young when he wrote the play and although his writing was muscular and modern, drawing its inspiration from American heroes like Sam Shepherd and Jack Kerouak, it was actually engaged in an argument with the past, with the Wales in which we grew up. We were at great pains while making the film to stress that *House of America* was not a complaint but a celebration and I think, that to a certain extent, we protested too much. Looking back – and hindsight is a wonderful thing – we were railing against a Wales that was already beginning to change, the Wales of our youth. (2002: 290–1)

The Wales that Evans refers to is one too satisfied with the limitations of its own dreams and which, in *House of America*, has produced Sid and Gwenny who can survive only by imagining themselves to be Jack Kerouac and his lover Joyce Johnson. Whilst the film is ambivalent about such appropriation of another mythology, allowing Sid and Gwenny's vision to be glorious at times as well as (literally) incestuous, it is ultimately doomed and fated to be dragged down by the 'real' world that they inhabit. It has inevitably been interpreted, probably correctly, as a crisis of individual identity acting as a metaphor for a crisis of national identity. When the individual/nation seeks to resolve such a crisis solely through the appropriation of the myths of a dominant alien culture then the result is inevitably tragic.

By the time the film was released it is arguable that Wales was already at least in the process of moving on. This is not to say that the film was an irrelevance, in fact it is possible to argue, as Evans tentatively does, that *House of America* in particular and Ed Thomas's work in general was an important part of the impetus behind such pre-millennial cultural shifts:

> It seems to me now that Wales is getting on with life and is less prone to arguing with itself about what it should be. Perhaps *House* was part of the process by which that happened, either as symptom or cause. But the situation was already changing as we made the film. (Evans 2002: 292)

Whilst Evans's work for film since *House of America* has seen him become a genuinely significant director who has managed to both continue making films in and of Wales as well as establishing an international career (his latest film *Snowcake* has just opened the 2006 Berlin Film Festival), Thomas's film aspirations have not yet recovered from the project that he turned to after *House of America*, though he has continued to produce work of distinction for theatre and, to some extent, Welsh television. Through a combination of factors *Rancid Aluminium*

(2000) came to be bracketed with a series of disastrous British attempts to make a film that would emulate the surprising success of *Lock Stock and Two Smoking Barrels*. One of its reviews in the national press has itself become legendary:

> Rancid Aluminium is the yardstick by which all things spiritual and temporal must now be judged. By universal consent, it is the worst film ever made in the UK. People who have seen it belong to an exclusive club. They cannot speak about the film, they simply shudder at its mention. (Peretti 2000)

Whether such hyperbole is justified is irrelevant here. The potential significance of *Rancid Aluminium* to the film culture of Wales lay in its having little to do with Wales at all except that it was produced and funded largely from Welsh sources. It had the potential in other words to show the way for Welsh film-makers that had aspirations to work in the mainstream in the way that British film-makers, in general, were being encouraged to do in the late 1990s.

The failure of *Rancid Aluminium* was in many ways surprising. The film was adapted from a successful contemporary novel written by James Hawes, a former lecturer at the University of Wales, Swansea, and Thomas's previous success in theatre and television suggested a creative talent that would bring an original eye to the project. More generous reviewers suggested that the film was a well-meaning, though ultimately very flawed attempt to parody the increasingly risible 'mockney' films that had proliferated in the UK at the time with its cast of rising British stars (Rhys Ifans, Joseph Fiennes, Sadie Frost, Tara Fitzgerald) being asked to perform in a selection of accents that seem to become more and more exaggerated as the film went on. Hawes (who wrote the screenplay from his own novel) was, though, far less generous and produced a thinly disguised satire on the process of making the film in a 'novel' called *White Powder, Green Light* (2002) in which the aspirations of some sections of the Welsh film and televisions are savagely sent up :

> It is the night of the Cymru-Wales Oscwr ceremony at the Millennium Stadium.
>
> The recipient of the main prize, the charismatic film-maker Richard Watkin (Rich) Jenkins, begins his acceptance speech, and the Head of Public Relations BBC Wales (English language section) is explaining the arcane proceedings to a female guest from Serbian Television. The puzzled foreigner asks why the film-maker starts his speech in Welsh when many people in the room obviously do not understand it.
>
> The cynical PR explains that 'everyone who can speak Welsh speaks in Welsh first here, love. In fact, a lot of people who can't speak Welsh speak in Welsh first here. Well, we all want promotion and grants and jobs, don't we? Same in Serbia, I bet.'
>
> (Quoted at http://icwales.icnetwork.co.uk/0900entertainment)

Hawes's jaundiced account both of the principal Welsh attempt to date to dip a toe into the kind of film-making that would bring international distribution and of the Welsh-speaking media establishment is, of course, contested. What is not in dispute, however, is that *Rancid Aluminium* was a commercial disaster and one that certainly encouraged the view that if a Welsh film culture was to have a future it was much more likely to lie within the confines of what Colin McArthur (in the context of Scotland) has referred to as 'poor cinema'. (McArthur 1992)

Whilst the attractiveness of the myth-making qualities of the film industry for a small nation with limited powers over its own economic destiny are obvious, Wales's current efforts to join any kind of global big league are currently more centred on efforts to realize a vision for a major film studio to be built near Bridgend than the encouragement of local film talent. If the so-called 'Valleywood' project is realized it will undoubtedly provide some kind of encouragement to those living in Wales and aspiring to work in the film industry, though whether this will mean projects with any real relationship to the country is open to question. For now it seems the possibility of another *Rancid Aluminium* means that 'theme park' Wales as a setting for the films of others is a more likely possibility than the country becoming a genuine originator of commercial cinema.

Ironically, though far more commercially and critically successful than *Rancid Aluminium*, *Human Traffic* (1999) has also proved a dead end for its Welsh debut director, though for different reasons. The release of Justin Kerrigan's film was seen by many as another kind of new dawn for cinema in Wales and prompted a review from Philip French in *The Observer* that made explicit connections between *Human Traffic* and emergent questions of identity related to the changing shape of Britain:

> Just as *Trainspotting* makes a clean break with the traditional Scotland of tartanry and kailyard, of Scott and Barrie, so *Human Traffic* turns its back on the Wales of male voice choirs and the whimsical humour of *The Englishman Who Went Up a Hill But Came Down a Mountain...* it seems more like an American picture than a British one; the influences working on it are Quentin Tarantino, Woody Allen, Bob Rafelson's *Head* and early Scorsese. (French 1999)

At first sight this might look like a leap from one kind of hegemony to another, until one begins to see that the specific Americans cited are themselves amongst the leading creators of a hybrid, independent American cinema resistant to the internal colonizing influence of Hollywood.

So what is the value to a postcolonial or post-devolutionary Welsh identity of the emergence of a young director who, if French is right, has most in common with American independent cinema (and perhaps with some of their models in Europe)? If the film is so unrecognizably 'Welsh' what can it mean for an emergent culture?

Well, to begin with, the film is not so much unrecognizably Welsh as Welsh with a style and wit that it wears very lightly. Set in Cardiff it justifiably makes its five central characters a diverse bunch on all levels, including cultural identity. What they have in common seems to be a lack of allegiance to any traditional idea of 'roots' and instead find their identity in the loosely conceived philosophy and easy-going friendships of the club scene which every weekend gives them '48 hours off from the world' as one character, Jip, puts it.

The still prevalent chapel-orientated moralizing dimension to the Welsh image (witness the previously discussed calls from church elders to ban the 'other Welsh *Trainspotting*', *Twin Town* when it was released in 1997) seems a million miles away as we are shown a Cardiff that responds to the drudgery of a Mac-jobs culture with a witty hedonism. To an extent this could have been Leeds or Manchester in the 1990s, except that it doesn't take itself as seriously and instead of a loud trumpeting of a city's trendiness we get an almost naïve revelling in the pleasant surprise that these pleasures are available here too.

In terms of form this is no British realist film either. The scenes involving the Cardiff clubs are the closest the film comes to embracing this aesthetic whilst the rest involves a hectic mix of pieces to camera, pure fantasy and mock-documentary. It is essentially a playful film, entirely in tune with its subject matter and it looks exactly as though it comes from the kind of Wales that seeks to throw off stale debates about identity.

In the scene in the film that most explicitly connects *Human Traffic* to the themes of this book, Kerrigan's characters take part in a fantasy sequence dreamed up by one of them, Jip, played by John Sim. As he contemplates the problematics of finding genuine points of identification in the world that he inhabits he is joined in a mass rendition of a mock new national anthem by the other inhabitants of the cavernous pub in which they are sitting. Without ever taking itself too seriously the scene makes explicit the gap between older expressions of Britishness and a younger generation for whom the last symbolic vestiges of empire are wholly meaningless. What makes Kerrigan's film doubly refreshing is that these are never replaced with other hidebound ideas of a new Wales, and instead we are shown a generation struggling with the profound questions of identity posed by their participation in a globalized culture of casual and alienated labour. As Martin McLoone puts it (in yet another comparison to *Trainspotting*):

> ... *Human Traffic* tries to do for Cardiff and Wales what *Trainspotting* had done for Edinburgh and Scotland. What is being questioned in both films, if not rejected outright, are traditional notions of Britishness, Welshness and Scottishness and the dominant regimes of imagery that the cinema has used to represent them. (2001: 285)

Though *Human Traffic* remains probably the most significant film, apart from Marc Evans's, the most conventionally successful director to emerge from Wales during the last decade is Sara Sugarman, whose earliest work was nurtured in the country through a combination of the lottery, the broadcasters and a number of short film schemes. Whilst Sugarman's current output is firmly Hollywood (her last film was *Confessions of a Teenage Drama Queen* (2004) starring Lindsey Lohan), her second feature, *Very Annie Mary* (2001), is highly relevant to the current discussion.

At one level *Very Annie Mary* foregrounds its Welsh identity to a much greater extent than Kerrigan's film. However this foregrounding is not straightforward and can be linked to the hybridity of Sugarman's own identity. Born in Rhyl and having spent much of her life in London as an actress, Sugarman began to return to both her Welsh and Jewish identities in oblique ways. To begin with she has set all her 'Welsh' work in the South Wales valleys, traditionally poles apart from the North Wales coastal strip that Sugarman comes from. It is perhaps this 'insider/outsider' tendency that has led to the affectionate, comic, almost surreal take on Valleys life typified by *Very Annie Mary*.

Taken at face value, *Very Annie Mary* dives head first into some of the staples of tired identity debates – singing, quirky valleys characters, close-knit communities, confinement of small-town life and so on. What makes the film genuinely interesting is how far Sugarman has been prepared to push the surreal humour. The presence of the Australian actress Rachel Griffiths in the lead does admittedly take us to a comparison with her big break, *Muriel's Wedding*, but also to Baz Lurhman's *Strictly Ballroom*. This is a film that hovers on the affectionate side of parody and in so doing opens up some of the things that are often part of Welsh identity when seen from the outside without resorting to the cosiness of quasi-Ealing comedy. Above all, it is a confident film, because it is unafraid of the traps involved in dealing with the stereotypes that it very consciously trades in. Significantly, the reviews that disliked it most saw its faults in relation to other current British films with social-realist pretensions (*The Full Monty, Billy Elliot* and so on) whereas, as Sugarman has acknowledged, her aesthetic is closer to Bergman than Ken Loach.

Whilst the tone of *Very Annie Mary* is predominantly playful (Sugarman persuaded the two rising male Welsh stars, Ioan Gruffydd and Matthew Rhys to play two gay characters, Hob and Nob) there is also a central narrative of oppressive patriarchy through the father who suppresses his daughter's singing talent through a combination of jealousy and a desire to have the girl skivvy for him. By the end of the film there is a sense of release and comparative freedom and it is one that does not involve the age-old route of marriage and family. In fact, the opposite is true as Annie Mary seems free to pursue both a singing career and her own idea of sexual fulfilment. Perhaps the most telling comparison to be made with *Very Annie Mary* is the Irish television comedy *Father Ted* (1995–97) of which Lance Pettitt has written:

> It was securely Irish, but expressed a strand of expansive, confident identity associated with the Irish in mid-1990's Britain. It addressed the derogatory stereotypes endured over generations by the Irish in English society, exaggerated them and sought to explode them... As Liam Greenslade has pointed out: 'There is a huge difference between being laughed at by the coloniser and re-possessing those jokes for your own purposes.' (2000: 196)

If *Very Annie Mary* never manages the sustained satire that *Father Ted* does in the context of an Ireland finally emerging from both the colonial shadow and the iron grip of the Church, it does however deserve its place as a small step on the road to casting off old identities, in particular those relating to the South Wales valleys communities that were the most obvious victims of power exercised at a distance during the last two decades.

The final major Welsh film I would like to consider is one that usefully raises the question of what constitutes a 'Welsh' film at all. *A Way of Life*, released in 2004 to great critical acclaim, was actually directed by Amma Asante, a young black British woman raised in Streatham in South London with parents that emigrated from West Africa in the 1960s. However, the film is set in the South Wales valleys and received a large proportion of its funding via the Lottery in Wales as well as the now defunct HTV. Asante has stated that she sees the film very firmly as Welsh and that she was inspired to write and direct it by what she saw as the complex identities of her own brother's children. They have a Welsh mother and a black father from Streatham, making them, in Asante's own words – 'half of everything you could possibly imagine' (Blandford 2004: 15). Asante's commitment to the project being rooted in South Wales was extensive, trawling youth drama groups and workshops throughout the valleys in order to cast with the kind of authenticity that she felt the project demanded. As a result she ended up with a largely young and inexperienced cast that gives outstanding performances which are crucial to the film's sense of place.

The film is also powerful and controversial both about the diversity of available Welsh identities and in its attempt to take an honest and sympathetic look at some of the underlying causes of contemporary racism. At the heart of *A Way of Life* is the murder of Turkish-born man, who has lived in the South Wales valleys for much of his life. One of the perpetrators is a teenage woman with a young child.

Asante's film therefore presents powerful challenges to reductive ideas about gender, race and ultimately nation as components of contemporary identity in Wales. In fact, the film dares to challenge the idea of Wales as a place of relative racial harmony, an idea that Asante herself admits that she had bought into before the film was conceived:

> I had also said something incredibly ignorant to Peter [Edwards, one of the film's producers] during the original meeting which was, 'You've got this long history of multiculturalism in South Wales, so surely you must be well ahead of the rest of the UK?, and he had said, 'Oh you would be surprised,' and I think that was probably the thing that really got him going, my assumption that everything must be so much better Cardiff because of its history. (Blandford 2004: 14)

Such assumptions have, in recent years, been effectively and interestingly scrutinized, particularly in the context of questioning the idea of postcolonial theory being applicable to Wales. Glenn Jordan, for example, quotes movingly from an interview conducted with a Cardiff woman born in the 1930s:

> I can remember I was very good at Welsh at school... Really good. I loved it. We had this Welsh teacher Mr –. He was going around the class this day asking everybody where they came from. Well, we were all from here.

> So... I said, 'I'm Welsh'. I mean as an eight year old, I wasn't thinking about anything. He asked me what I was: I was Welsh. And he said to me, 'How can you be Welsh? You're black! Black people can't be Welsh!' (2005: 65)

In the same vein Jordan quotes Charlotte Williams, herself one of the leading writers on the question of black Welsh identity and whose words so closely echo the starting point for Amma Asante's film:

> Poor old mixed-up Wales, somehow as mixed up as I was; confused about where it had been, what it was and where it was going, rapidly re-writing history to make sense of itself as some kind of monolithic whole and it just wasn't working. I love its contours and its contradictions. There is the north, '*Welsh* Wales' they call it, and a very different south, connected only in name... The Welsh and the English, the Welsh-speaking and the English-speaking, the proper Welsh and the not so proper Welsh, the insiders and the outsiders, the

Italians, the Poles, the Irish, the Asians and the Africans and the likes of us, all fighting amongst ourselves for the right to call ourselves Welsh and most of us losing out to some very particular idea about who belongs and who doesn't. How would we ever make sense of it? (Williams 2002: 169)

It is this affectionate, though critical, tone that *A Way of Life* tends to adopt. Though it shows us the ugliness of racial hatred and the exercise of both physical and psychological power by white men and women over their neighbours, the film's daring is to have us understand their position, though it does not encourage a tolerance of it. Its central narrative focuses on a white single teenage mother (a social grouping so viciously condemned by the Tory Welsh Secretary of State, John Redwood, on a visit to the St Mellons Estate in 1994) (http://www.timesonline.co.uk/article/), Leigh-Anne Williams (Stephanie James), whose life is defined by the relentless difficulty of sheer economic survival for herself and her infant daughter. Asante's story is, however, far from a sentimental tale of noble suffering and the nadir of Leigh-Anne's portrayal is a graphic scene behind a shabby pub as a middle-aged man has casual sex with a young girl 'sold' to him by Leigh-Anne. The fact that this is an act committed by a mother desperate to buy shoes for her child is visually counterpointed by Leigh-Anne standing nearby smoking as the vulnerable teenager is so brutally exploited. In this moment many of the central tensions of the film are encapsulated: a harsh existence in a post-industrial South Wales landscape which in turn produces the kind of brutal response that leads to a callous disregard for others and, ultimately, a vicious racist mentality. Asante's achievement is to secure our understanding and sympathy for such a position whilst never in any way disguising the pain of the victims of racism or hiding the irony of a marginalized people who themselves then turn upon the minority in their midst.

The film is explicit about the context of its tragic narrative being a search for identity, one that is frequently articulated as specifically Welsh. The Turkish neighbour, Hassan Osman, who plaintively asserts that he has lived in the valleys for thirty years and yet is still treated as an outsider, Leigh-Anne and her friends riding together in a car singing the Stereophonics 'A Thousand Trees' or the young boys that come in and out of Leigh-Anne's life starting to sing 'Bread of Heaven' only to break off in embarrassment all hint at a yearning for traditional forms of cultural identity only for them to be overshadowed by the relentless combination of poverty and racism.

There is no disguising the fact that *A Way of Life* is a brutal film. At its premiere in Cardiff, Asante was crassly questioned about the 'depressing' picture of Wales that the film offered and asked whether she couldn't have shown more of the beautiful scenery or added some jokes. I would argue that the contrary is true. *A Way of Life* is a welcome mark of a maturing culture, able to face its divisions, be critical of them and, therefore, open up new possibilities for being Welsh in the twenty-first century. The alternative is a complacent sentimentality and a reductive resort to a worn out identity based only upon self-congratulation and opposition to the English. By exploring the harsh problematics of racism in a Welsh context whilst at the same time offering understanding of its economic context, *A Way of Life* both explodes the myth of a cosily multicultural Wales centred on a sentimentalized 'Tiger Bay' as one the oldest mixed-race communities in Britain, and replaces it with a more honest plea for an inclusive, fluid Welsh identity, capable of offering a meaningful place to those excluded on the grounds of both class and race.

6

'An Evaporation of Certainty': England and Theatre

Until comparatively recently it would have been extremely rare to find any discussion at all of 'English' theatre. Or, more provocatively, the term English may well have been used, but synonymously, with the term 'British'. In the last decade, however, the idea of 'English' theatre distinct from theatre in the rest of Britain has begun, to a limited extent, to be part of accepted critical discourse. Aleks Sierz, who has been influential in characterizing British theatre in the 1990s as 'in-yer-face' (Sierz 2001), devoted an entire recent article to 'the State of English Playwriting', stating that

> Of course, in the past two or three years there have been plenty of good new plays in English, but most of them have been written by Scottish, Irish or American writers. (2004: 1)

This new sense of Englishness is partly the product of a new post-devolutionary sense of identity in the other 'British' nations and can be seen as part of a wider academic and popular concern with what the very concept of England can mean for contemporary life. Cultural commentators as diverse as Jeremy Paxman (1998) and Billy Bragg (http://www.billybragg.co.uk/words/words9.html) have, in widely differing ways, offered us versions, even new blueprints, of what is can mean to be 'English' in the new millennium, though it is reasonable to suggest that the issue remains, to say the least, very fluid.

In an art form such as theatre with a relatively high dependence on public subsidy, the impact of devolutionary tendencies has been much more tangible and visible since 1994 in when separate Arts Councils for England, Ireland, Scotland and Wales were established. The organization of subsidy for the arts in the UK could, therefore, be said to have anticipated the devolutionary spirit of the New Labour Government in 1997 by some three years, though arguably it is longer than that because of earlier experimentation with regional arts boards. (http://www.artscouncil.org.uk/documents/information/php74fniH.doc)

This new awareness of the potential distinctiveness of the theatrical traditions of the British nations was made manifest through a project initiated by Paines Plough Theatre Company in 1998. *Sleeping Around* (1998) was the result of the company commissioning one writer from each of the four British nations to collaborate on a play loosely based around the form and structure of Arthur Schnitzler's *La Ronde* (1897). The result is, as the Introduction to the published version says,

> a glimpse at Britain in the late nineties – a place where people still believe in the potential of a moment's true connection with another human being, in spite of being constantly compartmentalised and brutalised by the many pressures of modern living. (Fannin, Greenhorn, Morgan and Ravenhill 1998: i)

However, given the strategy of employing a writer from the different nations, the result has little to do with the cultural distinctiveness of any part of Britain. Only through one character, Lorraine, an air hostess, do we find any sense of a consciousness of which part of the UK she originates from as she describes her first sexual encounter with a boy called Dana 'because he could sing "All Kinds of Everything" with the gut twisting innocence of a wee Derry virgin'(Fannin, Greenhorn, Morgan and Ravenhill 1998: 39) By contrast, most of the play takes place in locations closely identified with the faceless anonymity of contemporary urban life and with the alienation experienced by those that work in the new 'service' economy that is purported to be Britain's future.

Two of the play's key motifs seem to be central to what this vision of Britain is about: at the start of the play, Sarah, a marketing manager for a multinational company, is admiring her handiwork in projecting a company logo onto the moon 'A capital share until the eve of the millennium, then Pepsi get in.'(Fannin, Greenhorn, Morgan and Ravenhill 1998: 1) As the play ends Sarah re-enters the stage for the first time since the opening scene and attempts to talk to Ryan who is employed in an all-night garage. The time-locked door comes between them and their conversation struggles to overcome the physical and psychological barriers that the play as a whole has been about. Sarah is obsessed with the marketing demographics that dominate her working life and the way that she views other human beings and Ryan is locked behind his perspex screen immersed in the fantasy fiction that helps the long night-shift hours to pass. At the very end of the play Sarah opens up in a rare moment of self-revelation and her exchange with Ryan takes us back to the start of the play's journey:

> SARAH.... when I was nineteen I wanted to be held very tender, very close, and I wanted someone to love me and I'd love them and they'd care about me and laugh with me and live with me and die with me. They'd stroke my hair, and touch me and hold me in their arms and tell me they were my biggest fan and I'd want them and they'd want me and they wouldn't sleep around. They'd just lie with me, stay still, stay with me, love just me... me... Do you think that's possible?
>
> RYAN *leans forward, as if almost to kiss her, thinking on the moment.*
>
> RYAN. You're weird.

RYAN *leans forward and steals another can off the shelf. SARAH stands watching him.*

SARAH. We're gonna light up the moon tonight.

A beat.

RYAN. (*sarcastic*) Wow.

Sarah turns and walks away. (Fannin, Greenhorn, Morgan and Ravenhill 1998: 72)

With this exchange the play ends in characteristic ambiguity, but what is clear is that there is a note of doomed longing for closeness, warmth and simple human contact. The oldest symbol of romantic love has been optioned by a multinational and become a simple screen onto which its logo is projected whilst Sarah's dream is rejected by the much younger Ryan as 'weird'. On the other hand the compulsion to keep trying survives and perhaps the rejection of Sarah's 'me' orientated vision of the lost romance of her past is not such a bad thing. Despite its genesis suggesting an emphasis on the cultural diversity of Britain, *Sleeping Around* is more about the encroaching power of the global and anonymous and as such is in tune with much drama from England in the last decade. Whereas work being developed in Ireland, Scotland and Wales would often, however obliquely, be touched by the urgency of a newly liberated debate over identity, English theatre is so often about loss and anonymity, despite the much-discussed vigour and energy of 'in-yer-face' theatre.

Whilst the 'England, Ireland, Scotland, Wales' genesis of *Sleeping Around* ironically resulted in a bleak urban landscape of hotels, airports and garages that could have been anywhere in Western Europe, never mind the UK, there are powerful examples of emergent 'English' voices that have embodied the end of a monolithic sense of Britishness in a variety of ways. Rebecca Prichard's *Yard Gal* (1998) is a relatively early example of a voice being given to the experience of young black women living in and around the violent gang scene in the East End of London. Though by no means the first play to recognize the multicultural nature of the idea of 'the English', Prichard's play, commissioned by Clean Break Theatre who work inside women's prisons, is a rare example within English theatre of the sustained use of street language and patois to get inside the worlds of two characters who come from a community who rarely have anything to do with mainstream theatre. In the context of 1990s theatre this amounted to an extension both of the idea of what theatre was about and of the idea of Englishness itself, leading Aleks Sierz to observe that

'At some performances, people in the audience called out, shouting advice to Boo and Marie. Unusually for the West End, there were many black people in the audience.'(2001: 228).

Though the play as a whole does not involve itself very directly with explicit questions of identity, Boo, one of the two characters, prefaces her telling of the story of her friendship with Marie with a clear statement of her view of how she sees herself in relation to where she lives:

BOO. Everybody be chatting about the violence and the guns and drugs on the east sides, saying we should get out, but uh uh. No way. I don't leave my roots at all. That's what I was born and brought up with and that's what I stay with. I'm a rude gal. I'm a HACKNEY GAL! And wherever I go everybody knows I'm there. And nobody touch me nobody talk to me and nobody come near me 'cos they cross me they know my posse cut them up one time, y' arrright! YARD GAL WE A RUN TING! SAFE. (Prichard 1998: 10)

Aside from the language and setting of Prichard's play Boo's speech above also draws our attention to the way that *Yard Gal* was not about 'victims'. Sierz identifies this as a strong tendency of late 1990s drama, part of its more general disturbance of traditional moral certainties:

One of the defining changes in nineties theatre was the demise of politically correct 'victim drama', where perpetrators were bad and victims good. According to Dominic Dromgoole, it was the Bush theatre's policy to put the aggressor onstage instead of asking the audience to spend its time being sympathetic to victims. By emphasising such troubling notions as the complicity of victims in their victimization, provocative drama became more complex, less ideological. Instead of a morally black and white world, theatre offered grey areas and ambiguous situations. (2001: 231)

It is possible to argue, then, that if the significant way in which Britain was 'breaking up' for the Irish, Scots and Welsh in the 1990s was tangible and constitutional, then for writers in England it was in a more metaphorical sense, as the theatre's role in challenging social and moral certainties once more asserted itself. This is, of course, not to argue that writers in Ireland, Scotland and Wales are only concerned with the idea of new national identities, but if the new possibilities opened up by the prospect of devolution offered a kind of quasi-public role to the writer in the new nations, then the theatre in England has a tendency to be much more about the loss of certainty in a variety of ways. This loss is self-evidently not always a negative notion and Prichard's play, amongst other things, is one of several that added up to a belated sense of racial inclusivity in English theatres.

Partly because of its role in Nicholas Hytner's attempts to change the nature of The Royal National Theatre, Kwame Kwei-Armah's *Elmina's Kitchen* (2003) has, more recently, taken on a particular significance in this respect. At the end of Hytner's first full season as Director, *The Guardian* published a highly positive assessment in which his efforts to redefine what 'national' might mean were central:

De Jongh [Theatre critic of the *London Evening Standard*] believes he has changed the National for the first time in its 40-year history. 'We thought Nick was a solid, middle-of-the-road theatre man and he has astonished us all. He realises that it is no good any more to spin out a repertory of classic and modern plays. People are looking for new things. You have to engage with the new forms, and all sorts of different audiences, the old as well as the young. *Elmina's Kitchen* was the first time I've seen a black audience at the National Theatre first night.' (Gibbons 2003 b.)

It would be wrong to overstate the importance of any individual production and Kwei-Armah would be the first to acknowledge the significant number of voices that have emerged from black communities in recent years. However, in a discussion about the shifting sense of the nation, it is hard to ignore the symbolism of *Elmina's Kitchen* at the Royal National Theatre. Kwei-Armah's play is also unapologetically concerned with popular perceptions of black British identity, particularly that surrounding the portrayal of young men:

> ... he wrote it for his eldest son; a dark love letter, voicing his worst fears. 'I wrote this as therapy, to say, "Son there is a whole strand in black youth culture that I'm having problems with; the idea that in order to validate your blackness one has to go through some form of criminality, or wear the dress of criminality."' (Hattenstone 2003 a.)

Arguably then Kwei-Armah's play takes a greater risk with the community it portrays whilst leaving itself open to the charge that it may reinforce reactionary views amongst the mainstream theatre audience. In the same interview, Kwei-Armah talks of a hostile reaction from a black actor who auditioned for the piece threatening to 'stand in the aisles' and 'boo with my family' if the play got its subject wrong. Kwei-Armah's response was combative and unapologetic:

> Listen my friend, I will stand up with the best of them outside when the demonstrations are going on and I will argue with them head to head, because as far as I am concerned our children's blood is consecrating the earth in Hackney and all over London and all over Britain, and what I want to do is create a catalyst for a debate. If you want to watch *Cosby Show* reruns go to the Paramount Channel. But that's not what I am about. (Hattenstone 2003 a.)

In the space between *Yard Gal* and *Elmina's Kitchen* there is a sense of two parallel shifts starting to take place. In the first case there has unquestionably been an intensification of the debate and productive uncertainty over questions of the 'national' and, optimistically, this is now reflected in a building on the South Bank of the Thames that has at least begun to reach out beyond its traditional audiences and contributors. Hytner himself could not have put it any more clearly when, on being appointed to run the Royal National, he stated that 'Any consensus about what our national identity is has evaporated in the past few years, and it is with that the National Theatre should start.'(Gibbons 2001 b.)

Moves towards radically different national theatres for both Scotland and Wales are one dimension to this, but Hytner's programming suggests he sees the idea in a much broader sense and that The Royal National Theatre, whichever part of Britain/England it stands for, has to reach out to the multi-cultural dimension of our national identities as writers and theatre makers have been doing for some time.

The second shift that has taken place concerns the cultural confidence of plays concerned with minority cultures. To some extent this comes through critical mass; as more black theatre is produced there is less of an onus to 'represent', to always offer positive representations from within the community, and *Elmina's Kitchen* is one example of this. As we saw above, Kwei-Armah has not been without his critics in the black community for the vision he presents, but there is surely optimism in the diversity of voices being heard and the audiences that are being reached.

Of course, *Elmina's Kitchen* is the tip of an iceberg and worth focusing on partly because of its role in Hytner's project to extend the 'national' in National Theatre, a policy that has also tended to encourage some of British theatre's older left of centre writers to return to various forms of 'state of the nation' address. In the case of David Hare this has simply meant a resumption of the role that he took on more than a decade ago when he produced a trilogy for the National on the Church, the law and the Labour Party. In the last two years, he has returned to similar territory in two plays, *The Permanent Way* (2004) and *Stuff Happens* (2005), both of which, in their very different ways, point to a radically changing sense of British public life.

Both of Hare's plays draw partly on techniques from so-called 'verbatim theatre' which in turn have been at the heart of an extraordinary series of works at the Tricycle Theatre in Kilburn, North London, that have come to be called the 'Tribunal Plays' and which draw on verbatim testimony from public enquiries and the like, all of which were the focus of enormous media attention. In the case of Hare, *The Permanent Way* deals with the consequences of rail privatization in the UK via the dramatized voices of some of those most centrally involved including, most tellingly, victims of recent disasters, whilst *Stuff Happens* examines the lead up to the 2003 Iraq war by putting on stage the politicians from the US and Britain who made the key decisions. At the Tricycle the subjects of the Tribunal plays have included the Scott Arms to Iraq Inquiry, the massacre at Srebrenica, the Stephen Lawrence Inquiry, the Hutton Inquiry and the Guantanamo Detention Centre.

The relevance to this particular discussion of the kind of work that seeks to offer up to scrutiny the intimate workings of the machinery of government and the exercise of power in this country (and sometimes internationally), lies principally in its attempts to use theatre as a means of opening up debates that the UK government show every sign of wanting to close down. In so doing, there is an implicit sense of an attempt to decentralize control, to refuse the traditional cover-ups of official enquiry and to return the power to examine the decision-making process to the wider population. Clearly, this is not an exclusively 'English' phenomenon (in the sense of excluding Ireland, Scotland and Wales), but it is at least partly a reaction to what is widely perceived as an increase in the power of the executive in this country at the expense of the power of the elected representatives in Parliament. In this respect, then, the phenomenon of the increase in verbatim theatre of the kind mentioned above can be seen as making a contribution to a national conversation which is opposed to a monolithic sense of the nation or national identity.

This interpretation is particularly pointed in those examples of such theatre in which direct questions are asked about the fracturing of British identity, or at least the fragile consensus that has traditionally held it together. In *The Colour of Justice* (1999) the reconstruction of the Stephen Lawrence Enquiry and the questions that it raised about the institutional racism of the Metropolitan Police exposed tensions which go to the heart of some of the components of British identity, particularly the theoretical objectivity of the police. As Richard Norton Taylor's careful distillation of hundreds of hours of testimony is enacted, what is exposed is not something as easily dismissible as the British National Party, but a failure of the very heart of what maintains British society to adapt to a changing sense of national identity and all that it now encompasses.

In Hare's *Stuff Happens*, we see played out not only the political manoeuvring that led to a war that the government has now acknowledged to be one of the major causal factors behind the July 2005 London bombings, but also the sense of Britain's greatly diminished influence on world events for all the posturing and talk of partnership with the United States. In the National Theatre production, the portrayal of Tony Blair (Nicholas Farrell) is predominantly weak, blustering and dominated by the sense that he constantly seems to have of his place in history. By contrast the Americans, including George W. Bush (Alex Jennings), are far more easily confident with even Bush's traditional Texan buffoon of popular imagination turned into an icily calm calculator, whilst Dick Cheney and Donald Rumsfeld are openly dismissive of Britain's real importance. *Stuff Happens* is not simply an anti-war play (in fact, it takes quite a lot of pains to give us the more rational of arguments that were presented in favour of the war) it is also tellingly a play about the delusion of the New Labour government under Tony Blair about Britain's status in the world. The great irony is that it is a delusion that has led to one of the great causes of an increasingly divided Britain in which it has become increasingly difficult to celebrate diversity and difference within the broad frame of national identity. Instead, calls for reappraisals of Britishness are made in an atmosphere of ethnic and religious mutual distrust, the causes of which are so chillingly enacted in *Stuff Happens*.

Occupying rather different theatrical and political territory, though still firmly linked to a fracturing consensus on British/English identity is *Playing with Fire* (2005), David Edgar's first play to be set in Britain since 1987. Given that so much of Edgar's early work was of the 'state of the nation' variety, both the long gap and the return to both the British setting and National Theatre appears to be further evidence of theatre's growing concern for the changing shape of British identity since the millennium and its intensification since 9/11 and the Iraq conflict.

Edgar's focus is far more domestic than Hare's and is therefore more explicit about the divisions that have opened up both within the Blair-led Labour Party and within the idea of Englishness itself. The play's central narrative focus is on a 'failing' Old Labour northern council authority and the attempts to reform it by a London-based high flyer who is the epitome of the London-based inner circle of New Labour. The addition to this uncomfortable collision of values is, of course, the racial tension that resulted in the real-life riots in places such as Burnley and Oldham earlier in the decade. The response to the London 'missionary' by the old-style councillors is, as one reviewer suggests, in keeping with satiric tone of the first half of the play. However, as the following summary from the same review suggests, the councillors' actions simply open up the deep divisions within the community leading to the play's much darker conclusion:

> They institute translation services, drop-in centres for people involved in 'anti-social public space behaviours' (ie prostitution) and faith festivals. All of these would be admirable, if paying for them didn't mean closing down hospitals and swimming pools, antagonising the white population and stoking up the hatred of the fascist Britannia Party. Resentment boils over during a holocaust commemoration.

Though hard on the spin doctor-inspired panaceas of New Labour, Edgar does not flinch from scrutinizing the stasis and complacency that has afflicted the Old Labour stronghold. What comes through most clearly is the enormous divisions that exist where spin would have us believe none exist. If an open flexible sense of national identity is to play a part in the future healing of a fractured society, then Edgar's play demonstrates what an enormous task lays ahead for those who have to try and define its fundamental values and parameters.

Whilst both the emergence of a number of black playwrights into British mainstream theatre and the revival of a more pointedly political theatre since the millennium have signalled a willingness to raise questions about British identity, it is appropriate that some critics remain slightly sceptical about the number of black voices genuinely being heard in English theatres. Deidre Osborne (2005: 29–9), for example, has written both of the remarkable upsurge in black 'English' playwrights since the millennium, but also of the enduring predominance of white, male artistic directors:

> The year 2003 develop in mainstream London theatres (although not the West End) through the staging of a number of high profile plays by Black British dramatists, a phenomenon that has continued into 2004. This indicates a shift *has* occurred towards perceiving Black British drama as commercially viable, moving away from traditional assumptions of its genesis and production as residing primarily within community or non-mainstream theatre contexts. Yet of the eleven plays staged during this period, nine were directed by white directors, primarily male. Whilst the staging of plays by Black British dramatists in mainstream London theatres might reveal an increasingly contested sense of the 'mainstream' and revisions of what has been perceived as the traditional theatre market, traditional theatre hegemonies remain evident. White men continue to remain at the helm despite the forays in cross-cultural programming with 'new' writing.

Despite such a cautionary tone, as well as Kwei-Armah, Osborne goes on to cite the work of those such as Debbie Tucker Green, Roy Williams and Sol B. River who are slowly creating a hybrid, distinctive black aesthetic through, for example, a variety of linguistic strategies, music, technology and dance forms. On the one hand, such work can be seen to sit 'outside' the idea of contemporary English identity as

> ... acts of theatre which break the bounds of the exclusions and delimitations of the codes of white mainstream society, acts which cross and re-cross economic, political and social boundaries, thereby transforming them, freeing individuals and communities by inspiring and provoking change in attitudes and behaviour to an acceptance of strangers and society.

But more ambitiously and optimistically they can be seen as fundamentally effecting a change in that identity itself, so that Englishness (and Irishness, Scottishness and Welshness) is changed and made endlessly fluid and adaptable. As Osborne suggests this becomes a significant contributor to the postcolonial condition as the previously colonized redefine the nature of the culture within which they assume their rightful place. Osborne quotes black writer and actor Lennie James on the shock of being seen as 'English' albeit from the perspective of another 'colony':

> In New Zealand I became an Englishman... in New Zealand, all the history of England was my history. When people interviewing me spoke of the long history of British theatre it was all mine. I was allowed to own it... I can't tell you how strange that sensation was. (2005: 29)

With all the appropriate caveats of the kind quite rightly suggested by Osborne above it can be safely asserted that the last decade has seen a powerful contribution by black theatre makers, especially writers, to the evolution of the idea of Britishness and especially Englishness. For all that, though, it was still remarkable that Helen Kolawole was able to write in 2003 that

There are more plays being written, produced or directed by black and Asian women than ever before in the history of British theatre. In fact, it is no exaggeration to say that our theatre is in the process of a quiet revolution with black and Asian women at its helm. (Kowale 2003)

The report goes on to discuss a role call of women who have contributed to this theatrical redefinition of a national theatrical identity. This includes a huge spectrum of work from the ultra mainstream such as Meera Syal's startling collaboration with Andrew Lloyd Webber on *Bombay Dreams* (2002) to the pioneering work with new writers that has taken place at London's Oval House, and everything in between including established writers such as Winsome Pinnock and Tanika Gupta and a younger group that would include Tucker Green, already mentioned above. Godiwala is among those who, despite its highly questionable aesthetic qualities, would particularly assert the importance of the 'moment' of *Bombay Dreams* as 'a sign of the widespread acceptance of British-Asian theatre... as it marked a boundary line that Asian theatre makers were able to cross'. In so doing, argues Godiwala, even kitsch mainstream work such as *Bombay Dreams* is able to incorporate aesthetic strategies which

> ... destabilize the political position of the English language and English drama in England, thereby decentring the imperial hegemony underlying English culture. British-Asian drama is one of hybridity as it fractures temporality and rehistoricizes... British-Asian theatre can be seen as a marriage of theatre forms of east and west as it is a hybrid and heady mix of two heterogeneous cultures.

However a number of critics and academics have been considerably more sceptical about the contribution of *Bombay Dreams* towards a new openness to Asian cultural practices in Britain. Jen Harvie, for example, follows a number of the newspaper critics of the show's London production in concluding that *Bombay Dreams* wants it both ways; on the one hand, revelling in the spectacle of Bollywood excess whilst also retaining a very western ironic distance which is mocking in tone:

> ... the production [*Bombay Dreams*] is deeply ambivalent about its relationship to Bollywood's conventions in a way that compromises its respect for the form. Its narrative logic concludes by rejecting Bollywood's utopianism, but its staging concludes by embracing that utopianism through joyous encores. The production dances a Bollywood two-step: it positions itself as intellectually superior to Bollywood, but it nevertheless exploits Bollywood's sense of carnival... This knowing attitude towards Bollywood – taking what it wants but indicating its shrewd disavowal of the form – suggests a classic Orientalist practice: *Bombay Dreams* indulges the Eastern form as a means of portraying its own superiority to that form.

Harvie and others see, with some justification that 'events' such as *Bombay Dreams* can simply be read as opportunism and clearly it would be an enormous mistake to conclude that during Nicholas Hytner's 'evaporation of certainty' over Britain's sense of its national identity there had been an unproblematic embrace of its genuinely multicultural nature. In 1999, Jatinder Verma, the co-founder of Tara Arts and a central figure in efforts to establish a multicultural theatre in Britain for almost twenty years, offered this proposition:

> The challenge of the coming Millennium, in society, as in theatre, is to embrace the Other: to learn how to become neighbours across divides of colour, language and sensibility.

Though this is in a sense a plea that is transnational, it clearly has implications for a multi-racial society such as Britain and, as Verma goes on to argue, they are implications that were not being fully addressed by theatre at the end of the century:

> Since the Second World War Britain has been transformed in colour, in sound, in taste by, specifically, non-European migrations. Yet our theatres as a whole, through their writers as much as their producers have scarcely reflected this tectonic shift in the nature of the country.

Helen Kolawole's article referred to above tends to suggest that there had at least been some semblance of progress in the period immediately following the Millennium, though, only a year before Kolawole was writing, her newspaper felt able to publish a piece asking bluntly: 'Is British drama racist?' which opened with the following paragraph:

> It is only a matter of time… before someone brings a case of racial discrimination against a British theatre. It may prove financially costly. It will also administer a profound shock to the theatre world's image of itself. (Allen 2002.)

Paul Allen's argument is based on cold statistics and addresses the almost complete lack of black workers in positions of power in British theatre:

> A survey of 19 organisations in range of art forms in 1998 found that 6% of staff were black and Asian, but that more than half of those worked in catering or front-of-house areas. Just one Venu Dhupa, then executive director of Nottingham Playhouse – held a senior management post. Ethnic minorities are variously estimated to form 10 to 15% of the population as a whole.

> While there has been a significant increase in the casting of black actors, backstage and office areas remain almost wholly white. You just don't see black managers or technicians. (Allen 2002)

Kolawole's piece suggests that there are signs of an upward trend in the presentation of black and Asian work that might in itself encourage a different level of participation in theatre at all levels that, as Allen suggests, is an urgent priority. However, there are some who would argue that such a concentration on mainstream or even small-scale theatre is to address questions of new British identity through theatre in entirely the wrong way. Barnaby King, in a short series of articles for New Theatre Quarterly, argued that the dominant culture in Britain was black culture but then posed the question of 'how much fair exchange occurs between Black and British culture, especially in regional theatres and communities'. (2000: 131) King's argument focuses on a study of the relationship between one major regional theatre, The West Yorkshire Playhouse, and its black community, but by implication it is also about the whole thrust towards the encouragement of greater representation of black culture on British stages. Essentially King argues for the prioritization of 'Black theatre initiatives' over what he calls 'culturally specific community regeneration'. The former he regards as being about assimilation whereas the latter focuses on putting resources into art forms that are primarily for the community to speak to itself and understand itself. Discussing the work of Culturebox, one community initiative in Leeds, King describes the radical idea of priorities around questions of identity that groups such as Culturebox seek to put on the agenda:

> Of primary importance is the content of the Culturebox, which should reflect the history and identity of the group. The form should be whatever best enables the content to be expressed, and something with which the participants are familiar and for which they have a sense of ownership... Communication with 'other' groups is secondary, and will only have meaning if the identity of the self is first expressed.(2000: 135)

Taken to its logical conclusion, such an approach has radical implications for a theatre that seeks to address new national identities in ways that extend far beyond race and ethnicity. Essentially it argues that in a culture with scarce resources the first priority should be to develop art forms that are culturally specific in very precise ways, rather than encouraging the high profile, or the mainstream to be inclusive. Of course, the naive answer is that both are important. It is surely not possible or desirable to deny the aspirations of third- and fourth-generation black writers, directors and producers to have their work play to the widest possible audiences and to help re-define institutions such as the National Theatre. Equally, the more radical project of organizations such as Culturebox is exciting in the way that it is likely to reach out far more widely and fundamentally within communities, offering the possibility of still more profound changes in the way we eventually view British identities. Official policy is clear enough: the Arts Council of England's theatre strategy includes the following:

> We expect the theatre community to develop work that speaks to the diverse audiences who make up this country today. This work is a priority for us. We want to see an increase in the workforce from the non-white population; a greater percentage of the audience for all theatre coming from a greater range of backgrounds... (www.artscouncil.org.uk./nextstage/national.html)

How best to achieve this may require a greater balance between the two approaches discussed above, though it seems evident that there is now an awareness at all levels that at a time when real conflicts of global proportions are so dangerously associated in the popular imagination with ethnicity, it is more urgent than ever that our sense of what it is to be English or British is broad and flexible. The theatre, particularly the subsidized sector, has to have a strong commitment to make its own contribution in diverse ways and these may have to include attempts to address the wider audience alongside the more radical function of theatre in addressing the more specific needs of communities.

Not only is the inclusiveness of major national institutions only one relatively small measure of a post-devolutionary impetus towards national re-definition, ethnicity is obviously only one measure of inclusivity. If the 1970s and 1980s are properly seen as the decades when women playwrights and other theatre artists broke through in large numbers, it is possible to also see the contribution of women to British national re-definition in the 1990s as having a particular significance. The work of women based in Ireland, Scotland and Wales is discussed elsewhere in this volume, but post-devolution, as Susan Basnett has said, we also have 'an increasing assertion of English identity – though this is proving more difficult to define than Scottishness or Welshness or Irishness...' (2000: 78). This new sense of an English identity is one to which a number of women have made a particular kind of contribution.

Discussing the writing of Timberlake Wertenbaker in the early 1990s, Susan Carlson clearly identifies the close association between Wertenbaker's dramas of female identity and that of England itself:

> It [*Three Birds Alighting on a Field* (1991)] is also a play focused on the idea of English identity; and as she [Wertenbaker] explores the lives of characters who bring together English, Greek, Romanian, Asian, and American backgrounds, she offers a play about contemporary England, a place in which the concept of nation is problematised and 'English' identity is consequently destabilised. (2000: 144)

Though writing well before the moment of devolution itself, Wertenbaker's work accurately reflects the problematics of national identity in England, and indeed Britain, particularly in the period following the false certainties offered by Thatcherism. Her contribution also draws attention to the way that the work of women writers has been central to postcolonial perspectives in a huge number of different contexts. In Ireland, Scotland and Wales women writers and theatre makers have often been at the forefront of the post-devolutionary theatre scene, though it is harder to discover recent women's voices that have attempted the extremely difficult task of writing about English identity in ways that are linked to new identities for women. Wertenbaker herself has spoken of what she saw as a more general decline in the range of women's voices to be heard in Britain as the 1990s progressed:

> I made a fuss about it recently because I felt women's plays were being marginalised again. There have been some bad years recently when not only could you not see any plays by women on the main stages you no longer even saw women appear on those stages. And in so far as theatre holds up a mirror of some sort, you began to fell women had no reflection. (Cited in Carlson 2000: 147)

Not everybody would agree with the extent of Wertenbaker's assessment, but work on 1990s British theatre suggests a re-assertion of a kind of theatricality that, superficially at least, is most commonly associated with masculinity, albeit a masculinity in crisis. The phrase 'in-yer-face theatre' has been mentioned previously and is expanded on extensively in the work Aleks Sierz (2001). Documentation of the phenomenon, in fact, usually includes women writers, most prominently Sarah Kane, but also Phyllis Nagy, Judy Upton, Naomi Wallace and Tracey Letts as well as Rebecca Prichard whose work is discussed above. However, there is little doubt that the overwhelming sensibility in this body of work by English writers lies outside what had come to be thought of as new strategies brought into theatre by the feminist writers of the previous two decades. Kane, for one, explicitly and aggressively rejected the idea of being thought of in terms of gender: 'I have no responsibility as a woman writer because I don't believe there's such a thing.'(Saunders 2003: 99), but at the same time there is a strong case for her work being seen as part of a new crisis of national identity and, moreover, one firmly linked to the ongoing crisis of sexual identity. *Blasted* (1995) was first performed before devolution itself became the constitutional articulation of one aspect of a 'new' Britain, but it can properly be seen as very much part of the same process of re-assessing the nation as plays that followed the formal 'break-up' of Britain. In its sheer impact, well beyond its original performance life, *Blasted* can properly be seen as one of the genuinely significant theatrical events of the last decade and as such has clear importance for this discussion. In the first full-length study of Kane's work, Graham Saunders explicitly articulates *Blasted*'s relationship to questions of nationalism:

> The play works on many levels, and while much of its dominant themes concern themselves with the relationship between Ian and Cate, and later Ian's personal agonies and partial redemption, its other dominant ideas focus around the question of nationhood. It is a play that asks uncomfortable questions about British identity, and in bringing a foreign war straight into a Leeds hotel room also asks questions about British engagement with a broader Europe. (2002: 51)

As Saunders points out, Kane makes Ian, the journalist at the heart of *Blasted*, Welsh by birth, but thoroughly English (in an old-fashioned imperialist sense) in his view of both 'Britain' itself and of Britain's relationship to the rest of the world:

> [To Ian] 'English and Welsh is the same. British' (3:41). But his sense of national identity is based almost entirely on a sense of racism – 'Hate this city. Stinks. Wogs and Pakis taking over' (1:4) – and racial purity: 'Come over from God knows where have their kids and call them English they're not English born' (3:41). (Saunders 2002: 51)

Kane's play, of course, makes Ian confront the potential consequences of his narrow nationalism in the most brutal possible way as the second half of the play introduces the soldier from the Bosnian conflict. As the soldier performs act after act of brutality on Ian, he represents the wider world that Ian's prurient parochialism has attempted to ignore, but also he represents one of the potential consequences of the idea of the nation becoming all-consuming. In a play that has generally been seen as being about a broader, more fundamental human propensity towards brutality, its passing references to ideas of English national identity are chilling. It is an identity inextricably linked to the cultural dominance of a particular kind of masculinity and in this Kane is inevitably linked to at least some of the 'in-yer-face' group mentioned above.

There is already enough written about the wider 'in-yer-face' phenomenon and Aleks Sierz in particular has done a valuable job in providing detailed signposts for the detailed re-evaluations that will inevitably come. Here it is possible only to make tentative connections between some of this work and the specific question of an emergent concern with English identity in the last decade.

Sarah Kane became a highly unwilling competitor in a game to nominate the theatre maker that would join the other artists that were supposed to have defined the end of the twentieth century in Britain. This ill-defined group often laboured under inappropriate titles including the now almost universally reviled 'Cool Britannia' which, for a brief period around 1998, until the spin moved on, was appropriated by the New Labour government in a whirl of parties at 10 Downing Street designed to show off the 'young' credentials of its members. Such media attention is difficult to cut through when attempting to assess the relevance of work in theatre to any new sense of a fractured Britain, but a number of commentators, including Aleks Sierz, have made valuable attempts to reflect on what seems to have been a powerful upsurge in new writing for the theatre during the 1990s. Some of this work is covered elsewhere in sections on Ireland, Scotland and Wales, and here there will be an attempt to assess the relevance of contemporaries of Sarah Kane to new questions of English identity.

The first thing to say is that the plays of writers such as Mark Ravenhill, Joe Penhall, Anthony Neilson, David Eldridge and Jez Butterworth have, in general, little explicit connection with a Britain that is 'breaking up' at all. If it is possible to generalize about their concern for identity it is in the area of gender and sexuality. However, it is clear that in certain respects that the concerns of these writers are connected to a rapidly changing world, one element of which is the changing identity of Britain as a nation and, post-devolution, the particular case of England. Sierz's fundamental explanation of the rise of what he sees as a closely connected group is based primarily on the scale of political change, both nationally and internationally, which produced a new moral and intellectual climate to which a new generation of writers could respond:

> ... the decade [the 1990's] was characterized by a new sense of possibility that was translated into unprecedented theatrical freedom. The fall of the Berlin Wall and the exit of Margaret Thatcher showed those under twenty-five that, despite the evidence of political ossification, change was possible; the end of Cold War ideological partisanship freed young imaginations. Youth could be critical of capitalism without writing state-of-the-nation plays; it could be sceptical of male power without being dogmatically feminist; it could express outrage without being politically correct. (2001: 36)

Though many of the 'landmark' plays of this generation of writers were written and first performed before the moment of devolution itself they are nonetheless connected to the evolving political climate that provided the momentum that led to devolution and all the implications that has for the idea of 'England'. It would obviously be wrong to separate this entirely from an altogether longer-term postcolonial sense of Britain, but the 1990s represented another change of gear after such a long period of a particular kind of conservative rule. Though the Major government remained in power it was clear by at least 1995 that it was a completely spent force and that there would be change, including the constitutional changes involved in devolution. The Irish Peace Process had already suggested a different stance on Northern Ireland. If anything could be said to have dominated thinking about the future of England as a meaningful construct it would be uncertainty about everything except perhaps the necessity to retreat from a culture so often identified with the assertion of power. Billy Bragg is just one of a number of influential cultural commentators who has discussed the need to reclaim the symbols of Englishness from those who have associated them with ugly, assertive masculinity and racism:

> Jack Straw's comments on the potentially violent nature of English nationalism may come to be seen as a defining moment in the search for a modern sense of English identity. Speaking in a Radio 4 documentary about what it means to be British in the aftermath of devolution, the home secretary shied away from the subject of a separate English identity by suggesting that there is something dark and dangerous lurking in the heart of England.

This instinctive reaction, that Englishness is a stone best left unturned, is not uncommon among liberal-minded people, woolly or otherwise. Sadly it is our squeamishness on this subject that has allowed it to become the preserve of the bigots and bootboys. Until the fair-minded majority of the English, who like to think of tolerance and a sense of fair play as national traits, can begin to evoke an inclusive identity for everyone who belongs to England, then it will be left to the Powellite right to declare who does and does not belong here. (http://www.billybragg.co.uk/words/words9.html)

Despite their so often being defined by the degree of onstage violence they portray it is possible to see that a number of key theatre makers of the 1990s were hesitantly part of the project to re-make England through their critiques of the masculinity that lay behind 'the potentially violent nature of English nationalism'. At one level Jonathan Harvey's accessible and populist work offers stories of struggles for gay identity in working-class settings, even venturing into the most traditional masculine territory of all, football, in *Guiding Star* (1998) set in a Liverpool working-class household profoundly affected by the Hillsborough disaster. By contrast, Mark Ravenhill's *Shopping and Fucking* (1996) is set in a much more rootless world of urban drifters where class is much less easy to define. In terms of overseas productions especially, *Shopping and Fucking* became one of the most frequently staged plays of the decade and thus one of the key theatrical representations of England. It shares with Harvey's work a concern for masculinity, but the similarity is strictly limited as Ravenhill's vision is much harsher and more cerebral. Sierz refers to it as a 'nineties boys' story' (2001: 130) intimately connected to the end of old certainties about the role of men in contemporary culture:

The play's gender confusions are about definitions of maleness: Gary the abuse victim who wants to die; Mark, the emotional dependent who is also a junkie; Robbie, the bisexual. In scene after scene, the boys foul up and it is Lulu the woman who holds things together. (2001: 130)

Alongside this depiction of the contemporary irrelevance of traditional masculinity runs an anger at the emergence of a culture where citizens have become mere consumers. In discussion with Sierz, Ravenhill makes the explicit connection with the world created by the older generation in the previous decade:

His play he said, was an implicit critique of Thatcher's dictum that 'There is no such thing as society'; if her vision was true, this is what you got, a 'cynical and hardened' attitude, angry that a 'sense of society has disappeared'. (Sierz 2001: 136)

Though, by the end, it is tinged with optimism for the future, Ravenhill's vision of contemporary culture is harsh but also full of doubt. It is, of course, not specifically about England as distinct from the rest of Britain, or, perhaps, the West in general, but in its focus on a directionless, rootless world struggling to discover anything of value outside of commodity exchange it is inevitable that it becomes a metaphor for an England devoid of the sense of purpose given to the other British nations through the project of re-definition and newly acquired power.

In *Some Explicit Polaroids* (1999) Ravenhill returns to similar territory to *Shopping and Fucking*, though, in a sense, more explicitly. He uses the device of a central character, Nick, being released from a long prison sentence in order to provide the audience with a distanced eye on the London into which Nick is released. Ravenhill's ambivalent vision of loss is global rather than specifically British – Nick' prison sentence was served for an act of politically motivated violence in the name of socialism (here very loosely defined) and he returns to a world where such values are seen as an irrelevance. The rootless world that the characters inhabit is very much the metropolitan centre and it appears as a place that is lost, one could say almost dispossessed.

Ravenhill wrote a piece very recently that, among other things, acknowledged the 'phenomenon' of the group of young writers to which his work belongs and the common sensibility which all they shared. Rightly he stops short of seeing the group as any kind of homogeneous movement, but in the context of this volume their depiction of a culture shorn of any direction except that of the consumer seems to have a connection to an England struggling to find an identity. Writing of all his work up to *Some Explicit Polaroids*, Ravenhill says:

> Nobody in these plays is fully adult. They are all needy, greedy, wounded, only fleetingly able to connect with the world around them. Consumerism, late capitalism – whatever we call it – has created an environment of the infant 'me' where it is difficult to grow into the adult 'us'. (2004: 311–312)

To his list of possible 'causes' of the environment he discusses, Ravenhill could have added what could be described as advanced postcolonialism. A Britain several decades after the end of Empire now faces a new phase of internal de-colonization and it leaves England, in particular, in a situation of great cultural uncertainty. Ravenhill and a number of the other key English theatre writers of the 1990s wrote of a world peopled with characters searching for any kind of identity. The idea of the national is only rarely mentioned, but the crisis of the nation is part of the fabric of the culture that they inhabit and the makers of 'in-yer-face' theatre can properly be seen as important to the efforts to re-invent English and British identity.

At the time of writing, the New Labour government has suffered a series of embarrassing reversals in its efforts to establish regional assemblies in England. Not the least of these was a huge majority vote against the idea in the North-East. The signs are that this will signal an end to the project of attempting to extend some measure of political devolution to the English regions, though London and other smaller cities will retain a mayor and, in London's case, its own assembly. Running counter to these setbacks for those who would wish to see the project of devolution continue has been a number of developments that have led to a revival of the fortunes of explicitly 'regional' theatre in England. In 2000, after a wide ranging Arts Council review of theatre in England, a new spending package was announced that made explicit reference to regional theatre:

> Chris Smith, the Culture Secretary, yesterday unveiled a bold rescue package for the arts, promising millions for the rejuvenation of an arts infrastructure devastated by almost two decades of neglect.

> The Arts Council will receive an extra £100m a year from 2003, the biggest increase in funding in its 44-year history. There will be smaller phased increases of £15m and £45m

before then, with a large portion of the money staunching the near meltdown in regional theatre. (Gibbons 2000)

Whilst on the face of it this represented a radical step towards English cultural devolution, commentators such as Jen Harvie have rightly drawn attention to the problematic link between such initiatives and New Labour's focus on the economic impact of the 'creative industries':

> ... New Labour's industrialization of the arts suggests for many very sinister implications, wrongly prioritizing art's commercial value over its social value, dangerously conflating the objectives of cultural and economic regeneration, limiting the right of artistic expression to those who can be economically productive, disempowering the people by transforming them from collective audiences and makers into individual and alienated consumers, and so on into an abyss of anti-social capitalist commodity fetishism. (2003: 22)

This pessimistic vision of New Labour's policies on the arts can, as Harvie herself goes on to suggest be tempered by consideration of the uses that arts practitioners themselves can make of the unaccustomed attentions of government:

> ... evidence suggests that in some situations, theatre planners and practitioners have exploited the government's interest and investment in the 'creative industries' to produce opportunities to make and distribute theatre practice that is impressively socially aware and democratic. (2003: 16)

Harvie actually uses Scotland as an example of what she means here, but it is worth considering for a moment whether the extra investment in New Labour's second term has produced 'devolved' theatre in England that has been strong and distinctive enough to be recognized as part of any re-invention of identity. Only a year after the announcement of the extra funding for regional theatre, and well before there had been much actual economic impact (though there would clearly have been a boost in long-term financial confidence), *The Guardian* ran a story proclaiming the return of the 'provinces' as a theatrical force:

> Regional theatre is drawing audiences from greater distances because cities north and west of the capital have become centres for talent. 'A lot of the best creative work is happening outside London and the capital's audiences are clamouring to see it,' said Rachel Coles of the West Yorkshire Playhouse. Hence the large numbers of regional productions and co-productions that premiere outside London then play to sell-out runs in the West End. *The Play What I Wrote*, a Kenneth Branagh-directed tribute to Morecambe and Wise currently packing houses in the West End, is a northern co-production that premiered at the Liverpool Everyman and Playhouse. (Chrisafis 2001)

From this description alone it is possible to see that the main way that this revival of English regional theatre is perceived is in its ability to please audiences at the metropolitan centre. The article as a whole marvels at the spectacle of Londoners travelling to previously unheard of venues and, as in the example above, celebrates work that originates in the regions but is actually good enough to pack them out in the West End! At one level there is nothing wrong in this, particularly if the high-end London transfers are used to underpin opportunities to see a wide variety of theatre outside London. However, the signs are that much regional success tends to be 'imported'; a recent *New Statesman* article praised the tenure of Michael Grandage at 'Sheffield Theatres' (a collaborative venture between two Sheffield venues: The Lyceum and The Crucible) by referring largely to his ability to bring in audiences by attracting established stars:

> His most important legacy is the creation of a new audience via a vibrant education policy and the snaring of box-office hits such as Joseph Fiennes, Kenneth Branagh, Diana Rigg and Derek Jacobi... (Coveney 2004)

The mention of 'a vibrant education policy' is clearly heartening, but the list of 'star' performers tends not to suggest any sense of distinctive local voices. In fact, as one would expect, the true picture is mixed. In a year's programming in Sheffield across three venues (the Lyceum also has a studio) there is a relatively heavy emphasis on star performers and staples of middlebrow theatre, but there is also Forced Entertainment in a large venue in the city in which they are based and even more importantly the 'Pyramid Project' designed to foster very small companies and new work. One such company has been Unlimited Theatre whose online production diary of a show called *Zero Degrees and Drifting* describes it as having its origins in 'a discussion about English identity and history'. (http://www.sheffieldtheatres.co.uk/index)

In comparable venues around England it is possible to find similar pictures. The Liverpool Everyman's artistic director is about to take 'a huge risk' (Coveney 2004) in celebrating the theatre's fortieth birthday with two new plays by new writers, though the strength of new writing remains in London and in exceptional touring companies such as Paines Plough. What has changed most in regional theatre in the last decade has been the sense of confidence expressed by the majority of artistic directors in contrast to the lengthy period of under funding and closures that happened in the 1980s and into the 1990s. In a piece entitled 'We don't have to whinge any more' in *The Guardian* in June 2004, the directors of the eight largest regional theatres discussed the prospects for the future and the impression is, for arts professionals at least, one of almost universal optimism. One comment by Simon Reade of the Bristol Old Vic is particularly telling in this context:

> Theatres are back in the hands of the artists again. Five years ago, we would never have dreamed of applying to run a theatre like the Bristol Old Vic, but the Theatre Review has given artists confidence that regional theatre is the place to be. I'd like to see the term 'regional theatre' abolished however. We ought to work on the European model of national state theatres. We're the National State Theatre of Bristol. (Hickling 2004)

It is tempting to see in this one sound bite loaded statement many of the contradictions contained in the whole concept of a devolved theatre in contemporary England. On the one hand the thinly disguised condescension implied in the idea that a regional theatre was now good enough for real artists to think of working in again, but on the other, the confidence that regional theatre need no longer define itself as such. Just as the aspirant national theatres of Scotland and Wales should not always and exclusively be looking inwards to questions of national identity so too can the 'regional' English theatres look beyond their remit to be national and international venues themselves. If, on the other hand, they ignore their region and, most of all, fail to nurture local voices, their role in the continuing project to imagine a genuinely diverse notion of contemporary England is severely diminished.

It has inevitably been more complex and problematic to discuss the notion of theatre in England as distinct from the rest of the UK in comparison to similar discussions about Ireland, Scotland and Wales. As has been apparent throughout this volume the very notion of a distinct English identity is at the present time extremely problematic, though attractive to many across the political spectrum, and because of the prevailing structures of power one is inevitably drawn into a discussion of 'Britain'. Whilst London remains the centre of UK cultural activity and we have a British (rather than English) Royal National Theatre on the South Bank, any discussion of English theatre will include much stronger resonances for the wider UK than those around the theatre of the other nations. What emerges most strongly from a complex picture, however, is a theatre that is, to some extent at least, restored to one of its most vital functions which is to question and unsettle conventional ideas about the distribution of power. In England, as well as the other three nations whose identity has more obviously shifted in the last ten years, I would argue that fundamental political change has been part of a revitalizing force giving impetus to this kind of theatre. Of course, such change has had to meet much larger influences, including the relations between Britain, the US and the Islamic world and the consequences of this for many of Britain's ethnic communities, but it also seems clear that a monolithic sense of Britain and, therefore, England, was powerfully destabilized by political change in the late 1990s and that theatre continues to respond to that through its unique capacity to perform the mutability of identity.

'PROTESTANTS DON'T WRITE PLAYS, YOU SEE': IRELAND AND THEATRE

The instability of the status of 'Northern Ireland's' devolved government has been reflected in recent theatre in ways that pull almost in opposite directions. On the one hand, there has been no appetite for any kind of 'national' institution in the north of Ireland as there has been in Wales and Scotland. Those that see such institutions as essential hallmarks of a mature theatrical culture tend to look from Ulster either south to Dublin or across to London to find national theatres which they can call their own if they so wish.

On the other hand, the 'Peace Process' and consequent movement 'back' towards some measure of political devolution to a Northern Ireland Assembly has seemingly been a factor in the emergence of a theatre both sides of the Irish border that has seen questions of identity close to the forefront of its concerns. This chapter is not therefore confined reductively to Irish writers working in Ulster, but rather looks at work that can be seen as contributing, however obliquely, to new definitions of Irishness in a post-devolutionary context. In many cases it can actually be difficult to define which side of the Irish border a writer genuinely belongs. As Mary Trotter has said:

> Many Northern Irish writers playwrights have received funding from the Arts Council both in Great Britain and the Republic of Ireland, and their works are regularly anthologised and critiqued as Irish, rather than British, dramas. (2000: 119)

There is also a sense in which the reverse is true whereby certain key Irish writers of the last ten years become 'British' through, for example, long stay residencies at one of the major national theatre institutions or, in the case of Conor McPherson, becoming central to the revived Royal Court, still for many the home of new 'British' writing for the theatre.

Inescapably the politics of Ireland, in general, but most pointedly in the north, have meant that identity is at the forefront of writers' concerns in ways that clearly have a greater sense of urgency than in the rest of the UK. If contemporary theory sees identity as, above all, contested, then in Northern Ireland in particular this has a distinctive force. As Trotter puts it:

> For Northern Irish writers, writing in the interstice between Eire and the UK, and finding their work influenced by both British and Irish cultural traditions and politics, the notion of national identity becomes complex indeed. (2000: 119)

It is, of course, not within the scope of this book to examine Irish theatre's concern with identity *per se*, but rather to examine its responses to developments within the last decade. More than in any other part of Britain dramatists and theatre makers have been involved in the bitter struggle for control of what Ireland 'is' for more than a century. What is being attempted here is the more limited assessment of how the theatre has responded to the specific changes in the 1990s that have once more promised to radically alter the relationship between what is constitutionally known as Northern Ireland and the rest of Britain. By extension, of course, this means Britain's relationship with the whole of Ireland.

Just as in the rest of Britain it is possible to find writers and other theatre artists in Ireland both responding in very direct and specific ways to the changing political situation as well as those whose work can be obliquely read as some kind of response. Among those who responded most directly to the ceasefires and subsequent 'Peace Process' is Christina Reid whose *Clowns* (1996) is a direct updating of the lives of some of the characters that appeared in *Joyriders* (1986), her bleak portrayal of the Belfast (more specifically the Divis flats) of the 1980s. Even the title of Reid's earlier work is a chilling reminder of a decade that saw the destruction by mass unemployment of communities right across Britain and the creation of one of the tabloid's most popular 'folk-devils', the young urban male that stole and raced cars, often with tragic results. Reid's narrative hammers home the bitter irony of the 'joy' part of that superficial label as her young characters experience the thorough inadequacy of one of the many employment schemes dreamt up by the successive British Tory administrations. Furthermore, *Joyriders* explores the particular edge that the phenomenon of stealing cars for pleasure took on in Northern Ireland when one of the characters, Maureen, is shot dead by a British soldier pursuing a stolen car.

Joyriders remains a powerful portrait of one of the many low points in recent Northern Irish history, but its vision of Belfast is undoubtedly a more sympathetic version of the monolithic view of the city that prevailed throughout the 1970s and 1980s. For many in mainland Britain it was also reflective of a highly generalized view of 'Ireland' perpetuated by a news agenda dominated by the traditional imagery of the 'Troubles' and drama (principally on television) that tended to work within the natural dramatic parameters of the conflict.

Clowns is no glib optimistic sequel either, though at times it attempts to catch the cautious optimism that gathered some momentum as the decade went on. Whilst not romanticizing the Belfast of *Joyriders*, Reid's later work is also cautious about new identities being foisted on the city by those anxious only to exploit its economic potential. As Trotter puts it:

> The old Lagan Mill which was the site of the employment scheme in *Joyriders*, is now a new shopping mall, a symbol of Belfast's burgeoning economic growth at the eve of the cease-fire. Yet the pristine mall, with its culturally non-specific stores and romanticised statue of a

millworking woman and her child in the middle of a fountain, reflect the way Belfast's true history – and the history of its workers – is being smoothed over by the hands of global capitalism. (2000: 127)

It is perhaps significant that in a decade that has seen a virtual avalanche of new Irish work produced in Britain that Reid's own work has not advanced. There is sense in which she deals unfashionably with an equally unfashionable view of what most want to see as a changing city. This is not to endorse this view, rather to speculate that Reid has been eclipsed by a generation whose work can more easily be absorbed by both theatrical and political shifts. There is perhaps a sense that work such as *Joyriders* and even *Clowns* are uncomfortable reminders of an identity that the image-makers are anxious to escape from.

For many in Northern Ireland one of the most striking developments in recent Irish theatre history has been the emergence of a major voice from the working-class Loyalist Protestant community in Gary Mitchell. Mitchell himself has consistently taken pains to distance himself from an overt political position; for example, when asked to contribute to a *Guardian* series on the state of 'political theatre' in Britain:

> To this day, I am asked in interviews to cough up the solution to the Northern Ireland problem, as though I were deliberately and selfishly keeping it to myself. Another question I am asked is: will I always write about Northern Ireland? My answer remains the same. I don't write about Northern Ireland. I write about people. (Mitchell: 2003)

Whilst entirely understanding Mitchell's motives and respecting his desire for recognition of the wider applicability of his thematic concerns, it is hard not to discuss his work as representative of political shifts in Northern Ireland when his characters are often not simply 'Protestants', but also members of loyalist paramilitary organizations. This is not in any sense to attempt to limit Mitchell's substantial body or work, but it seems clear that his vision of the world is at the very least highly coloured by an interest in what is now becoming of people who have invested so much of their lives in a struggle that has taken a radical new direction. What makes Mitchell distinctive, of course, is that his territory has been so rarely covered before, and it is highly unlikely that his rise to prominence is unconnected with the direction that Northern Irish politics has taken in the last decade.

Essentially Mitchell's work takes protagonists that no one else has wanted to touch except as vehicles for expressing another kind of politics altogether and attempts to open up the pain that has been covered by the bitterness of sectarian hatreds. He is obviously not the first Protestant to do this, but as he himself has acknowledged he is at the very least a rarity who is seen, to put it mildly, as an oddity within his own community:

> Protestants don't write plays, you see. You must be a Catholic or a Catholic sympathiser, or a homosexual to do that. No one in our community does that because playwriting is a silly pretend thing. (Gibbons 2000 a.)

Furthermore, Mitchell's has not always been a life lived observing the conflict from a safe artistic distance. Though now he professes his primary interest in people, he has also spoken about his immersion in Loyalist culture and values and earlier flirtation with paramilitary activity:

I grew up completely loyalist, completely Unionist, completely Protestant... I believed it all. I was very frightened of this Catholic monster that was raping my community and trying to kill us all. I tried to involve myself in the UDA and find out where the UVF was. I tried to play my part, I wanted to bring the war to them. I did some bad stuff to people to prove myself but I was racked with guilt. My conscience would never let me go to the levels of criminality you needed to. People put it down to a lack of masculinity. I was full of weakness but those weaknesses I now see as my strengths. I have an inability to break the law. I tried, but my conscience kept calling me back, and I question everything. (Gibbons 2000 a.)

Frequently, though not exclusively, his plays turn on divisions within the Loyalist community rather than sectarian violence *per se*, though it is often hard to separate the two. *Trust* (1999) is centrally concerned with the breakdown of trust within a family, but it is quickly apparent that the family becomes a clear metaphor for a post-cease-fire Loyalist community. Though the whole plot turns on a bungled deal over weapons and the characters are Protestant, there are no names of specific Loyalist groups (unlike some of Mitchell's other work). This tends to make the play a more abstracted dissection of the mechanisms by which trust between human beings is undermined rather than an examination of who and what is to blame for the failures of the Peace Process.

Perhaps more than the central family itself, the character in *Trust* that is most poignantly emblematic of a changed Britain as it manifests itself through the politics of Northern Ireland is Trevor, a member of an unnamed Loyalist paramilitary organization, recently released from prison after thirteen years inside. He visits Geordie, a small-time paramilitary leader, on a vague mission to get something to do, some kind of 'work':

TREVOR. I just thought I'd call round and see how the land lies so to speak. Things have been kind of quiet for me Geordie. Since I got out like there's been nothing.

GEORDIE. What do you mean nothing?

TREVOR. There's been nothing for me. Nothing for me to do like.

GEORDIE. Work you mean.

TREVOR. Aye, work like. I need to get some. You know, its just me and my Ma and all but like I need to get something extra for Christmas coming up, like, you know what I mean? I was thinking of maybe trying to see the kids and you know she won't let me like unless I've got something for them. You know.

(Mitchell 1999: 20)

The poignancy of Trevor's situation, a supposed anachronism in the 'new ' Belfast, is heightened moments later when Geordie and his wife Margaret suddenly seize him and frisk him for a concealed recording device. Trevor is both confused and outraged at this, the play's first revelation of a specific loss of 'trust':

GEORDIE. Look, Trevor, you're not long out, you're short of money and you suddenly appear at my door and come into my house and start asking questions. Now put yourself in my place. Do you hear me Trevor?

TREVOR. I know what you mean, But for fuck's sake, it's me, like. Thirteen fucking years. Thirteen fucking years. Thirteen fucking years and you think I'm going to come out and... I can't even fucking say it. I'm fucking disgusted, Geordie, I really fucking am.

GEORDIE. Well, look I'm sorry, Trevor mate. It's a sign of the times, the Police are all over us these days. You just can't be too careful.

(Mitchell 1999: 23)

What Trevor has served thirteen years for is never discussed, Mitchell is more interested in the sudden sense of loss being experienced by whole sections of his own community alongside the more celebrated benefits of fitfully sustained cease-fires. Trevor proves later in the play that he remains capable of both extreme violence and stupidity, but Mitchell's skill is in making him remain sympathetic, largely because of his sheer inability to comprehend the changes that have left him so isolated and without a discernible place in the new world. Trevor ultimately becomes a pawn in the vicious struggle between Geordie and his wife over the best way to deal with their son Jake, who is, of course, the future, a future that at the end of the play can only be secured by betrayal.

Mitchell's is not a romantic view, but ultimately one that makes an implicit plea for those left behind by the shifts in British and Irish politics. It is also one that continually reminds us of the enduring role of class in creating identity and power relations even in a culture where religion has for so long been the apparently defining factor. In a rare scene that takes the play outside the suffocating domestic space that is Geordie and Margaret's home, Mitchell sets us up to expect a moment of symbolic importance by having his characters arrange a clandestine meeting at the Knockagh Monument. As the English soldier Vincent says, 'A monument to remember all the people of Antrim who died fighting in the great war side by side with Englishmen...' (Mitchell 1999: 50), but Julie the working-class pragmatist looking for any way out of the limiting world in which she finds herself has a different view. She doesn't see the venue for the meeting as being selected by the paramilitaries for anything other than practical reasons and dismissively debunks the monument's symbolic importance:

JULIE. They didn't pick this place to make me nervous or sad. They picked it because hardly anybody would ever come near this place. Hollywood would have suited you better; that's what they didn't like about it. But here, this is... you might get people once a year coming away up here on a Sunday morning or something, but that would be it. Other than that. Some nights you get fellas bringing their girls up for a shag in their car. That's why they call it Knockherupagh Monument.

(Mitchell 1999: 50)

If anything Mitchell's next play, *The Force of Change* (2000), is more explicit still in its examination of what many of his characters see as a dying culture. In this play Mitchell is altogether more explicit about the specifics of the conflict as he presents a relentless picture of the Royal Ulster Constabulary as torn apart in its attempts to shake off a past contaminated by its association with Loyalist paramilitary activity. In a series of diatribes during the interrogation of a UDA member, Bill Byrne, an old-school RUC detective, vents his feelings about what is happening to Northern Ireland. Speaking to Stanley Brown, the UDA suspect, he says:

> BILL. Your organisation is changing too and there's nothing you can do to stop it is there? See I know like you know that there are other more important people out there, causing all these changes. Changes that affect you and me both. Changes that affect our culture, our identity, our country. You know the people I'm talking about.

(Mitchell 2000: 49)

Just a few lines on and Byrne makes explicit what he and, by implication, so many of Mitchell's 'lost' characters think is driving change in Northern Ireland:

> BILL. I don't think it is a peace process for a start. I think it is a Nationalist process. I think its playing into the hands of the enemies of Ulster. I don't believe David Trimble when he says that the Union is safer now than it ever was. I don't believe the Irish Government when they lifted their territorial claim over Northern Ireland. But I do believe Gerry Adams when he says that this a stepping stone to a United Ireland.

(Mitchell 2000: 49)

Bill's diametric opposite in the RUC is Caroline Paterson, a modernizing officer who is both ambitious and determined that the force loses its inward looking macho culture and its close identification with the Protestant paramilitaries. It is through Paterson that Mitchell is able to offer one of his many speculations on the potential of women or, in more abstract terms, the feminine to contribute to a genuine future for a culture so weighed down by a particular vision of masculinity. At least one reviewer was quick to compare Mitchell's portrayal of a woman police officer struggling with a deep-rooted patriarchal culture with the high-profile TV series *Prime Suspect* (1991–) (Gardner 2000), but the context here makes the gender power struggle a clear parallel to the political one. Because Mitchell's work principally gives voice to the fears of the Protestant community this becomes a highly complex collision of ideas. It is a commonplace in postcolonial art to link contemporary gender politics with the politics of postcolonial societies, but in Mitchell's case his most articulate voices are not raised against a colonial power in any accepted sense of the term. If there is an identifiable oppressor for Mitchell it appears to be the distortions of truth and loss of faith in fundamental human values that have been the consequences of the bitter sectarian struggle in Northern Ireland and it this 'colonizing' effect that the woman police officer in *The Force of Change* struggles against as much as gender prejudice. At one point in the play Paterson is discussing her pessimism about her promotion prospects with Mark Simpson, a relatively sympathetic colleague:

MARK. I worked with a Catholic Detective once. You think you have problems. This guy thought everybody was watching him, everybody was out to get him.

CAROLINE. But surely he must've been right.

MARK. No, what I'm saying is he thought it was everybody and all the time. Not just when promotion boards came round.

CAROLINE. How long ago was this?

MARK. That's not the point.

CAROLINE. If you're going to sit there and tell me that nobody was out to get this Catholic guy then... (*Almost laughs*).

MARK. Caroline, lots of people were out to get him, of course they were, it was a different world back then.

CAROLINE. Oh of course I forgot we've got peace now, we've got progress. Mark, if that's what you want to believe then go ahead and believe it, but don't talk to me because I live in the real world.

(Mitchell 2000: 45)

Despite the fact that Paterson and her RUC colleagues all remain Loyalists to different degrees there is also throughout the play what has been called a 'parity of disesteem':

Rather than choosing to venerate or simply accept unionism and nationalism we should be attempting to deconstruct and transcend them. Perhaps the time has come for a little more parity of *dis*esteem. (Coulter cited in Llewellyn Jones 2002: 142)

Whilst *The Force of Change* is powerfully pessimistic in its depiction of the depths of bitterness being experienced by a demoralized police force, there is also a sense of change, of something monolithic beginning to crumble. If there is hope it is here in this faint flickering of new identities being forged that do cut across some of the older divisions. Even David Davis, a younger detective constable and in some ways one of the most hostile to Caroline Paterson, is able to say to the UDA prisoner:

... When I look into your eyes I see a reflection of every IRA man you claimed to be protecting us from. I see old men closing their shops and going home penniless because you took their profit and more. I see old ladies cowering in fear trying to forget what they witnessed in case you or your cronies came back to make them forget permanently.

(Mitchell 2000: 76)

The terrible footnote to this brief account of Gary Mitchell's work is that in late 2005 he and his family were forced into hiding after multiple death threats from paramilitary groups in his own community. (http://enjoyment.independent.co.uk/theatre/news/article334858.ece) This has led Mitchell to publicly declare the depth of his pessimism about the Peace Process and to allege that the scale of continuing sectarian violence is far greater than official accounts would have the wider world believe. Whatever the truth behind the appalling situation in which Mitchell and his family find themselves, it stands as powerful testimony to the more dangerous and potent relationship between theatre and identity in the north of Ireland as compared with any other part of the UK.

A much more optimistic, though arguably highly sentimental, view of the changes in Northern Ireland was offered by another writer with their roots in the Protestant community, Marie Jones, in *A Night in November* (1994). Jones has since gone on to achieve huge commercial success with a succession of accessible plays, many of which are concerned to a greater or lesser extent with questions of identity. However, none deal as explicitly with the slow emergence of the possibilities for a new vision of what it means to be either 'Irish' or from the north of Ireland than *A Night in November*. The play is about class and aspiration as much as about sectarian divisions and the world that the central character inhabits is almost that covered by Mike Leigh in the endlessly revived *Abigail's Party* (1977). Fairly rapidly, though, Jones reveals that the main problem facing her protagonist, Kenneth McAllister, is not the suffocating atmosphere of vol-au-vent-dominated soirees and all the petty snobbishness of golf club membership: at a football match between Northern Ireland and the Republic at Windsor Park, Belfast, McAllister experiences an evening of such bitterness and hatred that it shakes his fundamental belief in the validity of his own identity as Protestant British citizen living in Belfast. Worse still he experiences the bigotry and hatred with especial force because a lot of it is being bellowed in his ear by his father-in-law. When McAllister tries to mildly protest that it is only a game of football, Ernie, the diehard loyalist replies:

> ... well let me tell you they may luk like mere innocent futball players but as far as I am concerned they are representing the I.R.A. get it... the Irish Republican Army, understand, Republic of Ireland, same thing, if they are prepared to sully themselves by playing under banner of the Republic of Ireland I don't give a shite, if they are from Stoke on Trent or bloody Blackpool because to me they are representing the men that blow up our peelers or kill our soldiers... and what is more, as far as the Protestant people of this province are concerned they are... Fenian scum.

> Dirty Fenian scum... (*Chants*) There's only one team in Ireland.

> (M. Jones 2000: 71)

That McAllister undergoes a kind of road to Damascus conversion not only to tolerance of Catholics, but to a new kind of Irish identity is both acceptable and enjoyable within the play's broad comic framework. What undermines this to some extent is McAllister's seeming discovery that Catholics and southern Irishman all live a life of free-spirited self-expression in stark contrast to the repressed Prods that he is forced to live amongst. One evening he gives Jerry, a Catholic colleague, a lift home from work, the first time he has ever been either in West Belfast or inside the home of a Catholic:

... and inside Jerry's house was a whole other life, a life I'd never known, a life of disorder... books upside down in their bookcases, not in order of size or colour... Debrah's [his wife] order from the book club... burgundy leather bound classics... never opened, but they suit the bookshelf, match the wallpaper, blend in with the carpet, books that can't be allowed to vary just like the fitted kitchens...

... and there in Jerry's house, books of all shapes and sizes, books that look read, had dog ears, piles and piles of them and I was jealous of Jerry and his disordered life and his higgledy-piggledy books.

(M. Jones 2000: 83)

In a play that suggests a radical rethinking of Irish identity, particularly for Protestants, this seems a serious flaw and a re-erecting of the kind of barriers that Mitchell would later respond to from a Protestant perspective. To set against this, in terms of theatrical form, Jones' work is in certain ways bolder and arguably more in tune with a theatre responding to a new sense of fluid identities. A Night in November is written for a single actor playing only one man, but who enacts numerous other identities as he tells his story. During the course of the play his experience leads him to will another kind of identity for himself into reality and by extension a new kind of community for Ireland. The play's demands on the actor make the performative nature of identity integral to its structure so that we see the possibility of change enacted before us. The play's closing lines are a triumphant declaration of optimism, written at a time when the future for the Protestant community was looking more fluid than at any time for two decades. Having left his family to go to New York to follow the Republic of Ireland team in the 1994 soccer World Cup, Kenneth has just experienced the exhilaration of the team's famous triumph over Italy in a crowded bar only to be told of another atrocity back home involving the slaying of Catholics by Protestant paramilitaries. His response to this amounts to a willing into being a whole new hybrid identity for himself and any of his community that care to join him:

... tonight I can stand here and tell you I am no part of the men who did that... I am not of them any more... no, no-one can point the finger at Kenneth Norman McAllister and say, these people are part of you... tonight I absolve myself... I am free of them Mick... I am free of it, I am a free man... I am a Protestant Man, I'm an Irish Man.

The End.

(M. Jones 2000: 108)

Since A Night in November Jones has become a hugely successful commercial playwright whilst continuing to be a major contributor to the response made by theatre makers to the changed situation in the north of Ireland. To take just one more example, her most commercially successful play to date has been Stones in His Pockets (1999), which is not only set in Kerry in the Republic of Ireland, but which is not overtly concerned with the politics of the north in any way at all. It is though very much a play about the struggle for Irish cultural identity and its commercial appropriation by various forms of media and marketing campaigns and as such is worth discussing as a high-profile contributor to the rich mix of recent work that has helped forge the way the wider world sees a changing country.

Stones in His Pockets, like *A Night in November*, requires the actors to perform a number of different roles, so, again, the act of taking on identities is foregrounded as one of the play's key structural elements. Beyond that, though, the play is itself about the 'performance' of Ireland itself as its setting is in and around the making of an American film set in rural Kerry. The film is, of course, a hilarious set of historical clichés involving picturesque peasants digging turf and finally celebrating one of their own marrying the rich woman at the 'big house' thus enabling them to keep their land. The play is therefore an ironic contributor to what Margaret Llewellyn-Jones, drawing on Colin Graham's work, has called the 'new authenticity' in Irish theatre, a trend which has clearly been a factor in the enormous popularity of certain kinds of Irish work in both London and New York in the last decade (2002: 126). 'New authenticity', Graham argues, has been produced by what Llewellyn-Jones summarizes as:

> ... post-colonial market forces, which have both mythologized and celebrated 'the authentic' through 'a process in which the authentic is commodified, reproduced and re-told'... as for example, through tourism, 'heritage products' and certain kinds of TV programmes, especially those shown in Britain. (2002: 126)

Ironically, it is possible to argue that the exponential growth in such products has been facilitated by the Peace Process and resultant political changes and this is especially true in the rest of Britain. There has been a slow and not always welcome journey from the predominant mythology of Ireland being urban and paramilitary to it currently being that seen in the likes of *Ballykissangel* (BBC TV series 1996–2001). For some this would be suggestive of progress, but as *Stones in His Pockets* demonstrates there is a clear danger in swapping one kind of colonization for another.

As with most of Jones's work, *Stones in His Pockets* ends on a note of romantic optimism and in this case it is through the resistance of the main characters, who are employed as extras on the movie, to the hegemonic control of the image producers that have come to this part of Ireland, a resistance that Llewellyn-Jones argues is linked to Bakhtinian notions of carnival:

> ... these extras, who have begun to feel estranged from themselves by the fabricated, simple, subjectivities of the film-maker's version of their identity, are now able to begin to re-constitute themselves by taking charge of their own story, and reversing, in Bakhtinian carnival style, the hierarchy of teller and told. (2002: 129)

This is an attractive vision, but feels slightly exaggerated in its optimism. There is some sense of the two main characters taking charge of their own narrative journey as the play closes, but it is a limited kind of control that they manage to exert. The 'reversal' that is central to *Stones in His Pockets* starts with a chance remark by Charlie that the filming could be stopped to allow the extras who are all local to attend the funeral of a young man who has committed suicide. This is seized upon by the other central character, Jake, near the end of the play:

JAKE. No listen, remember what you said earlier when the Director wasn't going to stop for the funeral, you said, sure stick it in the film, this is the movies you can do what you want... You are right Charlie, it's only a story... if it was a story about a film being made and a young lad commits suicide... in other words the stars become the extras and the extras become the stars... so it becomes Sean's story, and Mickey and all the other people of this town.

(M. Jones 2000: 54)

The symbolic value of seizing control of the people's story is a seductive one in the context of a discussion about the direction of Irish identity. However, it should be treated with caution as both Jake and Charlie have been set up by Jones as attractive dreamers whose respective journeys have involved disappointment and failure. This is not to completely deny the optimism which comes from their defiant rejection of the patronizing view taken of them by the film crew, but it should at least provide a question mark.

If the play is primarily critical of restrictive external visions of what Ireland 'is', it should be noted that the Irish themselves do not escape criticism for their complicity. The description of one character, Simon, the film's first Assistant Director, as an 'ambitious Dublin 4 type' (M. Jones 2000: 8) is an amusing nod in the direction of the pretensions of those products of the 'Celtic Tiger' economy happy to trade in the patronizing mythologies of their birthplace in order to capitalize on the boom in demand for 'Oirishness'. More innocently, Mickey, a local legend in his seventies, boasts constantly of being the last surviving extra of *The Quiet Man*, a Hollywood vision of the Irish from another era.

The sheer scale of *Stones in His Pockets* commercial success, considering its modest origins, has made it one of the most widely circulated narratives of Ireland since the Good Friday agreement. As such it offers an essentially playful vision of fluid identities resistant to monolithic external definitions. At the same time there is also a clear sense of dependence on some forms of commodification of the culture and it remains an open question how far this is something that is well controlled by the Irish themselves and how far it is simply a new mutation of colonial influence. Though the play is set in Kerry, its resonances for the situation in the north are clear in that it is, above all, a play about the control of identity and, moreover, one about the need to resist definition from outside.

Exceeding even Jones considerable commercial success by a comfortable margin, both Martin McDonagh and Conor McPherson have made the largest contribution to the huge presence of Irish playwrights on the main stages in both the UK and the US. In their very different ways, they can both be said to have contributed to this period in which both broad definitions of 'the Irish' and the relationship of that construct to the rest of Britain have been in such a state of flux. Of the two it is McDonagh whose work has proved the more controversial for a number of reasons. These can best be summarized as his apparent tendency to trade on images of Ireland on both sides of the current border that are uncomfortably close to those used by outsiders in the kind of crude satires of Ireland and the Irish that have tended to circulate in the UK for generations. There is, however, a strong case for arguing that McDonagh's work is actually representative of a cultural trend that is, in fact, the opposite of a retreat into the past and which bears witness to a new cultural confidence that enables certain representations to be reclaimed, whereas they would have remained taboos for Irish writers in the recent past (see Llewellyn-Jones 2002: 97).

McDonagh's *Leenane Trilogy* established him in both the Republic and the UK through a series of co-productions between the Royal Court and the Druid Theatre Company who premiered all three plays in Galway. Eventually hugely popular with audiences on both sides of the Atlantic, there is little doubt that at least some of that popularity rested on the comic value of the petty details of a rural life presented as restricted in the extreme. This restriction is most often expressed through the characters' obsessions with these details in the form of brand names such as 'Complan' or 'Kimberley's' biscuits (McDonagh 1999: 1). Garry Hynes, the play's original director, sees McDonagh's vision of Ireland very much in terms of an opposition to any attempts at fake authenticity and a return to traditional Irish settings for comic purposes. In an interview with Cathy Leeney, Hynes, in fact, rails against what she sees as the identity of a changing Ireland being put in the hands of the Tourist Board:

This town now seems to be a set version of Irishness. That's what it is. There's a gap between that and what we are. I don't know what's happening in that gap and I don't know how wide that gap is; but it's worrying. It worries me that the centre of Galway is effectively a tourist centre. It's not a living centre of a community. It's brought great wealth, great opportunity, but it seems to me we haven't even begun to think of the consequences of all this, and it's getting too late to be able to do anything about it.

(Chambers et al. 2001: 206)

However she sees McDonagh's work as opposing this trend, taking the clichés of a Synge-inspired version of rural life and creating something altogether darker which is intimately connected with the contemporary 'performance of Irishness':

There's the issue about Martin and authenticity – the response that his is not Irish life now and its not Connemara life. Of course it isn't. It's an artifice. It's not authentic. It's not meant to be. It's a complete creation, and in that sense it's fascinating. (Chambers et al. 2001: 204)

Aleks Sierz in appropriating McDonagh for his generation of 'British' 'In-Yer-Face' playwrights goes further still in asserting his essentially postmodern nature. McDonagh, he argues, is the ultimate critic of the trade in nostalgia and far from trading on a mythical version of the West of Ireland from the safe distance of his roots in Camberwell (McDonagh's critics are quick to draw attention to his south London upbringing), he is actually the leading Irish satirist of nostalgia:

Instead of directly showing modern Ireland... McDonagh prefers pastiche. Instead of following other writers – Declan Hughes, Dermot Bolger, Conor McPherson – into urban settings, he parodies the tradition of bog, blarney and poteen. McDonagh's Ireland is postmodern in its grotesque exaggeration, in its isolation in a globalized world, and in its knowing nods and winks at Irish culture... A mythical place – the West of Ireland – is deconstructed with meticulous attention to detail. Scenic beauty becomes constant rain, folksy charm is really inbred ignorance, the old-fashioned village is isolated and full of hatred, and the family a nest of vipers. This postmodern irony is not only entertaining, it also delivers a stinging criticism of nostalgia. (2001: 223–4)

In *The Leenane Trilogy*, McDonagh makes very few direct connections with the impact of the political changes in the north. The work is, though, important in the context of this book because of its extremely wide circulation and consequent influence on the perception of a changing Ireland in a wider world. Whether it is part of a new sense of cultural confidence, some of which emanates from the possibilities offered by the Peace Process or whether it is exploitative of a general demand for commodified Irish culture remains open to question. From time to time, however, references to the politics of the north do surface and in *The Beauty Queen of Leenane* there is a telling comic exchange over the Birmingham Six:

RAY.... Although no fan am I of the bastarding polis. Me two wee toes they went and broke on me for no reason, me arsehole drunk and disorderly.

MAUREEN. The polis broke your toes, did they?

RAY. They did.

MAUREEN. Oh. Tom Hanlon said what it was you kicked a door in just your socks.

RAY. Did he now? And I suppose you believe a policeman's word over mine. Oh aye. Isn't that how the Birmingham Six went down?

MAUREEN. Sure, you can't equate your toes with the Birmingham Six, now, Ray.

RAY. It's the selfsame differ.

(McDonagh 1999: 53)

Such a satirical approach to the pomposity and pretension that he sees as surrounding much paramilitary activity, of course, anticipates the extended and controversial take on the subject that McDonagh produced in *The Lieutenant of Inishmore*. He once professed 'indifference to larger political issues' asking an age-old and highly contested view question about audiences: 'Why should anyone pay ten or twenty pounds to be lectured at for two hours?', but in a play that was to prove his most controversial to date this did not prevent him from engaging in a ruthless satire on the factionalism of Republican paramilitary groups that is one of the most direct dramatic responses to the changing shape of the country since the Peace Process began.

Though its central character is a member of the Irish National Liberation Army, the play is in the same very broad black comic tradition as *The Leenane Trilogy* and, apart from a single scene, the setting remains remote and rural. What is obviously different is that several of the characters are not simply employed on the land, but active in real named organizations and, as a result, the satire is not in any sense generalized. One is reminded at times of the kind of dialogue used to hilarious effect on the popular UK TV show *Father Ted* (1995–98) whose central technique was to put the most ludicrous discussions into the mouths of supposedly 'serious' central characters, in this case priests, and crucially they would have no sense of the ridiculousness of what they were saying. In *The Lieutenant of Innishmore*, the discussions have the same mix of the surreal and utterly banal, but the objects of our derision are not country priests, but men (and women) who are committed to the use of force in support of political change in the north. More specifically, the central character, Padraic, is part of a group whose activities have become more focused because of the participation of both Sinn Fein and the 'official' IRA in various forms of negotiations with the British and Irish governments.

If the play was simply a satire on INLA and the various other 'splinter' groups that have proliferated since the ceasefires began in the mid-1990s, then, to an extent, it is uncontentious in all except the sheer quantity of graphic violence that McDonagh puts firmly down stage centre. However, one is inclined to agree with Mark Lawson's description of *The Lieutenant of Inishmore* as 'a very rare example of a play liberal in content, but conservative in politics' (Lawson 2001), a judgement that Lawson goes on to justify by reference to the play's final scene:

> A final comic twist – involving the live cat – leads to the realisation that the sickening killings have been entirely pointless and based on misunderstanding. 'So all this terror has been for absolutely nothing?' asks one of the few living characters. 'It has,' his fellow survivor replies.

> This could, I suppose, be interpreted as supporting the position of republican breakaway groups towards the peace process – all that killing was for this – but it seems to me more likely that McDonagh if offering an Ulster twist on the Borges put-down about the Falklands war: 'Two bald men fighting over a comb.' (Lawson 2001)

Whatever one finally thinks of McDonagh's reading of the politics in the north of Ireland there seems little doubt that *The Lieutenant of Inishmore* is a play that would probably not have been written without the changes that took place in Northern Ireland throughout the 1990s. It is a play that is, apparently like McDonagh himself, immensely confident in its opinions and judgements and perhaps it is this that has been the most important impact of the Peace Process to date, to liberate controversial voices and allow cultural diversity to contribute to new versions of Ireland. According to another piece in *The Guardian* in the year the play was first produced, 'Both the National Theatre and the Royal Court turned down the script saying they "did not want to endanger the peace process"', whilst McDonagh himself declared that he would be 'seriously pissed off' if the INLA 'were not angered by the play' (Gibbons 2001 c.). All of this adds up to a sense of involvement with political change that is rare in UK theatre and one that is intimately connected to the imperative to reinvent cultural identity in an Ireland that is being reshaped metaphorically if not yet literally.

As mentioned at the start of this section, one could not hope to discuss all the work that is of relevance to a post-Peace Process Northern Ireland. One of the key phenomena in all UK theatre in the last ten years has been the sheer volume of Irish work that has emerged either from entirely new writers, and, to some extent, it is inevitable that this will be seen in the context of the changing shape of the two countries. Conor McPherson's work has become a phenomenon in its own right with *The Weir* instantly taking on classic status, whilst Frank McGuiness has continued to confirm his status as a world-class writer with work that has generally related to political change in oblique ways from the long perspective of plays set in the past. Llewellyn-Jones summary of recent Irish theatre sees McGuiness's *Dolly West's Kitchen*, for instance, as one which:

> ... embraces American, European, English and Irish identities from both sides of the border... reconciling 'a postcolonial cosmopolitan internationality with the ties of tradition and locale' (1999: 147)

McGuiness himself has been specific in suggesting that part of the driving force behind both his own new work and his translations of European classic texts has been to assert the separate nature of an Irish voice from a generalized British one. In a revealing interview with Joseph Long, McGuiness discusses his translation work:

> Joseph Long: There is a major part of your work, over the past twenty years, which is comprised of translations or adaptations of European plays. I think you see this as an intrinsic part of your own writing, as part of your function as an Irish dramatist, to re-appropriate these texts, and not just as a service of translation.

> Frank McGuiness: Absolutely. It's also a liberation. Irish literature has always been far too much defined in terms of its relationship with English literature. It's been part of the taming of the Irish by the English to do that.

> (Chambers et al. 2001: 305)

But if McGuiness's work is predominantly related to broader questions of Ireland, there have also been more specific, if ambiguous, references to the changing situation in the north. In the same interview with Long, McGuiness discussed directorial readings of his *Mutabilitie* (1997) which is clearly about Anglo-Irish relations, but is set in 1598 and features Edmund Spencer and William Shakespeare as characters. Long puts it to McGuiness that Trevor Nunn's original Royal National Theatre production had created an optimistic ending:

> Long: In that production, the child became the centre of a gesture of giving, there is an exchange of food. But as you wrote it, the ending is ambiguous, even negative.

> McGuiness: More ambiguous than negative I think. The weapons are still on stage. When the Irish lay down their weapons, the weapons still remain there, on the stage...

> Long: That's a fairly clear reference isn't it, to the present-day situation in Northern Ireland?

> McGuiness: Yes. There's a flicker of hope, but that's all. It can be very easily extinguished. But it's still there. There is a flicker of hope.

> (Chambers et al. 2001: 301)

Conor McPherson's work, whilst so often seeming intensely personal, can also be seen as reflective of a period of fluctuating identities but, also, mainly through the international success of *The Weir*, as making a major contribution to a high-profile period for theatre relating to Ireland and, thus, a contribution to a new sense of Ireland on world stages. His work can only be read in the most oblique terms as directly relating to change in the north but, in terms of a sense of postcolonial identity and Ireland in general, his plays frequently depict a male crisis of identity that could be seen as linking his work to the very different and much more direct commentaries of Gary Mitchell. Whereas Mitchell shows us men whose whole purpose in life has been left behind by the changes in Northern Ireland, McPherson's lost souls inhabit a much more abstract landscape, but are still cast adrift by crises in the definition of their roles as husbands, fathers, breadwinners and pillars of the community. The relationship between colonialism and patriarchy is a well-trodden theoretical path as Ashcroft, Griffiths and Tiffin make clear:

> ... both patriarchy and imperialism can be seen to exert analogous forms of domination over those they render subordinate. Hence the experiences of women in patriarchy and those of colonized subjects can be paralleled in a number of respects, and both feminist and post-colonial politics oppose such dominance. (Ashcroft et al. 2001: 101)

The other side of this, of course, is the impact on notions of masculinity in a postcolonial context, particularly one where armed struggle has been part of the recent history. McPherson's central male characters frequently inhabit a territory that is no longer sustained by any of the apparent sureties that made up the totality of Irish identity but, on the other hand, they are also often tormented by the ghosts of the past. In *Shining City* (2004), his first play after a four-year gap, we have a character haunted by the ghost of his recently dead wife, but also by the more vivid ghosts of his own failures and disappointments. For comfort he visits a lapsed priest who is now some variety of counsellor. It is hard to avoid the sense that McPherson is offering us an Ireland where the rhetoric about Celtic Tiger economics and Dublin as a leading European capital does not yet satisfactorily sustain a culture struggling to redefine its relationship with so many old certainties: the Church, Britain, its rural mythologies and, of course, the six counties in the north. However the analogies are barely detectable and flicker into life only through the use of the lapsed priest and the odd veiled reference to the harshness of contemporary city existence. It is the relentless sense of struggle on the part of the middle-aged male characters, across a number of McPherson's plays, to just make sense of their role in the world that suggests that he is interested in the impact of a fast-changing world.

It has to be recognized, though, that McPherson himself has gone into print to assert his detached bewilderment at the way that a changing Ireland is read into his work:

> Although I had never set out to write consciously about my country, my work seemed to suggest Irish issues to certain critics. Maybe that's understandable, given the relationship between our countries...

> ... all I was trying to do was write plays that hold your attention, make you laugh and hopefully engender a sense of community between the work and the audience. I wasn't concerned with geography or politics...

> ... People of my age grew up with a confused detachment from the violence in Ireland... Our childhood grasp of what was going on has probably shaped the sense of bewilderment many

of us still feel. We were raised in a democratic republic where successive governments moved further and further away from any claim on the North. (McPherson 1998)

Although one can entirely understand McPherson's difficulties with being so easily labelled, it is also his very desire to distance himself from questions of identity that give his work a clear relationship to the climate of change in which he writes. If words such as confusion and bewilderment crop up frequently when he attempts to define his own politics, then it is no surprise to find his plays peopled by characters who feel in these ways about their role in life itself. McPherson's is a world shorn of grand narratives of heroism and struggle, instead his male characters must grope towards glimmers of hope and limited understanding which makes his writing utterly of its time.

The above account, particularly at a time when new writing on both sides of the Irish border has flourished, can be defined as well by its omissions as inclusions. All that one can hope to do is draw out some of the key trends and discuss some of those that best exemplify them. There are some omissions, however, that are too glaring to pass unnoticed. Central to these are the names of certain key companies that worked in the north during the 1990s and in the present decade. A number of the works and individual writers discussed owe a great deal to some of these companies, but in a number of cases the total sum of a company's work is more significant than the individual parts might suggest. Charabanc Theatre Company, which functioned in Belfast between 1983 and 1995, is often best known because of one of its founders', Marie Jones, subsequent individual success. However, this does no justice to twelve pioneering years when the company continually worked to break down barriers, particularly for women theatre makers who wished to stay in Northern Ireland to work. In many ways their work was part of (and contributed to) a shift in the political landscape that the Peace Process was able to build upon. As Helen Lojek has said:

Perhaps it is the awareness of multiple perspectives and delight in their creative clash that typically kept Charabanc plays from being regarded as political. It's hard to hoist a flag over them. They do not belong to one of Northern Ireland's divided communities more then another, despite the Protestantism of the company members. They offer no pat solutions or even conclusions. Multiplicity and lack of dogma are, in fact, their politics

(1994: 94)

The most significant company, in terms of new work, still working in Northern Ireland, is Tinderbox, based in Belfast. Tinderbox has produced new work by Mitchell and Jones as well as by a range of significant writers that have not been discussed here, including Daragh Carville, Owen McCafferty and Tim Loane. One of their highest profile projects was *Convictions* (2000) produced for the Belfast Festival and performed in various spaces inside the disused Crumlin Road courthouse. The employment of site-specific strategies has not been as important in recent Irish theatre as it has in, say, Wales, but here the use of what was once seen as a potent symbol of the Anglo-Protestant domination of Ulster was seen by most critics as, in itself, a powerful statement of political change. The production not only moved around the various parts of the court building but also employed seven writers to produce seven short pieces all performed in different rooms as follows: Daragh Carville (*Male Toilets*), Damien

Gorman (*Judges Room*), Marie Jones (*Court Room No. 20*), Martin Lynch (*Main Hall*), Owen McCafferty (*Court Room No. 1*), Nicola McCartney (*Jury Room*) and Gary Mitchell (*Holding Room*).

Margaret Llewellyn-Jones quotes Mary Holland in *The Irish Times* as suggesting that the play was so significant that it 'could help to liberate both communities from the past', but also Susannah Clapp in *The Observer* who took the view that at least parts of the production ran the risk of 'turning horror into heritage'(2001: 161). On the whole, though, Clapp's view appears to be in the minority with many seeing the play as the embodiment of the spirit of political change:

> The production was of now. It was an Irish, Northern Irish, Ulster, nine and six county piece. It was never claimed by one or the other. It is written that way in the Good Friday Agreement, nearly in stone. (Llewellyn-Jones 2002: 161)

It is perhaps understandable and totally forgivable in a culture so desperate for hope that many of the claims for the piece are exaggerated and, four years later, it is easier to see that. However, this should not be allowed to undermine the contribution of Tinderbox which has continued to look for new work, much of which is about intelligently responding to the possibility of change and the potential of fluid identities which are not exclusively Irish or British.

The work of Dubbeljoint Theatre has, to some extent, been represented through the discussion of Marie Jones' work, though it is important to add that this company has also been committed to what their own website calls:

> ... a democratic theatre approach for the local writers. With all future productions, we hope that we continue to fulfil the ideals on which the company was founded: to create sharp, funny, provocative, and popular theatre that is accessible and attractive to the whole island. (http://www.dubbeljoint.com/)

The last phrase, of course, will carry most weight with a number of people in Belfast, but equally important to the company has been the commitment to work with the West Belfast community in which they are based. This strong identification with their roots and the socio-economic difficulties surrounding them appears to have lain behind a bitter and high-profile court case over the rights to the hugely successful *Stones in His Pockets*. The company's website remains convinced that not enough of the great wealth that came from London and New York productions found its way back into the company and, by extension, the community and the blame is laid firmly at the door of Marie Jones. The tone of the press release is perhaps a strong reminder of the deep divisions between those, on the one hand, that might see hope for a 'new' Belfast in the high-profile success of plays by Jones and her contemporaries and, on the other, those who would prioritize the limited resources that theatre has in support of giving voice to impoverished communities.

Whilst the work discussed so far encompasses a very wide range of dramatic strategies it would be fair to say that the picture is dominated by the play text, usually in a form that can be published and read. There are, however, younger companies that have established themselves in the last decade that are more easily identified with physical, visual and devised traditions.

These include Kabosh, Big Telly and Ridiculusmus. Of the three, it is perhaps Kabosh that has involved itself in work that has some relationship with political change through their tour of Owen McCafferty's *Mojo Mickybo*, though the piece has only a tangential relationship to the current situation. Collectively the emergence of a new generation of companies with aspirations to push a little harder at the boundaries of theatrical form can perhaps best be seen as itself a mark of a society that has begun to open up and seek to be free of the burden of always needing its art to discuss its central defining feature.

In many ways the majority of Ridiculusmus's work is as far removed from a theatre defined by the Troubles as it is possible to be, though one of their shows, *Say Nothing* (2000), did offer a bizarre take on the Peace Process. The company has, though, made its name principally through comedy theatre and 'events' that owe more to European art than the social-realist dramas most often associated with an outsider's vision of Belfast. Ridiculusmus, which currently consists of two people, David Woods and John Hough, has also been linked with the kind of TV comedy exemplified by *The Fast Show* or *Little Britain*. It is perhaps appropriate to close the chapter on that note; a Northern Ireland theatre scene capable of producing one of the most innovative small companies in Britain today.

Hard to define, Ridiculusmus's blend of influences from high modernism (they quote liberally from Beckett in their publicity material) and popular contemporary comedy are testimony to at least some kind of expanding sense of possibility in the north of Ireland. Whilst it is obvious that the existence of a handful of companies working in ways that defy easy definitions is not in itself evidence of fundamental change, it is equally obvious that they represent a real desire for the performing arts in the north of Ireland to break out of its perceived obligations to represent sectarian division. In attempting to move away from the 'burden of representation' that is referred to so often in this book, companies such as those briefly mentioned here can be seen as part of a theatrical future that, whilst it is unlikely to cast off its vital role in creating narratives of the conflict, might also assert its right to a more pluralist theatre that is capable of encompassing forms of expression that have been largely submerged by what has been seen as the urgencies of the political context.

No More 'Cultural Cringe': Scotland and Theatre

The last decade in Scotland has, in common with the UK, in general, been a strikingly productive time for new writing for the stage. Many of the writers prominent during the period have also written for television and for the cinema, and their work for these other media is sometimes discussed elsewhere in this volume. The group includes both writers who have established their strong international reputations relatively recently such as David Greig, Anthony Neilson, Stephen Greenhorn, Zinnie Harris, Nicola McCartney and David Harrower, as well as voices that were established rather longer ago but who have continued to flourish in a changed Scotland, such as Rona Munro, Liz Lochhead and Sue Glover. In addition, innovative companies such as NVA, Boilerhouse and Suspect Culture who are engaged in a variety of theatre practices less reliant on text have produced work that has contributed to Scotland's standing as a place where innovation in artistic practice is flourishing,

The relationship between the work of this group of writers and companies and any sense of new emerging Scottish identities naturally varies enormously according to the individual cases. There are clear instances when national identity is very explicitly on the agenda, such as Greig's *Caledonia Dreaming* (1997) or the various components of TAG Theatre's *Making the Nation* project (1999–2002). TAG, widely described as Scotland's 'national' theatre for young people, describes the latter on its website like this:

> Between 1999 and 2002 TAG worked with over 25,000 young people aged 7–25 throughout Scotland and abroad delivering a diverse programme of eight performance and participatory projects. TAG sought to raise debate amongst young people, by engaging them both intellectually and emotionally in issues surrounding the developing nation and by exciting them through the mediums of drama and theatre to engage with the political process.

(http://www.tag-theatre.co.uk/index)

Clearly, then, in the immediate post devolutionary period, theatre makers made what were sometimes very direct contributions to the explicit project of 'nation building', albeit in this case through very open and participatory means. More commonly, however, the sense of the new nation is present metaphorically and in ways occasionally hotly disputed by those claiming to have a hotline to the writer's 'intentions' (Scullion 2001: 389). However, there is little escaping the sense of expectation that seems to have surrounded theatre in Scotland, almost more than any other art form:

> Of all the art forms, theatre is traditionally the one most closely associated with ideas about nations and nationhood. At its simplest, theatre is a public arena where people who live in the same place, and usually speak the same language can come together to share experience; to recognise dilemmas, identify conflicts, laugh at enemies, celebrate achievements or mourn great losses. It's no accident that in capital cities all over the world, since the rise of nation-states as our most important political communities, national theatres have tended to stand cheek by jowl with presidential places and parliamentary buildings as symbols of the national community. (Macmillan 2003: 4)

Encouragingly, however, the single dominant theme that emerges from writers, companies, critics and the academic community is the sense of real dialogue and debate. In some ways this is not so different to the rest of the UK, particularly Wales with the nearest thing to a parallel political situation. If anything, though, the level of reluctance to accept any attempt to 'fix' a new post-devolutionary identity is stronger in Scotland. Again and again in the work of both theatre makers themselves and those that write about theatre practice, the recurrent sense is of a 'conversation' and virtually always that conversation uses the plural 'identities' rather than 'identity'. There are some, of course, who would rather that these questions were not of any concern at all and that artists in Scotland could be free of any perceived responsibility to contribute to a sense of an emerging nation. Most though are more realistic and there appears to be a widespread consensus that while a monolithic definition of Scotland is undesirable, it is also inevitable that theatre makers cannot help but make a contribution to what Nadine Holdsworth has called ' a re-imagining of what constitutes the nation' (2003: 25). Some may do this more consciously and explicitly than others, but at one level there is a sense that all who make theatre in Scotland or about Scotland at a time when the national culture is fluid and so constantly scrutinized can be seen to be engaged in that re-imagining.

It is, of course, no surprise that a debate about a Scottish 'national theatre' has re-surfaced at such a time as Macmillan suggests above. Parallel debates will be discussed in the sections on Wales and Northern Ireland, but in a way that is perhaps reflective of both a greater degree of political autonomy and a more advanced sense of cultural confidence Scotland has, at the time of writing, taken a bolder step in trying to define what a national theatre might be. (Though in fairness, Wales already has a Welsh language company.)

The boldness of the Scottish version of a national theatre lies in its refusal to opt for the traditional model of a large building-based single company alongside any real or metaphorical 'presidential palace'. Instead, the Scottish Executive allocated an initial £7.5m of funding to establish a theatre that was a 'commissioner' and would draw principally on Scotland's existing talent in order to produce work that could happen anywhere across the country. To add to this the announcement of the first director of the Scottish National Theatre also defied any sense of a narrow jingoistic approach. The successful candidate, Vicky Featherstone, is not Scottish and has worked principally with the radical new writing of Paines Plough. Significantly, Paines Plough has successfully worked with many of the generation of new writing talent to come out of Scotland such as David Greig and Gregory Burke.

There are, of course, those whose vision of the 'national' does not allow for the celebration of this kind of progressive vision. Eddie Jackson, chair of the Federation of Scottish Theatre (a key partner for any Scottish national theatre), is on record as detecting 'a sense of disappointment that they [the board of the National Theatre] weren't able to appoint from within the existing Scottish theatre community or from the Scottish diaspora' (http://www.timesonline.co.uk/article/0,,2090-1310869_1,00.html) and it remains to be seen whether Vicky Featherstone's undoubted vision can win over the people she has to work with. What is apparent is that the post-devolutionary vision for theatre in Scotland has taken an unpredictable turn away from a narrow vision of the nation.

What appears to be happening, even in the sphere of 'official' Scottish theatre, is the embrace of a post-devolutionary idea of the new nation that accords with the view expressed by Thompson and Fevre that 'the realities of national identity, and hence of nations themselves, are both contestable and often contested.'(1999: 39). If the practice of the new National Theatre in Scotland begins to live up to its earliest actions, then it will be an institution that attempts to serve the whole country at both the practical and symbolic levels. Structurally the new theatre is designed to operate across the country whilst the early artistic vision will be supplied by someone who in terms of gender and cultural identity lies firmly outside the establishment.

There appears to be a recognition then, not simply of the reality of Scottish theatre traditions, which as Macmillan says have tended to be built upon 'diversity and strong local identity', but also of the undesirability of a concept of the nation that demands strong, monolithic institutions in the service of forms of nationalism that have been so destructive in less stable parts of Europe in the last decades of the twentieth century.

Of course, many are wary of the very idea of a national theatre project of any kind in Scotland, just as they have been in Wales and elsewhere. What is perhaps finally a persuasive argument is that at a time of debate about cultural identity, theatre has to find ways to make itself significant. It has to do this to secure funding, but also to make sure that its distinctive ways of exploring the territory between the global and the national and the national and the local are fully recognized and engaged with. As Macmillan's perceptive summary of the debates around the national theatre puts it:

> In the past 25 years. Scottish theatre has made a contribution to the enrichment, modernising and radicalisation of ideas about Scotland and Scottishness second only to that of Scottish literature in the same period. Yet the average Scot – even the average well-informed Scot – often has very little idea that there is any significant theatre produced in Scotland at all. (2003: 4)

In addressing this question by producing a national theatre model that defies centralization and regional hierarchy and, in turn, appointing a forward-thinking woman to oversee the project,

Scottish theatre's contribution to the new nation is already encouragingly radical in the institutional sense.

At the time of writing, the new National Theatre of Scotland has been launched with a 'production' that is very much in keeping with the institution's radical structure. *Home* (2006) is, to begin with, not one piece of work but ten, produced across Scotland in spaces not usually used for theatre in Aberdeen, Caithness, Dumfries, Dundee, East Lothian, Edinburgh, Glasgow, Inverness, Shetland and Stornoway. The ten venues each host a show by a different director who, in turn, has collaborated with other artists according to the kind of work to be produced.

The use of non-traditional spaces is, of course, designed to emphasize the democratic intent of the new institution whilst broadening its base and profile. It has also had the effect of rooting the first commissioned work by the National Theatre in the lived experiences of the very diverse parts of the nation in which it is performed. To take just one example, the show in Shetland is performed on the Northlink ferry, sitting in the dock at Lerwick between fifteen-hour voyages. Amongst other things, it uses the stunning device of a hundred fiddlers playing in the cavernous car deck of the ship as part of an experience that explores the emotional role of the journey home for the people of this most marginal of Scottish regions.

Home is then an extremely strong statement of intent on the part of the new National Theatre and its artistic director. It is the absolute opposite of a building-based symbol of national status and prestige and genuinely makes an attempt to convince a wider audience that theatre is something much broader and more inclusive than they might have otherwise thought. In so doing, the project also gives the strongest possible signal as to what the theatre's contribution might be to the long-term project of national definition. In one sense it could be seen as inward looking as it discusses 'home' but, in fact, the result is far from navel gazing as its sheer diversity and vitality takes in such a variety of formal influences and applies them to unexpected contexts and locations.

There is of course no room for complacency. It is far from certain whether simply taking interesting and radical theatre to unlikely places will actually entice people in to watch. One critic sent to observe one of the first-night shows certainly had his doubts:

> Whether Scotland was picking up on the collaborative spirit of the occasion is another matter. After a decade of debate and wrangling, sealing a century of dreaming and scheming, all eyes weren't exactly on the NTS [National Theatre of Scotland] this weekend. If perishingly cold weather didn't keep people indoors, the Scotland v England rugby clash certainly did. As I stood shivering from 'head to tae' in a wind-blasted wasteland beneath a Glasgow tower block, I couldn't help envying those stay-at-homes. (Cavendish 2006)

Of course the man from the *Daily Telegraph* would be unlikely to be the most enthusiastic advocate of such an open and eclectic version of the idea of the 'national', nevertheless, with long-standing Scottish companies being forced to close because of cuts in Arts Council subsidy, the new National Theatre will have to work hard to justify its annual absorption of around £4m of public money. At this point it can only be said that it has at least made a radical start that is inclusive, not only in terms of geography, but also artistically. Its first project is concerned with the nation, but in ways that open up the question rather than attempt to close it down and in the UK context it is an exciting project.

In some ways the new National Theatre is picking up the spirit of much of what has been happening in Scottish theatre for more than a decade. Reading a range of critical views on Scotland's particularly rich vein of new theatre work during the last ten years, one immediately picks up on, as mentioned above, the profound sense of debate over what theatre has to offer the country. Whilst much of the disagreement remains implicit, at times differences have become much more open and even bitter. Even before the election of the Labour government in 1997 that began the process of devolution, there surfaced arguments over funding that would divide those that would see themselves as being part of an engaged Scottish theatre. Dan Reballetto, writing about Suspect Culture, describes one eruption of hostilities involving the late John McGrath:

> These debates found particular force in 1996 when the Scottish Arts Council simultaneously granted revenue funding to Suspect Culture and cut funding to Wildcat. Without singling out Suspect Culture by name, John McGrath grumbled in the *Herald* that money had transferred from political work to 'theatre for west end yuppies'. (2003: 62)

Rebellato makes clear where his sympathies lie and he goes on to reinforces his view of Suspect Culture as taking an infinitely more tenable position with regard to the idea of the radical in contemporary theatre by referring back to debates at the end of the 1980s. Such debates could be described as comparing an older left-wing theatre of the kind typified by Trevor Griffiths to theatre that Vera Gottlieb saw as being dominated by 'mysticism; the irrational; violence, whether physical or verbal; impotence, and an abdication and surrender to "dark forces", whether undefined or anarchic'(cited in Rebellato 2003: 63).

In the context of post-devolution Scotland, then, Suspect Culture's contribution to any definition of a new national culture is ambiguous and oblique. The company deals with questions of identity, but not in a way that has direct links to questions of the nation or national culture. Rather, they frequently address the absence of identity as any kind of reassurance. As Rebellato puts it:

> Typical settings for Suspect Culture shows are what Marc Augé has called 'non-places', spaces brought into being by the rapid expansion of communication and transport characteristic of globalization. Such places are anonymous, functional – airports, shopping malls, hotels, bars, motorway service stations... (2003: 64)

On the rare occasions when Scottishness is mentioned directly, it is parodic, 'glimpsed only in logos, stereotypes, cultures reduced to the images in the travel agent's brochure' (Rebellato 2003: 65)

For some, typified by John McGrath mentioned above, Suspect Culture's refusal to be explicit about the politics of their work is a frustration and an indication of an elitist theatre surrendered to fashionable metropolitan values. For others such as Rebellato they contribute to the making of a new Scottish culture precisely by looking outward and possibly more importantly by making unashamedly 'difficult' theatre that has powerful roots in cultural theory as well as contemporary visual and physical traditions of theatre and movement.

It is, though, a distortion to represent Scottish theatre as so polarized. After all the writing energy behind Suspect Culture is provided by the same David Greig that supplied 7:84 (admittedly the post-McGrath model) with *Caledonia Dreaming* (1997), his own most explicit contribution to the national identity debate. Additionally, Greig, writing in *The Independent* at the time of the 2002 Edinburgh Fringe Festival, said of McGrath:

> The wellspring of the Scottish tradition of experiment is found in the work of an Englishman, John McGrath. In a sense, McGrath is the single individual most responsible for shaping the bones around which Scottish play-writing has grown. Political, experimental and poetic – it's all there in *The Cheviot, the Stag and the Black, Black Oil.* (Greig 2002)

Remarkably enough, then, the leading light of the new generation of post-devolutionary Scottish theatre pays homage to what many would assume was his diametric opposite in terms of an approach to the way that theatre contributes to debates about the direction of the nation. Greig is, though, anxious to generously attribute the much-documented strength of new Scottish writing for the theatre to the previous generation who had to write in much less culturally optimistic times in Scotland. This generosity is probably a more accurate reflection of the way that the theatre community speaks to itself and to the wider world than any sense of division. There are huge differences between the companies and between the new writers, but more often than not this is celebrated as reflective of the grown-up state of Scottish culture rather than provoking spats over what should be the 'authentic' voice of the nation. Greig does actually attempt to identify what he sees as unifying the group that has come to prominence in the last decade:

> So what does the tradition consist of? What defines the new Scottish playwriting? All of them are unafraid of structural experiment and collaborative work... The other key link for me, is poetic. Every one of the writers I've mentioned has a very distinctive voice. Their plays carry the sense of language handled with the poet's care. (Greig 2002)

For Greig, the Scottish theatre community has responded to devolution less through the direct address of issues around identity, culture and nationhood and more through developing a theatre that is free to experiment, to be challenging, even difficult, in a spirit of confidence. In doing so, they have cut their ties with what many still see as the mainstream social-realist strand of British theatre and, instead, now look to Europe and beyond for their antecedents. What is more, argues Greig, this phenomenon has not been born from the recent momentum towards a 'new' Scotland, but rather has built on something much older and which grew from the failed devolution referendum in 1979:

> The new generation of Scottish writers didn't come out of nowhere. The roots of the current success lie primarily in the Eighties, and in the incredible groundbreaking and beautiful play-writing of Chris Hannan, Liz Lochhead, Ian Heggie, John Clifford, Simon Donald and John Byrne. These playwrights, writing in the immediate aftermath of a failed devolutionary referendum in 1979, and in an atmosphere of distinct cultural cringe, forged a new,

confident, bold language of theatre in Scotland. A new theatre that was, I believe, in part responsible for devolution eventually arriving. (Greig 2002)

This is an attractive vision and certainly not without truth, but it probably goes too far in key respects. Whether theatre played any part in hastening devolution is impossible to judge very accurately, but it is salutary to consider that the widely derided *Braveheart* arguably played a more significant, certainly a more direct and visible, role. More contentiously, though, it is highly debatable whether the central thrust of a new Scottish theatre is quite as unified in difference as Greig's account suggests. In a limited sense, of course, all writers have a sense of language, but in terms of the priorities behind their writing there are perhaps more 'divides' than Greig implies. In another piece in *The Guardian* coinciding with the production of his own translation of Camus' *Caligula*, Greig takes his point about the distinctiveness of new Scottish theatre still further through an attack on what he calls 'English realism':

> This English realism, this 'new writing' genre which has so thrived in subsidised spaces over the past 40 years, attempts, as one of our leading playwrights put it, to 'show the nation to itself'. It seeks out and exposes issues for the public gaze. It voices 'debates' rather like columnists in the broadsheets. Its practitioners are praised for their ear for dialogue as though they were tape recorders or archivists recording the funny way people talk in particular sections of society and editing it into a plausibly illustrative story. English realism prides itself on having no 'style' or 'aesthetic' that might get in the way of the truth. It works with a kind of shorthand naturalism which says 'this is basically the way I see it'. Distrustful of metaphor, it is a theatre founded on mimicry. In English realism, the real world is brought into the theatre and plonked on the stage like a familiar old sofa. (Greig 2003)

Greig's view has, of course, been the academic and, to an extent, critical orthodoxy for some time now, what is new is the attempt to distance the dominant 'English' tradition from that of post-devolutionary Scotland. It is an understandable stance to take for an immensely talented writer who, probably not through his own choosing, has often become something of a spokesman for his generation of theatre makers. His work, both just before and after devolution became a political reality, has been identified almost more than that of any other writer with efforts to, as Nadine Holdsworth puts it, 'challenge inflexible notions of the Scottish nation and Scottish cultural identity'(2003: 25) and for Greig this means looking away from England and attempting to portray a Scotland looking towards Europe (France seems to be particularly singled out in the article quoted above) (Greig 2003), and a respect for ideas and intellectual traditions that have rarely taken hold in 'Britain'.

This said, whether he likes it or not, David Greig remains constantly identified, even by his most passionate supporters, as both the leading theatrical force within the new Scotland and a leading voice in the articulation of contemporary Scottish culture in the rest of the UK and beyond. In this respect, he can be compared to someone like Ed Thomas in Wales, a voice sought out by political as well as theatrical commentators. As Dan Rebellato has put it:

> David Greig is a central figure in an extraordinary flowering of Scottish playwrights that emerged to international acclaim in the 1990s. Championed by the newly built Traverse Theatre, Edinburgh, playwrights like Greig, David Harrower, Stephen Greenhorn and Chris

Hannan created a fiery stage poetry with which to present contemporary Scotland to the world, mixing a powerful sense of its history with profound care for its future.

This renaissance of Scottish playwriting coincided with a revival of Scottish nationalism after the dog days of the 1980's culminating in a vote in favour of a devolved Scottish parliament in 1997 and the inauguration of that body two years later. (2002: ix)

Though Greig's work is clearly and unambiguously associated with the Scottish dimension to the break-up of an older Britain he cannot, as Rebellato goes on to say, be seen as 'straightforwardly nationalistic', quoting Greig himself as saying that 'any playwright who tells you they're a nationalist is either a bad playwright or a bad nationalist.' (Rebellato 2002: ix). Rebellato is rather inclined to see Greig's work as conscious of the place of a small nation such as Scotland in an increasingly globalized world with both the advantages and disadvantages that marginalization can bring. A sense, perhaps, that Scotland is already practiced at the art of survival in the face of economic forces seemingly bent on the destruction of its distinctive national identity through two centuries of English exploitation.

One of Greig's earlier works for the Traverse, *Europe* (1994), is seen (alongside Stephen Greenhorn's *Passing Places* (1997)) by Nadine Holdsworth as central to the way that Scottish theatre before and immediately after devolution 're-imagined' national identity in a truly global context. For Holdsworth, the two plays

Explore how local, national and global events necessitate a re-imagining of what constitutes the nation... these plays challenge inflexible notions of the Scottish nation and Scottish cultural identity by presenting both in constant states of production which are never complete and subject to the play of history, culture and power. (2003: 25)

Greig's *Europe* has most frequently been read as a response to the Balkan wars, but Holdsworth quotes Greig as stating that 'if I had my time again, I would call the play Scotland. That border town could just as easily be Motherwell.'(Cited in Holdsworth 2003: 27). To anyone with knowledge of *Europe*, such a statement is not surprising but mildly shocking, nevertheless, as Greig makes explicit the idea of such a close connection between the genocide and related atrocities that followed the break-up of the former Yugoslavia and contemporary Britain. The connection between *Europe* and the Balkans is, however, oblique and suggested, rather than explicit, and Greig's story of drifters, both exploiters and exploited, is deliberately set in a no-man's-land, a border crossing and abandoned railway station where the express trains speed through on their way to somewhere else. Holdsworth's reading makes clear the relationship between such a place and the most influential contemporary theoretical writing on nations and nationalism:

By presenting a town in a state of flux, Greig suggests the unreliability of fixed notions of place and nation and how this forces inhabitants to invent myths of continuity to counteract the constant process of reinvention that actually occurs. A treatment that resonates with Benedict Anderson's account of nations as 'imagined communities' and Bhaba'a assertions regarding the 'nation as narration', which both stress the act of bringing a nation into being through creative processes. (2003: 29)

As the play closes, its universality is enforced as two of the characters are once more moving on, and they dream of all the different cities across Europe that they might go to. Whilst there is an element of optimism as the two individuals have survived and left behind a place of destruction, there is also the bleak reminder of how close the destructive forces of nationalism that were unleashed in the Balkans are to Vienna, Moscow, Paris and all the other destinations they name. After the murderous fire that is at the play's climax, Berlin, one of the arsonists, describes how a government minister visited the previously anonymous town to see the destruction of the station and that 'For one day, for one week... maybe even for a month. Everybody knew the name of our town.' (Greig, 2002: 89). We are, of course, reminded of the small towns in the former Yugoslavia, suddenly famous as the site of a terrible massacre and of the terrible price of identity and recognition.

Three years before the vote on Scottish devolution, then, David Greig was at the forefront, not of those opposing aspirations towards a new Scottish national political identity but, rather, of those seeking to see it in a much more sophisticated and ambiguous context than separation from England. Like his friend and contemporary, Sarah Kane, the re-emergence of fascism and genocide in places that had become package holiday destinations was a powerful formative influence that met a newly energized call for political devolution in the UK head-on and produced warning notes that could act as an antidote to gung-ho nationalism.

Apart from *Caledonia Dreaming*, perhaps the least typical of all his work, all Greig's engagement with a new sense of national identity has been in a similarly oblique vein to that in *Europe*. Often his work is about the essential difficulty of making and maintaining human connection and, therefore, by extension of forming meaningful communities. In *The Architect* (1996), the central figure is confronted with failure of his designs to work 'on a human level', whilst in the memorably titled *The Cosmonaut's Last Message to the Woman He Once Loved in the Former Soviet Union*, there is the powerful metaphor of the cosmonaut stranded and abandoned in space able to try only one more attempt to communicate with a woman he loved by destroying his space vessel and himself. In both plays there are constant reminders of the context of the rapid pace of globalization and the virtual shrinking of the world through the power of technology, a feature well summarized in scene from *The Cosmonaut* set in a bar in rural France; Bernard, an eccentric Frenchman set on monitoring the activities of aliens, conducts an angry comic exchange with the Proprietor full of invective against American cultural imperialism which starts with his reading a newspaper:

Bernard: Have you seen this?
             The Americans want to write the word 'Pepsi' in space.
             A giant advertisement
             To say 'Pepsi'.
             Every night it will compete with the moon.

Proprietor: The moon has nothing to sell.

Bernard: Give me a whisky

Proprietor: It makes good business sense.
             Scotch or Bourbon?

Bernard: Don't give me any of that filthy Bourbon.
I'll smash it over your counter.
Give me a Scottish malt.
(*He toasts*)
Death to the Americans!

Proprietor: I like Americans.

There follows a comically angry exchange as the two men exchange invective on both sides of the argument concluding with Bernard's gloomy prediction:

Bernard: One day, I tell you this, there will come a time when all the stories humanity has ever told will have been made into films set in American high schools.

(Greig 2002: 243–5)

That such an exchange is on the periphery of the play and takes place between two eccentric characters in a bar on the periphery of modern Europe is, in a way, typical of Greig's approach to the question of national identity. In many ways it is every where in his work, but it is always oblique and surfaces in ways that are often comic and which deflect any sense of earnestness or a traditional concern for the survival of any essential Scotland.

Outlying Islands (2002) has a take on what some might call English imperialism that is superficially reminiscent of the Ealingesque Welsh film *The Englishman Who Went Up a Hill But Came Down a Mountain* (1994). Both works deal with the initially comic culture clashes that occur when representatives of London-based officialdom encounter the apparent 'primitivism' of the inhabitants of the remoter parts of the UK, when they are dispatched to such places on official business. In Greig's play the officials are duped into thinking that their survey mission to a Scottish island has an ornithological purpose whereas it slowly emerges that the work is linked to an anthrax experiment. As is the case in Bill Forsyth's *Local Hero* (1983), the simple schema of oppressed locals exploited by the forces of imperialism and international capital is disrupted by the complicity of the local tenant farmer, Kirk, who is set of exploiting the situation for his own personal gain regardless of the long-term consequences for the island. Greig's handling of any reference to contemporary politics is light touch, to say the least, but the engagement with issues of periphery and centre, not say chemical weapons in the context of the year of its first production, makes the play clearly of its time, despite the comic delight in period language and other detail.

Much more recently, Greig's play *Pyrenees* (2005) intriguingly takes up some of the threads of *Cosmonaut* after a gap of nine years. Ironically enough, it was commissioned as part of a Paines Plough series entitled 'This Other England' which set out to explore the shaping force of language on identity. In Greig's play a man is found alone in the Pyrenees having lost his memory and the play centres around attempts to help him reconstruct an identity. Again, there is the metaphor of the reconstruction of a personal past, the rebuilding of memories, unavoidably connected (in the context of the Paines Plough series, quite explicitly so) to questions of national identity in a bewildering, shrinking globalized context.

Of late it is common to read astonished accounts of the sheer volume of David Greig's work and at his age it is astonishing to read that he has written thirty-seven plays for the stage. Much more important in this context, however, is the way that he has constantly re-cast the idea of writing about questions of Scottish identity in the era of devolution. In doing so consistently and in such a variety of ways he has probably made one of the most sophisticated and important contributions to the development of a 'new' Scottish culture and the way that it is viewed, particularly outside the United Kingdom.

Like Ed Thomas's *House of America* in Wales, Stephen Greenhorn's *Passing Places* touches (albeit more fleetingly) on the problematics of a renewed sense of national identity in the context of the hegemonic power of American popular culture. However, with a self-conscious irony, it takes on a structure with its roots firmly in Hollywood, that of the road movie, in order to journey around a multi-faceted contemporary Scotland. By the time he wrote *Passing Places*, Greenhorn had already been part of an explicit project by Paines Plough to explore a contemporary Britain on the point of political fracture by commissioning writers from England, Ireland, Scotland and Wales to produce *Sleeping Around* (1998). His work was already therefore associated with a largely comic exploration of the everyday meaning of identity, and *Passing Places* takes that a stage further. What Greenhorn's play has in common with *Europe* is a mistrust of essentialist identities, something which the 'road movie' format allows him to demonstrate as his characters encounter clichéd versions of Scottishness which are inevitably seen as, at best, part of the picture.

Holdsworth describes the first production of *Passing Places* at the Traverse as beginning with 'a giant projection of "greetings from Scotland" accompanied by four scenic postcard images, ironically juxtaposed with the environment of Motherwell that opens the play.' (2003: 35), whilst the play's structure allows its characters to experience such ironies at first hand. This is, though, no savage satire and, to some extent, the excesses of tourist board Scotland are treated affectionately and somehow part of the journey. What is celebrated, perhaps, is diversity and a willingness to engage in exploration at a significant historical moment. Mark Fisher, one of the most active journalistic supporters of a distinctive Scottish theatre, saw the first run of *Passing Places* like this:

> Behind the gags and the quips, the trivia and the pursuit, *Passing Places* is really about that foreign country we like to call Scotland. In these devolutionary days it's fashionable to talk about a nation as a homogenised entity, as if all eyes were focused on a single goal. Without tub thumping or getting especially polemical, Greenhorn gently points out that if Scotland has a glory, it is in its diversity not its similarities. (1998: 12)

Fisher's comments refer to the journey undertaken by Brian and Alex, the two main characters, as they explore a Scotland beyond the decimated post-industrial landscape that is their 'home'. Greenhorn presents their experience as one of an awakening to the realities of any idea of a Scottish identity in a globalized culture, though not necessarily experienced as simple disillusion. Instead, the play's conclusions, such as they are, seem to be that whilst the nation state is one unavoidably powerful point of reference, it cannot also be a prison. Brian and Alex, as the play closes, have both embarked upon new 'journeys' that will undoubtedly have profound consequences for their respective selves, and Nadine Holdsworth very usefully links

Greenhorn's presentation of these journeys with Greig's more oblique depictions of a search for a stable identity amongst characters more obviously and explicitly displaced by the forces of both globalization and nationalism. In both *Europe* (and by extension much of Greig's other work) and *Passing Places*, Holdsworth sees an advocacy of what she calls:

> ... an almost utopian state in which multiplicity is openly embraced; where disaporic communities are welcomed for the skills and knowledge they bring and compatibility is judged on the identification of common concerns as opposed to mythic notions of shared ethnic origins and national character. They [the two plays] propose a nation that is never static, always in process, proud of its heritage as well as its increasing heterogeneity and, above all, one that can surprise and provoke engagement beyond the confines of a restrictive and potentially damaging nationalism. (2003: 36)

If Greenhorn's work is not from the so-called 'English' naturalist tradition that Greig dismissively refers to above, it is certainly closer to it than Greig's own work and is part of the reason for seeing Greig's polemic about the nature of recent Scottish theatre as attractive, though too narrow and prescriptive. Probably further still from the centre of what Greig sees as a new, almost postcolonial Scottish tradition, Gregory Burke's phenomenally successful *Gagarin Way* (2001), whilst not conforming to the vision of 'English' theatre offered above, certainly presents a recognizable Scottish community shot through with a new generation's take on the experience of class at the so-called 'end of history'.

Gagarin's Way could be said to be at the heart of what many have seen as a re-imagining of an older vision of a working-class male Scotland which was the flip side of tartanry and kailyard in the making of the myths of twentieth-century Scotland. On the one hand, it is set firmly in the masculine territory of an 'older' Scotland but, on the other, its dark humour suggests a restless search for an adequate way for this world to cope with the enormous changes that have been forced upon it. Burke's own, half tongue-in-cheek, description of the play provides a sense of this angry, cynical, deadly serious search for an adequate means of finding a new identity for vast numbers of people seemingly abandoned by history at the end of the twentieth century:

> I wanted to write something about the twentieth century and I wanted to write something about economics and I wanted to write about men and it turned into Gagarin Way. A comedy. I didn't expect it to be a comedy but when you consider the themes which emerged when I wrote it – Marxist and Hegelian theories of history, anarchism, psychopathology, existentialism, mental illness, political terrorism, nihilism, globalisation and the crisis in masculinity – then it couldn't really be anything else. (2001: iv)

In the Scotland of 2001, there is, of course, something quite conspicuous missing from this list, and Burke's scepticism about any emerging or changed sense of Scottish national identity is manifest by its total absence from the play apart from two brief exchanges. In the first, Eddie, who has kidnapped what he thinks is a key executive of a large multinational company (Frank), mocks the power of the new Scottish parliament by drawing on the age-old myth of Scotland 'ownership' of North Sea oil:

Eddie: And while we're on the subject... (*to Frank*) when day I get my fucking oil rig?

Frank: I'm sorry... I...

Pause

Gary: (*to Eddie*) What the fuck are you on about?

Eddie: When day I get my oil rig?

Pause

Tom: Your oil rig?

Eddie: Aye. My oil rig. Ken... fay the new parliament. The one they're building. The one that's gonnay give us (*shouting in Braveheart style*) freedom. When day they cunts start divvying up the crude? That's been what? Two? Three year? Havenay had as much as a fucking barrel.

(2001: 65)

It is left to the earnest and naïve student, Tom, to actually ask the question directly only a moment or two later:

Tom: (*to Frank*) Do you... do you, you know... think that devolution's been a success?

Pause

Frank: (*looks at Gary and Eddie*) Obviously not.

(Burke 2001: 67)

The idea of devolution having even the most passing relevance to the lives of the inhabitants of the old Fife coalfield where the play is set (the title comes from a real street in the village of Lumphinnans) is therefore treated in the most dismissive way possible, and the play quickly returns to what it sees as the only real power in the world, that of the multinational. A recent article on Burke further reinforces his lack of identification with any idea of a 'new' Scotland and relates it to the time he spent as a child in Gibraltar:

Burke's chronic sense of dislocation comes out of those six years in Gibraltar and his cynicism about myths of national identity was reinforced on his return 'home' to Dunfermline, where he was slagged for being 'English'. He took on the colouration of the local vernacular as a matter of survival. (Renton 2005)

Whether or not Burke's experience as a 'forces child' in Gibraltar was as precisely formative as this interview asserts is open to question, but in a more recent play, *Straits*, Burke draws on this period of his life and again displays his antipathy to national identity as a liberating force. Describing the period when the play was set, the early 1980s, Burke says:

> Gibraltar went into overdrive during the Falklands War,... Everyone supported Argentina. It was a really schizophrenic place. After the border with Spain closed, the community's strengths and fault lines became even more pronounced. There was a siege mentality. The British sort of coalesced, and there was a lot of feeling against the Spaniards. The British kids were calling the Spanish kids 'spics'. A pack mentality took over. (Cited in Renton 2005)

For her first major success on the stage, Rona Munro also chose to operate in a place that many view as one of the last remnants of British imperialism. In Munro's *Bold Girls* in 1991 this use of a setting in the dying days of Empire is much closer to home as it focuses principally on the very ordinary lives of a group of women in contemporary Belfast. It would perhaps be wrong to strain too far the parallels between the Belfast of dying old-fashioned masculine politics and Munro's native Scotland, though her work has consistently engaged with ordinary women's experience alongside representations of traditional masculinity, often in communities undergoing profound change. However, though it is hardly ever explicit, Munro's work can at least partly be seen as belonging to a tradition in which the emergence from colonialism is inextricably linked to issues of gender, though rarely in ways that are easy to quantify or disentangle. Munro's comparative lack of profile, even after a long and prolific career, was attributed by one authoritative source to 'a colonialist attitude to Celtic myth, culture and language' (Scullion 2000: 70), whilst the wider audience she has reached through work for film and television (such as *Ladybird, Ladybird* (1996)) are likely to see her work primarily in populist feminist terms.

As always such descriptions are reductive and Munro's work for *Dr Who*, for example, suggests a much more eclectic and pragmatic writer whose stage work has become a less significant part of her output in the last few years. Equally, though, it would be wrong to suggest that she has no significance amongst the group of playwrights that have created such a prominent role for Scottish theatre in the era of devolution. As Adrienne Scullion has argued, 'in challenging the conventions of gender, women artists... also challenge the conventions of representing the nation' and it is within these parameters that Rona Munro's work tends to fall.

Munro's most successful recent play for the stage, *Iron* (2003), centers on a female character, Fay, who is serving a life sentence for the brutal murder of her husband. After a gap of fifteen years, she is visited by her daughter, Josie, who was aged eleven when the murder took place. Munro's play, though powerfully focused on female experience, never reduces its narrative to a simplistic treatise on the defensibility of female violence within abusive relationships. On the contrary, the play seems much more interested in the prison experience itself and the impact of this on individuals and their family relationships. Though, on the face of it, little to do with any contemporary sense of the nation, it is possible to see Munro's play as part of a reworking of traditional Scottish masculine territory from a female perspective. What Duncan Petrie calls 'the culture of machismo and violence that prevents many "hard men" from growing up' has been something of a staple of Scottish dramatic fictions in the twentieth century, with Peter McDougall's television adaptation of the autobiography of convicted murderer Jimmy Boyle, *A Sense of Freedom* (1980), perhaps, its most prominent example. Munro's play nearly twenty years later can be seen at least partly as a response to such a tradition and to the wider implications for Scotland of a cultural dependence on such mythology.

As Adrienne Scullion has suggested, particularly in the case of women playwrights, '... because of the orthodoxies of Scottish cultural practices and criticism, when challenging the conventions of narrative or of gender representation, artists also challenge the conventions of representing and responding to the nation.'(2001: 388). In Munro's case, not simply in *Iron*, but also in her other major success, *Bold Girls*, and, indeed, across much of her output, this has meant challenging, often not from a conventional feminist standpoint, orthodoxies around conventional gender relations and their centrality to the mythology of the Scottish working class. Furthermore, as her collaborations with 7:84 suggest, Munro has most often attempted to work within popular and accessible forms, her tales of ordinary female lives opening up areas of Scottish (and more broadly British) experience which in turn contribute to the redefinition of the nation.

Adrienne Scullion has herself made a significant contribution to such a redefinition through critical work that has opened up precisely this kind of territory to a wider academic audience. In a key article that has already been referred to a number of times she cites three plays by women, all produced in 2000, that have contributed in their different ways to a new questioning of the nation from a particularly female perspectives. She argues that Zinnie Harris's *Further than the Furthest Thing*, Sue Glover's *Shetland Saga* and Nicola McCartney's *Home*, either directly or through metaphor and analogy, are all examples of the progressive tendency of a large number of theatre writers in Scotland over the last decade to seek ways of talking about the nation that are not limited to the outmoded and narrow definitions of the past. Instead, Scullion argues that

> ... devolution will shift how we create and imagine and represent Scotland. I would argue that theatre-makers working in Scotland – and my examples here have been the playwrights Harris, Glover and McCartney – do aim to meet the challenges of a new cultural and political Scotland. And that they have done so by adopting a dramaturgy, by telling stories that are both international and outward looking *and* essentially and immediately committed to work within and about Scottish society. (2001: 388)

Glover's *Shetland Saga* is by some way the most direct of the three as it takes an example of identity within Scotland, that is in itself as marginal to the new metropolitan image beloved of the Scottish Executive as Scotland itself has been in relation to London. Furthermore, a number of Glover's characters are Bulgarian sailors involved in fishing off Shetland, and the relationship that they have experienced in relation to the Soviet Empire adds a further dimension to the sense of communities and nations engaged in the struggle to forge new and meaningful and flexible identities after the collapse of old certainties.

Harris and Glover's respective approaches are, as Scullion acknowledges, altogether more oblique. In Harris's case, she uses a South Atlantic island (very like Tristan da Cunha) whose population is subjected to forced evacuation as a consequence of a volcanic eruption. Their resettlement in the UK inevitably raises profound questions of cultural identity and marginalization. McCartney, on the other hand, writes about the family and in such a way, in

Scullion's formulation, as to draw inevitable parallels with contemporary questions about the nation:

> McCartney unsettles the idea of family, recreating it as flexible, re-imagining it as a community that can shift and alter and evolve, and can then tell new and different stories. Home, for McCartney in this play, is a place that evolves and changes as much as any other community or identity. And, I would suggest, this flexibility in the nature and the purpose of family is remarkably unfamiliar in Scottish drama. (2001: 387)

Whilst it is unwise to focus any examination of theatre work in contemporary Scotland too obsessively on a concern for the nation, it has been interesting to see that the ambitious first project undertaken by the National Theatre of Scotland also focused on the diversity of meanings contained in the idea of 'Home' (as discussed above). As Scottish playwrights embrace a new freedom and an easing of what has been referred to as the 'burden of representation' it is clear that the evolution of what it means to be at 'home' in the national sense will remain a potent idea for some time to come. McCartney's dark and unsentimental exploration is a significant contribution to the range of ideas that theatre makers have contributed during the last decade.

Although her most recent work has been less concerned with the idea of the nation, it would be perverse to leave any discussion of contemporary women writers and their contribution to theatre's role in shaping identity without mentioning the work of Liz Lochhead. Mentioned above by David Greig as one of the key figures that paved the way for the current generation through her pioneering work during the 1980s and 1990s, Lochhead's work for the stage is focused on women's experience and, in her best-known plays, the recovery of that experience from a writing of history that has largely obscured it. Probably the key text in this respect is *Mary Queen of Scots Got Her Head Chopped Off* (1989), which is widely seen as one of the most significant works for the theatre to have emerged from modern Scotland. As Scullion puts it:

> *Mary Queen of Scots* is typical of Lochhead's dramaturgy in its representation of the cherished and hegemonic myths of Scottish national identity, its explosive feminist re-setting of both 'legitimate history' and popular culture. (2001: 98)

In *Mary Queen of Scots*, Lochhead both offers a re-reading of a key episode of the history of relations between Scotland and England and an example of the reclaiming of theatrical language for both feminist and nationalist purposes. The latter can be most obviously seen through the use what Lochhead herself refers to as 'Scots English'. As Greig suggested above, Lochhead (and others) paved the way for the contemporary explosion of ways that the theatre contributed to the ongoing definition of new Scottish identity and, what is more, did it during a much more hostile and defensive historical moment.

At the time of writing, early in 2006, one of the most significant Scottish theatre companies of the last twenty years, *7:84* (Scotland), looks like it will become the highest profile theatre company yet to fall victim to the Scottish Arts Council's shift of emphasis to project funding in order, as they see it, to assist the individual artist. *7:84*'s view, of course, is that this comes dangerously close to ignoring the audience and further exposing the fault lines at the heart of

Scottish theatre. It is also a sign that, post-devolution, funding for Scottish theatre has been no less fiercely contested than it was before. The demise of *7:84* follows the collapse of Wildcat theatre earlier in the decade, suggesting perhaps that John McGrath's pessimistic view of a new orthodoxy (see above) maybe coming to pass, despite the avowed pluralism of the National Theatre project. This, in turn, is almost certainly too simple, though there seems little question that the kind of engaged theatre of the kind typified by *7:84* and which has traditionally flourished in Scotland is struggling to retain its hold within the new funding regime.

In 2002 Mark Fisher re-asked a question that he first posed in print in 1995 – 'What is so special about Scottish theatre?' – His answer is in many ways frustrating because he finds a theatre 'built on nothing if not plurality' (Fisher 2002). For Fisher it is David Greig that epitomizes that plurality because, he argues that, ironically, 'there is no overbearing Scottish tradition to constrain him'. For Fisher, the strength of theatre in Scotland in the mid-1990s was the lack of a unified past.

Whether or not one subscribes to Fisher's view, in a post-devolution Scottish theatre we can certainly see a healthy lack of an overarching response to the changed political situation in Scotland. There has been neither a unified flag-waving response to devolution but, also, not simply a rather grand artistic distance. There is plenty of evidence of both artists and policy-makers seizing on the idea of a 'new' culture that politicians at least give the appearance of valuing. The responses are indeed various, but so plentiful and internationally recognized as to make it no coincidence that they are springing from a new and relatively confident culture. In theatrical terms this is a situation best summed by one of the most consistent champions of Scottish theatre, Joyce Macmillan:

> Joyce McMillan, theatre critic for The Scotsman, says: 'Things have definitely changed recently. During the Eighties and Nineties, before the Parliament, there was a sense that most Scottish writers were conducting some kind of dialogue about Scottish identity. Now there's a strong group of young writers, at the top of which I'd put David Greig, Douglas Maxwell, David Harrower and Anthony Neilson, who have all got completely different things on the go.'

> The kind of self-confidence engendered by the march towards devolution has, she argues, almost led to a feeling that 'we're cool enough, postmodern enough and mature enough not to be spending a lot of time thinking about being Scottish'. (Cavendish 2002)

Macmillan, looking to the future, rightly emphasizes, the way that Scottish theatre makers have revelled in the freedom to not think about being Scottish, whilst unavoidably contributing to a project of self-definition. It is a largely optimistic picture which, when coupled with the developing vision of the National Theatre of Scotland, gives a strong sense of a diverse, though unified, artistic vision amongst Scottish theatre makers. On the whole, this may be the right note on which to close, though equally tempting is the warning note that is sounded by the inability of the new funding regimes to find a place for the likes of *7:84*. The coming years, as the coalition that is likely to run the Scottish Parliament continues to mutate, will demonstrate whether or not the kind of relationship that companies such as *7:84* established with audiences across Scotland can so easily be replaced as a small but significant part of the process by which the nation is able to continue the democratic conversation that is the essence of national self-definition.

Behind 'The Façade of Cool Cymru': Wales and Theatre

In ways that are perhaps more fundamental than in any other part of Britain, the recent history of theatre in Wales has been inextricably linked to debates about 'performance' and its relationship to conventional building-based theatrical practices. This tendency can, in turn, be related to the stated desire, often passionately expressed, to develop what one leading practitioner has called:

> ... a new, vibrant and distinctive theatre tradition in Wales, one which is relevant and responsive to the perceptions, experience, aspirations and concerns of a minority culture and a small nation and which is more than just a pale reflection of English theatre convention. (Adams 1996: 55)

In Wales, then, it is possible to see what is perhaps a stronger and more explicit relationship between theatre and debates around national identity than in the rest of Britain, a relationship that was clear well before the run-up to the 1997 devolution referendum and which continues today in ways that are endlessly mutating.

What many have argued about Wales in this context, and it is helpful to rehearse this a little here, is that the country has very little in the way of what might be termed a theatrical history, but equally it possesses an almost uniquely varied history of 'performance' in the widest sense. In a recent special edition of *Studies in Theatre and Performance* devoted entirely to 'Nationhood and Performance in Wales', practically all the articles use this precise point as part of their various investigations into one dimension or other of theatre and performance in contemporary Wales. Lisa Lewis's piece, for example, seeks to distance most Welsh-language performance in particular from mainstream British theatrical tradition:

> ... performance in Wales can easily be defined as something other than a set of devices and techniques for staging or presenting plays (that is, a vehicle for the exposition of dramatic

literature). Performance may include poetry, quotation and stories, including the sophisticated poetic and musical forms that lie at the centre of Welsh-language performance culture. Performance may include techniques found in forms such as the *noson lawen* (of sketches and sing-alongs), *twpathau* (barn dances), *eisteddfodau* (cultural events on a local or national scale incorporating all kinds of performances), and the oratory and singing taught at chapel and school. Behind these performances lies a drive that is at the core of Welsh language identity and the way that it is constructed and performed. (2004: 167)

Whilst Ceri Sherlock asserts that:

Wales is a performative culture and increasingly its perception is as such, as the land of song, sport and language/words – in recitation, sporting prowess, choral singing, poetry, preaching, oratory, *cerdd dant*, rock concerts, dance, acting, singing, painting, creating installations, erecting public art, making theatre and in all manner of creative public assemblies. (2004: 152)

It is, therefore, possible to see that questions of national identity, as expressed through live performance in Wales, are debates about the value of building-based theatrical traditions to the new nation. Conversely these commentators argue in favour of the far greater relevance and applicability of diverse performance traditions that are more firmly rooted in what is a distinctive national culture.

Such ideas are, of course, not new to Wales. It is ironic to many that whilst the 1980s and early 1990s saw Wales develop an international reputation as the home of some of the boldest experiments with theatrical form and context in Europe, the latter half of the 1990s and political devolution saw this tradition in steep decline as funding cuts and other factors saw many of the companies disappear.

It is perhaps helpful at this point to discuss briefly some of the things that have been lost because of this disappearance. The inevitable starting point for such a discussion is the company Brith Gof which became internationally recognized during the 1980s and early 1990s as one of Europe's leading innovators, particularly through their site-specific work and, particularly relevant to this discussion, for their attempts to make fundamental connections between their work and the nature of the national and cultural identity of Wales.

Although Brith Gof's best-known work involved their use of large urban spaces (of which more below), their earliest attempts to connect with the material conditions of Welsh culture and history focused almost entirely on the rural context of the Welsh-speaking heartlands of the north and west. As Heike Roms puts it:

The company's early work wove together elements of Welsh literature, folklore and history with physical actions that were derived from everyday patterns of work, play and worship and objects that were taken from the paraphernalia of traditional rural life. (2004: 181)

In work such as performances based upon the collection of Welsh myths known as the *Mabinogi* (1981–1983) and *Rhydcymerau* (1984), Brith Gof sought to deal with the threat of the loss of a Welsh national culture conceived principally as Welsh-speaking and rural. However, as Roms goes on to discuss, by the late 1980s, Brith Gof's work had become much more focused upon the more recent urban and industrial history of Wales as refracted through the devastation of the economic conditions of the present. One of the common links between these two periods, however, was Brith Gof's preference for spaces outside traditional theatres as sites for their work (though they have frequently worked in theatres as well). Some of the reasons behind this are pragmatic, in that many areas of Wales simply do not possess a theatre of the kind that Brith Gof might have sought. Much more importantly, however, Brith Gof sought to explore a connection between the spaces in which they worked and the local and national community's values and preoccupations. During the early work this meant rural locations as described by one of company's founders, Mike Pearson:

> We went to live and work in a small village in West Wales, and began to think about manifestations of theatre that were not theatre-bound. We were making performances for farmhouse kitchens, for the Post Office counter, and so on... I think it would be the venues in which a Welsh, particularly a Welsh rural audience, would feel more at ease – rather than sitting in dark rows in a theatre. (Cited in Kaye 1996: 209–10)

However, the better known later work used large-scale ex-industrial sites such as a disused car plant for *Gododdin*(1988–9) or the closed steel works at Tredegar for *Haern* (1992). This later work did not, though, abandon the concern for the ancient roots of Welsh culture as the company saw them, rather the performances continued to draw on the mythological and attempted to forge connections between the devastation of contemporary post-industrialization

> ... by bringing together the ancient and the modern, the rural and the industrial, the English-speaking and the Welsh-speaking aspects of Welshness, united as common victims of the cultural and economic exploitation of Wales by England. (Roms 2004: 182)

At this point, though, it is essential to state Brith Gof's distance from the propagation of any essentialist notion of Welsh national identity, in opposition to England. The evidence, both from the totality of their work and from direct statements by members of the company, is that they both saw national identity *per se* as a highly contested, problematic concept and, moreover, that they strongly advocated the idea of Wales looking beyond England to Europe for a context for its emerging identity as a nation. Discussing one of their most prominently 'Welsh' performances, Jen Harvie makes precisely this point:

> *Gododdin* remembered and constituted a strong and often positive narrative of Welsh identity as linguistically and culturally rich, loyal, creative, innovative, and brave, whether in the face of war, environmental onslaught or economic decline. It did not, however, present an entirely sense of national identity that might then be seen as fixed or, indeed, exclusive and xenophobic. McLucas [a key member of Brith Gof] argued 'The idea of an authentic Welshness which speaks for the heartland is a myth' (2005: 50)

Fascinatingly, as Harvie goes on to discuss, the dangers of such ideas of essentialist nationalism were reinforced when *Gododdin* was performed in Germany where such ideas have an altogether more immediate recent history. A production which had started in the site-specific context of a post-miners strike Wales, which in turn had helped to rekindle ideas of a postcolonial Welsh 'nation', took on very different meanings in a country so haunted by a recent history of imperial expansionism.

As the moment of actual devolution got closer, Brith Gof's work became, at least on the face of it, still more specifically concerned with ideas of national identity. Far from pursuing narrow questions of Welsh identity their attention now appeared to focus on the problematics of crude nationalism, particularly in the British context. This could be seen at its most explicit in their 1996 show *Prydain: The Impossibility of Britishness*. Heike Roms quotes the following sentence from *Prydian*'s programme notes: 'After the break-up of former Yugoslavia can the idea of nation have any credibility when unspeakable acts were committed in its name?' (2004: 186), though goes on to say that, in fact, *Prydian* was less pessimistic about the idea of the nation than this would imply. Instead, as Wales anticipated the first Labour government since 1979 and the prospect of devolution, the show offered a new model upon which to base ideas about the constitution of identity itself. This was, above all, never to be an identity that was fixed or given, but rather endlessly negotiated by active citizens, something inscribed in the performance itself by the fact that each night 50 tickets were available to 'audience participants' who became crucial parts of the performance.

Though one of its key members, Mike Pearson, has continued to make fascinating work in collaboration with Mike Brookes and others, most recently around the idea of the contemporary city, it remains ultimately ironic that a company whose work had been so concerned with a highly sophisticated exploration of national identity should effectively cease to exist at the very moment of devolution. Heike Roms, in an article referred to a number of times already, makes an interesting case for the recent work of the Pearson/Brookes partnership, taking Brith Gof's concern for the national into a new era of the potentially post-national citizen. However, it is indisputably the case that the latter has rarely reached out to an international audience interested in the resonances from Wales for those interested in the contemporary burning questions of national identity in the way that Brith Gof's work has regularly done over the previous decade.

Brith Gof, then, stands as an example of the way that theatre in Wales in the last two decades showed itself both capable of reaching out beyond Britain to become part of the European avant-garde, but also to be seen as part of the urgent quest for self-definition during some of the darkest moments of Wales's post-industrial history. Since devolution itself there is a strong case for saying that a preoccupation with institutions, among them a 'National Theatre', has rather bedevilled the development of theatre in Wales. With notable exceptions this has reduced the scale of the ambition of theatre's involvement with any project of on-going redefinition, and too often public discussion has revolved around conflicts over funding or buildings rather than the ground-breaking theatrical imagination displayed by Brith Gof (and, of course, some if its contemporaries such as Moving Being or Man Act).

One such exception is the highly original body of work by the one-time *Brith Gof* performer Eddie Ladd. Ladd's work during the last two decades has often shown an overt interest in the ongoing project to continuously reinvent Wales but through such startlingly oblique and inventive conceits as to make all connections with stale debates about identity seem irrelevant.

Often hard to define, and frequently making redundant the boundary between theatre and live art, Ladd's work has memorably encompassed Brian de Palma's 1993 film *Scarface*, the lives of Leni Riefenstahl and Maria Callas and a long-lasting concern for her rural West Wales roots on her family's farm. It is through such unlikely eclecticism that Ladd has worked, often with the aid of advanced technology, to continuously explore a version of a Welsh identity that has little to do with hackneyed traditional iconography. To its great credit, Ladd's work is very hard to define, but there are recurring questions around the relationship between her sense of the performative culture of West Wales where she grew up and, in particular, the apparently monolithic American popular culture that surrounded it. However, there is no simple liberal opposition to American cultural hegemony with *Scarface* especially coming across as a highly complex, technically demanding homage to the performance of Al Pacino in the tile role. Ladd's work offers a vision of Wales which can be home to the most ambitious work in the performing arts which embraces huge demands on the actor's body alongside a fascination for technology, and her award from NESTA in 2002 acknowledged the international significance of her approach. That such an acknowledgement should come to an artist that has remained committed to a continuing exploration of the unfolding story of Wales, its languages and questions of identity is testament to how the best recent Welsh performance work is able to use the case of Wales to reach out and speak to those in all cultures that see identities as fluid and part of a complex narrative journey.

However, as suggested above, work by Eddie Ladd, and those like Marc Rees, Sean Tuan John and *Earthfall* who have worked through the kind of visual and physical languages that frequently see their work characterized as 'dance', has, since the moment of devolution itself, become somewhat drowned out by the sheer volume of antagonistic debate raging around control of the nation's official cultural agenda. The dominance within such a debate of the idea of a national theatre which is discussed in detail below has, in turn, led to what has to be seen as at least a partial retreat within Wales from its strong tradition of experimentation in theatre. What follows is an attempt to assess what has happened in its place as the cultural life of Wales has become more and more of direct interest to elected politicians seeking to use the arts as part of a wider nation-building strategy.

To begin with the bloodletting, it now seems ironic that the theatre community in Wales began what we might see as its postcolonial life with a series of impassioned and very public rows that included questions in the Westminster parliament and a symbolic coffin paraded through the streets of Cardiff. Both these events were sparked by different dimensions to the Arts Council of Wales's, now notorious Drama Strategy, which among things proposed a drastic halving of the number of companies providing young people's theatre in Wales as well as merging the two companies charged with developing new writing for theatre in both Welsh and English. There was also a drastic reduction in the number of companies receiving revenue funding from the Arts Council and casualties of this policy included Brith Gof amongst many others.

The response to the Drama Strategy was in many ways extraordinary. As well as the events already mentioned, the outcry from the artistic community was sustained and well publicized. Rarely, one suspects, have the pages of the Western Mail [the main English-language Welsh daily newspaper], or even the regional news bulletins, been so infiltrated by a debate about arts policy of any kind. There are a number of different ways of reading this, of course, but in the context of the immediate post-devolution atmosphere it is tempting to see it optimistically. That is as a sign of an arts community with a new sense of its own identity, seeking to make policy-makers more open and accountable. To an extent they succeeded: even though key parts of the strategy remained in place there were dramatic reactions to the public protest. The first of these was the direct intervention of the new Welsh Assembly Government in asking the Arts Council to suspend implementation of its Drama Strategy, one of the first major steps in the devolved Government's move to be much more proactive in the area of cultural policy. On the 1 December 1999, a statement of opinion was issued as follows:

> This Assembly believes that the Arts Council for Wales should defer its decision on its proposed Drama Strategy until after the Assembly has completed is own review of the Arts. We believe that if the Arts Council for Wales proceeds with its new strategy at this stage, it could run counter to the Assembly's priorities. (http://www.theatre-wales.co.uk/news/index.asp)

The restraint of the official language hides the significance of such a direct intervention and this was simply the beginning. Nine months of continued public criticism and an Assembly commissioned report into its management later and the Arts Council's Chief Executive, Joanna Weston, had resigned amidst much acrimony. It is clear from various claims and counterclaims that internal divisions within the Arts Council were partly responsible for the resignation, but it is equally clear that the National Assembly's role was also very prominent. The Assembly had begun to flex its muscles in the sphere of public policy and it has continued to do so ever since.

At the time of writing, in early 2006, the Arts Council of Wales is involved in yet another very public row with the Assembly Government, this time over what the former sees as yet another breach of the so-called 'arms length' principle underpinning the relationship between government and arts funding in the UK. Though the latest exchange is over the appointment of the Chief Executive of the Arts Council, what really underlies the dispute is the Assembly Government's decision to take direct control over six of the largest revenue clients of the Arts Council of Wales, including two of the best funded theatre companies, Clwyd Theatr Cymru and Theatr Genedlaethol Cymru.

In the absence of real economic power, then, the Welsh Assembly Government has placed a great deal of public emphasis on the power of culture. In its *Culture Strategy for Wales* it continually make reference to the role of culture in establishing and enhancing a Welsh identity both within Wales and abroad, whilst the section on theatre explicitly states its belief that a strong Welsh culture needs both 'flagship companies' working in both Welsh and English as well as a successful community-orientated sector.

Whatever the outcome of such a strategy, it is abundantly clear that theatre in post-devolutionary Wales, alongside other art forms, is being put close to the heart of government policy. Clearly there are enormous dangers involved as well as some potential benefits as the arts struggles to compete with the urgent economic priorities of health and education. At the time of writing, the tendency within Wales is to be pessimistic about the institutional handling of theatre, particularly English language theatre. In the context of this discussion, however, it remains fascinating to see politicians explicitly acknowledging the importance of theatre at the start of the digital age, even if their plans for it provoke deep suspicion in the arts community.

One of the clear consequences of such direct political interest in theatre, especially in an emergent nation, is the overemphasis of the importance of symbolic structures and buildings. The companies and institutions that the Welsh Assembly Government has taken under its direct control are, quite obviously, considered institutions likely to enhance the reputation of Wales internationally and to help develop a sense of national identity at home. Part of the same thinking underlies the endless debate about a 'National Theatre' that has raged in Wales for decades but, which, since devolution, has taken on a new significance. Whilst in 2005 a Welsh language National Theatre Company exists and a building is being developed (in Carmarthen), the arguments over an English-language version go on, and on. That there should be one organization is enough to induce an attack of the vapours in some quarters.

For many though the whole idea of a national theatre in Wales runs counter to the genuine cultural identity of the new nation:

> The 'trophy art' mentality is an English construct and is inherently alien to Wales and its culture, and the clamour for national theatres in Wales is an attempt to impose a centralised vision on a nation of communities. (Sherlock 2004: 151)

As the same writer reminds us, the most recently developed state national theatre in Europe (at the time of writing in 2005) is in Serbia, a stark reminder of the dangers of reliance on the imitation of grand imperial symbolism. However, there are other models, notably the highly innovative one adopted in Scotland (discussed elsewhere in this volume), which are capable of accommodating the distinctiveness of Welsh (or any other) performative culture, and it is surely in this direction that Wales must look if the energy-sapping discussions are to end. However, it is fair to say that at the time of writing, the arguments seem polarized between, on the one hand, those who see a powerful political imperative toward the creation of national institutions (in a nation with limited power over more traditional material concerns) and, on the other, those who see the idea of imported models as inevitably diversionary and opposed to the 'real' business of artistic endeavour:

> *So why a National Theatre?*
>
> Because it sounds good? Because it fits in with Assembly politics? Because it avoids thinking about theatre as an art form, as a practice, as a profession? Because it make life easier for the decision-makers? Because it can create status without any test of quality? Because it pretends that Wales has an established English-language theatre tradition?.... Take your pick. (Adams 2004: 92)

So far, then, we can see that post-devolutionary Wales has, in one sense, taken theatre very seriously, though many would argue that the overall sense is of the loss of the vibrancy of the country's well-developed experimental, largely physical theatre tradition. One rather simplified way of looking at recent Welsh theatre history would be to say that the significant 'events' have moved towards a middle ground. That is a territory that has enabled a number of young Welsh playwrights to have their work play at prominent London fringe venues as well as tour in Wales and, perhaps just as significantly, to appeal to different audiences within Wales. When I say significant events, I am talking about those that have gathered attention, in the press, in terms of audience numbers and, which, have provoked debate both within the theatre community and amongst audiences that have witnessed them. It hardly needs saying that none of these things is any mark of artistic success, but here we are talking of the kind of theatre that has, so far, seemed to define the postcolonial context both inside Wales and to a wider world, and it is in those terms that I propose to examine it.

Again, ironically, considering the levels of angry debate that have surrounded its funding, it has been in the field of new writing that many of the 'events' have taken place. Until the Arts Council's decision in 1999 to only fund one new writing company, both Made in Wales in English and Dalier Slyw in Welsh had struggled to build a new writing tradition for Wales under conditions arguably less favourable than any other part of the UK. With no building dedicated to new writing and persistently low levels of funding, both companies struggled to maintain a consistent, high-profile public output, though both had moments of success. Outside the two principal companies there were also many examples of innovative new writing work, often in the area of theatre for young people (see, for example, Greg Cullen on Theatre Powys or the work of Charles Way) (Cullen1997: 132–152), though it mostly proved difficult to sustain.

As we have already seen, many even argued that it was a positive and distinctive feature of Welsh theatre that it had no strong new writing or 'literary' theatre tradition, and, instead, Wales had fostered both experimentation and theatres closely linked to communities, particularly for young people.

However, and against the odds, from the mid-1990s until its closure in 1999, Made in Wales, in particular, began to maintain a rather more consistent public output that is highly relevant to our current discussion. What is also relevant to a discussion about forging identities is that a significant part of that output has been published. In the introduction to the first of two volumes of *Made in Wales* plays from the late 1990s, the artistic director, Jeff Teare, makes his project pretty explicit:

> Well, they are Welsh plays and they are concerned with identity but not in the usual Welsh theatrical manner. The cultural identity of *Safar* is somewhere between Pakistani and British Asian, the identity discussed in *Gulp* is sexual, and *Happiness* deals in social and existential self rather than national. Three Welsh plays in one volume not about definitions of Welshness, good grief! (Teare 1998: 12)

Teare had come to Cardiff in the mid-1990s from the Theatre Royal in Stratford East, a theatre that had prided itself in attempting to build relationships with its local audience in London's East End. He clearly saw the theatre being produced in Wales at that time as being very restricted in the range of people it addressed and, by extension, limited in its definitions of what it is to be Welsh at the end of the century. In his introductions to both volumes of plays, he continually snipes at what he saw as the narrowness and parochialism of the theatre establishment, particularly with regard to racial identity:

> *Giant Steps* by Othniel Smith was very much part of my attempt to give Made in Wales' work a multi-cultural perspective. The first thing I did with the Company in 1995 was to set

up a multi-cultural writers workshop and my first actual production with Made in Wales was a show-case of these writers' work.

How large a task I had set myself was soon revealed by a phone call to ACW. By 'multi-cultural' they assumed I meant 'Welsh and English speaking'. When I explained that I was mainly talking about Welsh writers from non-European backgrounds I was met with a long silence. (Teare 2001: 11)

In a sense, we have here a very interesting set of tensions around the issue of postcolonial identity, a director from the London fringe arriving in Wales seeking to drag the fundamentally heterogeneous nature of Welsh identity kicking and screaming onto stages in Wales and beyond. Predictably, the results met with very mixed reactions and many questioned the theatrical as well as intellectual sophistication of much of the work. Arguably, the most positive dimension is that, at times, the company could claim to have reached out to new audiences who saw something for the first time in a Welsh play that was part of their experience of living here. Typical of this was *Gulp* by a young Cardiff writer, Roger Williams:

It was generally considered to be Cardiff's first professionally produced young, out gay play, referred to by the press as a 'cultural milestone'. The audience at Chapter was predominantly under 35 with many first-time theatre attenders. (Teare 1998: 11)

Teare's tenure at Made in Wales coincided with the run-up to devolution and ended not long after the Assembly came into being, but the work produced during that time is expressive of a strong tendency that we will see again in film and television drama and from other producers of theatre during this period. That is a desire to rid Welsh drama of the burden of old debates about Welsh identity and the Welsh nation, to somehow connect Wales to a more 'modern' and youthful wider world and in so doing demonstrate that Wales is a place with far more possibilities than had previously been thought.

In the context of debates about the postcolonial situation of Wales this tendency poses interesting questions. On the one hand, it would appear that the aspiration is for young artists to ignore the historical and cultural specificities of Wales and simply take on forms that fit more easily into the demands of a wider industry. In the case of theatre this sometimes meant the text-based, small-scale neo-naturalist tradition that has tended to be the dominant form, as Teare suggests, not only in London but in Dublin and Edinburgh as well.

Here, clearly, the linked concepts of hybridity and mimicry come into play. Made in Wales critics would argue that it largely produced work that did simply 'mimic' that being produced anywhere in the UK and ignored the more radical formal possibilities that had been so prevalent in Wales during the 1980s and early 1990s. On the other hand, the company's explicit project to work with writers in Wales from communities that had hitherto been largely ignored could be argued to have extended the definition of who Welsh theatre was 'for'. By implicitly linking the subordinate nature of black and gay communities within Wales to the subordinate nature of Wales to England, the company could be said to have been very much part of a postcolonial spirit to re-define and re-invent.

The successor company to Made In Wales and Dalier Slyw – Sgript Cymru has, to some extent, extended this tradition, though arguably its output has been less self-consciously concerned with 'minority' representation and more with careful processes of script development, so that the final product is more fully 'crafted' in both literary and theatrical terms. Like Made in Wales, it has also seemed to prioritize the production of new Welsh writing outside Wales and has had high-profile success, particularly with two plays that had extended London fringe runs and consequent press attention. Both were by young writers relatively new to theatre and neither is overtly concerned with Welshness at all, though they clearly contain identifiable Welsh characters and references.

Crazy Gary's Mobile Disco by Gary Owen and *Art and Guff* by Catherine Tregenna were, to some extent, presented as a kind of 'package' which helped to maximize publicity and create a minor stir around Welsh playwriting getting in on the 'Cool Cymru' act. What seemed to unite them was not so much their concern for Wales, as much as the (by now) well-trodden ground of masculinity. Perhaps this is not surprising coming from a country seeing the last rites read over most of its remaining heavy industry. Of the two, *Art and Guff* appeared closest to the new writing tradition of the London fringe; reviews most often made comparisons with both Pinter and the cult film *Withnail and I*. *Crazy Gary*, on the other hand, relied on a monologic, storytelling tradition, with three voices giving us stories that gradually revealed their connection with each other.

What these plays represent, then, is a particular approach to the postcolonial context, or in some cases the anticipation of it. That approach I would define as attempting to establish a Welsh presence within a particularly strong British tradition, one that had in the 1990s been given a new 'cool' and vigour by a generation of what Aleks Sierz has immortalized as 'In-Yer-Face-Theatre'. The approach, by and large, ignores the idea of a distinctive Welsh tradition either in terms of form or content, instead it seeks to demonstrate that talent exists in Cardiff, Swansea and Wrexham as it does in London and Leeds. It attempts to ride a wave of post-devolution confidence and through that a new, youthful brash identity for Welsh theatre.

Since the premiere of *Crazy Gary's Mobile Disco*, Owen in particular has become, arguably, the most successful playwright to emerge from Wales in more than a decade. The route to such success is also instructive about both positive and negative dimensions to the development of theatre in Wales in the post-devolutionary period. On the one hand, Owen has clearly escaped the so-called 'burden of representation' mentioned elsewhere in this volume and so often bemoaned by artists working in minority cultures. His work has come to be seen as having little to do with Wales in any direct sense and his most high-profile success has been through commissions and collaborations with the likes of Paines Plough and the Royal National Theatre. More negatively, it is sadly true that Owen is better known amongst regular metropolitan theatregoers than he is in his native South Wales, where the opportunities for his challenging brand of non-naturalistic, linguistically inventive new writing remain very limited, though he remains an occasional collaborator with Sgript Cymru.

With a Methuen collection (Owen 2005) to his name and an international reputation, Gary Owen is one of the highest profile successes of recent Welsh theatre and in most ways it is a matter of celebration, and, perhaps, a maturing culture, that he stands as living proof that it is possible to be a young Welsh artist and not be overtly concerned with the identity of the nation. Mark Jenkins would not claim to a 'young' anything, but belatedly and deservedly he has also enjoyed international success as a playwright after being virtually ignored in his native Wales over two decades. What Jenkins shares with Owen is both a welcome published collected edition of his work (Jenkins 2004) and a huge range of concerns in his plays, none of them overtly Welsh. Jenkins's work is almost invariably biographical and his range is huge, taking in, for example, Richard Burton (obviously his most Welsh subject), Karl Mark and Orson Welles, though, until very recently he found it desperately hard to get a production in Wales. The irony of this has not been lost on Jenkins and his comments on the way theatre in Wales has generally treated him and others has resonances across a culture where theatre has often been used as a rather limiting kind of battleground in the project of national redefinition. Speaking of his long, internal exile and very recent 'discovery' in Wales in contrast to his international success, he says:

> Surely there is some kind of lesson here for those of us concerned with theatre in Wales. One lesson is this – the small unassuming door, the one closest to the writer is the hardest one to enter, whereas on the other side of the planet the imposing portals of the Sydney Opera House are open. It's an irony, and I believe I know why. Theatrical gatekeepers in this neck of the woods have been laying down 'agendas' for Welsh writers and have been busy outlining 'collective' visions for Welsh theatre. All this instead of listening or reading. (Walford Davies 2004: 275)

In their very different ways, then, both Jenkins and Gary Owen have become examples of post-devolutionary Welsh theatre, discovering both challenging text-based theatre and the fact that it is possible to be a Welsh playwright and write and something beyond Welsh identity. However, in the scale of things, these are glimmers, and the twin forces of under funding and political interference from an overanxious Assembly government remain powerful obstacles to the future development of a body of work for theatre in the English language continuing to emerge from Wales.

There have, however, been theatrical 'events' in the last decade that have sought a much more direct engagement with Welsh identity, less through the subtle development of form and more through an open confrontation of the devastating social and economic problems facing the new Wales Assembly. For example, both Patrick Jones's *Everything Must Go* (1999) and Helen Griffin's *Flesh and Blood* (2000) were generally seen as theatrically crude and naïve by the Welsh theatre community, but, particularly Jones' play, were also seized upon for their value in defining an emerging Wales. Jones's close relationship with The Manic Street Preachers through his brother, Nicky Wire, obviously contributed to this, and sections of the London press were quick to link the play to the Manics' very direct political agenda. In both these plays we are a long way from lazy descriptions of a confident European-orientated agenda, culled from a casual stroll around Cardiff Bay. Jones, in particular, has been happy to explain his mission, stating in interviews that his play,

> attacks so-called Cool Cymru, the idea that Wales is suddenly sexy. We're so apathetic, so used to accepting second-best. We're down on our knees grovelling to foreign investors, be they Japanese or Korean, who come in and use us as fodder. I'm not xenophobic and I don't

want to romanticise the mines, but they did stitch communities together and factories fracture them (Sullivan 1999)

Griffin's view is perhaps less direct, but equally sceptical about the confidence of one version of the postcolonial agenda. Her play examines, through one Swansea family, the darker side of nationalism and its links to racism. As one reviewer put it:

Hidden behind the façade of Cool Cymru lies a Wales ravaged by unemployment, racial tensions and fear for the future. Helen Griffin's first full-length play wrestles with all these ideas in this bittersweet black comedy, using one Swansea family as a metaphor for a nation. (Watts 2000)

Both plays are valuable correctives, short-term fixes maybe in fluid cultural climate, but a long way from the aspirations of those that have been most ambitious for a genuinely distinct theatre from Wales.

Similarly concerned with the colonial relationship between Wales and England, but theatrically far more ambitious and distinctive, is the considerable body of work written by Ian Rowlands and produced mainly by the small-scale touring company Theatr y Byd. Whilst often highly dependent upon a dense, allusive use of language, Rowlands work is also highly visual, sometimes the result of formal collaborations with artists, and always dense with powerful metaphoric connections between the personal situations he focuses on and the state of the Welsh nation. As David Adams suggests:

Rowlands's concern is the state of the nation. But as with other writers describing the relation between colonising power and oppressed nation he talks not about politics but sexual relationships. Like Doris Lessing (in an African context), Toni Morrison (in a black American context) or Margaret Atwood (in a Fourth World Canadian context), Rowlands makes men and women, the dominator and dominated, analogous to the coloniser and colonised. (1999: 252)

Adams goes on to argue that Rowlands similarly adopts a postcolonial strategy with regard to language in the way that he writes (usually) in English, but in a form that is distinctively Welsh and furthermore that he distances himself from what Adams sees as the traditional English form of theatre, naturalism:

... he [Rowlands] also abrogates and appropriates theatrical convention by subverting the traditional naturalism of English theatre. He emphasises the Welshness of his plays by reference to place names, food, cultural history and so on, and by using Welsh. (1999: 252)

Whilst the last sentence is undoubtedly true, the first, I think, betrays a common anxiety amongst critics interested in the emergent British nations to pin down and assert difference in their artists when the truth may be more allusive. To suggest that a rejection of realist/naturalist forms is in itself a postcolonial act is, apart from anything else, to misunderstand the diversity of both English theatrical tradition and contemporary British culture. Whilst the allusive poetic quality to Rowland's work undoubtedly connects him to a wider European avant-garde tradition, this implies a rejection not so much of Englishness *per se* and more of the simplicities of nationalistic debates that rely heavily on contemporary 'reality'. One such simplicity, of course, frequently draws upon the colonial power as the only useful reference point through which to define the new nation, and Adams's analysis of Rowlands's theatrical strategy is in danger of submerging it under the dead weight of this binary opposition.

For all its dense metaphoric language and visual imagery, though, Rowlands's body of work taken as a whole is as substantial a contribution to recent Welsh theatre as any other writer. It is also a complex and passionate attempt to address the issues surrounding an emerging nation whilst at the same time attempting to transcend the contemporary situation. His most critically acclaimed work, such as *Blue Heron in the Womb* (1998), tends to be that in which the politics of contemporary Wales seem barely there at all, only to surface through almost casual asides and the sudden explosion of the Welsh language as the play reaches its climax. At other times Rowlands is far more direct, never more so than in *New South Wales* set on the day of the Welsh devolution referendum in 1997 in which a travelling Welshman is determined to return home to greet the birth of the new nation. So desperate is he to do so he hires a taxi all the way from London in order to arrive in time thus starting the journey that constitutes the play's entire length. What prevents the play becoming an uncharacteristically crude piece of sentimental nationalism, however, is the lead character's acute sense of the fault lines running through his culture. The play cannot help but end optimistically as a real and metaphoric dawn breaks over Cardiff Bay, but along the way we hear that 'The only thing the Welsh can agree upon is what they're not – not English.'.

Equally heavy with the loaded symbolism of one day in recent history is Rowlands's earlier *Marriage of Convenience* (1996), which is set on the day of the marriage of Charles, Prince of Wales, to Diana Spencer in 1981. The context of such a celebration of all the pomp of 'British' imperialism is used to powerful effect in this monologue that focuses, above all, on feelings of exclusion: from family, community, nation and language. The monologue belongs to Alex (a character that appears a number of times in Rowlands's work), born to a Welsh-speaking family in the largely English- speaking Rhondda Valley and who later suffers at the hands of his English-speaking stepfather. In the run-up to the 1997 election, as the prospect of devolution came back on to the British political agenda, Rowlands's play produced powerful resonances, not only in Wales but across the UK, as it toured to Scotland and Ireland. As one artistic director put it:

It struck a chord in Glasgow. Identity, nationhood, language, tradition – all the old clichéd questions suddenly coming to life in a passionate monologue that filled the Tron stage with a multitude of Welsh characters, mountains, families, vistas – in the context of the distant and self-important nuptial solemnities. It struck a chord with the Glasgow audiences socially and politically... (Brown 1999: 85)

In an interview in 1998, Ian Rowlands light-heartedly discussed with the interviewer whether Wales could really cope with the prospect of there being a whole clutch of new writers for the stage coming to the fore:

'People ask me if I'm disillusioned that Wales can only have one prince – meaning Ed Thomas', he says with a mischievous smile. 'But my reply is that Wales would not have had Owain Glyndwr without its Prince Llewellyn' (Evans 1998)

The (no doubt ironic) hyperbole can perhaps be excused by the somewhat heady context of anticipating devolution, but it cannot disguise the fact that Welsh theatre (and to an extent film and television as well) has revolved around the very considerable figure of Ed Thomas to an extent that he probably finds mildly embarrassing. There is absolutely no doubting his talent and influence on a range of younger writers, directors and producers (including Rowlands), but there remains the nagging sense that his ubiquity and pre-eminence across the full range of Welsh media is not only a reflection of his considerable gifts and political vision, but also something of a commentary on the lack of emergent companions. In some ways this does not do justice to those such as Dic Edwards, Charles Way or Greg Cullen who feature alongside Thomas in Hazel Walford Davies's valuable attempt to give turn of the century Welsh theatre some shape and substance (Walford Davies 1998), though the truth is that it is only Thomas that has managed to sustain the kind of output that has made him the kind of significant cultural commentator that is called upon whenever London sees what it would regard as a flicker of life in contemporary Wales.

Since the first of the many incarnations of *House of America* back in 1988 Thomas has become steadily more and more acknowledged as the principal mythmaker for a Wales stirring into new life in the era of devolution. His contribution on film is discussed elsewhere in this volume and here follows a brief discussion of the way that his work for theatre has made a major contribution to the idea of a profoundly changed Britain.

Though Thomas is in no sense a directly 'political' writer in the manner of the 1970s generation of English 'state of the nation' dramatists such as David Hare, Howard Brenton, David Edgar or Trevor Griffiths there is also little doubting the fact that, after a decade spent in London, his work back in Wales has been constantly linked to a concern for the future state of his country. In turn, this has meant, as he surely hoped it would, that his work has contributed, perhaps as effectively as any artist has a right to expect, to the way his country imagines itself. For Heike Roms, who has written on Thomas's work a number of times:

> Thomas's entire oeuvre has been motivated by the ardent belief that the art of theatre may have the capacity to save a culture from drowning in insignificance. In Thomas's case, this hope of rescue is aimed at the culture of Wales, a culture which, in his own words has been 'paralysed by lack of self-esteem and lack of confidence'. (Roms 1998: 131)

In Thomas's earlier work, most notably *House of America* this lack of self-esteem was seen to manifest itself largely through a tendency to try and take culture 'off the peg', as it were, mainly from America. As the play went through its many re-workings, its tone became less censorious and Thomas's understanding and identification with those who sought escape from the post-industrial landscape in the iconography of the US cultural industries came through more strongly. This was particularly true of the film version released just before devolution (and which is discussed more extensively in Chapter 5).

In the period since devolution, in a way that is far more obvious amongst contemporary Scottish writers, Thomas's work has moved further and further from an overt concern with nation and identity, though it remains possible to argue that these are still central both to his own writing and the overall ethos of his multi-media company, Fiction Factory. This has also meant for Thomas a welcome retreat from the position that he held in the contemporary Welsh cultural scene at the start of the Millennium and described, rather acidly by one critic, like this:

Celtic cultural identity? Ask Edward Thomas. A Welsh arts renaissance? Wheel on Edward Thomas. The referendum debate? Cue Edward Thomas. Edward Thomas, soundbites supplied. Instant summaries of the problems of inferiority and self-deprecation. And delivered with authentic Welsh lyricism and eloquence. Many more people have heard Edward Thomas talk about re-inventing Wales, rebuilding confidence in the Welsh voice, breaking the silence than have ever seen his plays... at best a committed but hopelessly romantic rent-a gob. (Adams 1998: 145)

Thomas's pre-eminence as a contemporary cultural commentator was hit fairly hard by the reception given to his debut feature film *Rancid Aluminium* (1999), though he remains a justifiably respected figure who has maintained a steady output for television as well as theatre in recent years. It is even possible that the fall from grace that was *Rancid Aluminium* was something of a blessing in disguise in that it revealed the somewhat absurd pressure on Thomas as a spokesman for post-devolution Wales. The work for theatre that has followed has therefore been far more speculative, both theatrically and in terms of the future of Wales, and some have argued that it promises a greater range to come, free from what Thomas himself has frequently referred to as 'the burden of representation'.

In his first play after the election of New Labour in 1997, *Gas Station Angel*, Thomas remains clearly interested in Wales, but it is an interest that has retreated further than ever beneath a dense layer of metaphor and a journey into the land of the fairies. It is also, arguably, a more hopeful play as his younger characters learn to fully embrace the possibilities of magic and fantasy as essential ingredients in a new future – for themselves, but of course we are inevitably led to think, for the country.

This, though, was far from any glib hymn to the possibilities on offer as the moment of self-determination arrived for Wales. It is a play that could be seen to be about 'spaces' or 'gaps' as one exchange between the characters seems to indicate:

ACE: You speak Welsh?

BRON: Yeh. You?

ACE: Only when I was small. *(PAUSE)* I like Welsh.

BRON: Why?

ACE: Because it's got gaps.

BRON: What kind of gaps?

ACE: Like its not all hard and fast; like there are rules but there are still gaps... like to fill in, the meaning... you got to work the meaning out for yourself...

(Thomas 2002: 368–9)

As the exchange goes on Bron compares the language to jazz and in so doing connects the conversation to the play's advocacy of a life lived through an imagination that is responsive and capable of improvisation, qualities that he has frequently recommended to Wales itself. As a play partly about a house about to fall into the sea, it is inevitably also about margins, not in the traditional postcolonial sense of 'marginalized', but about the joy of the margins in a globalized, commodified culture.

Many of the London reviews of the 1998 Royal Court production of *Gas Station Angel*, so ironically made reference to the kinds of stereotypes that ensured that Neil Kinnock would never become Prime Minister, as a review of a more recent revival spells out:

> Welsh Rabbit, Rabbit, Rabbit, mocked the Guardian headline-writer when Ed Thomas's play was first produced by The Royal Court in London, neatly conflating their Cymrophobia, their bourgeois suspicion of lyrical language and their celebration of being an unashamed Londoncentic arbiter of cultural taste – rabbit being one of those famously cockney rhyming-slang words for talking too much… part and parcel of the colonial mindset that helps explain which English (unlike Scots or European) critics just never got Ed Thomas.

> (http://www.theatre-wales.co.uk/reviews/)

In fairness, there is a case for saying that *Gas Station Angel* could be considerably shorter, but its attempt to take Thomas's journey in search of a Wales that has a genuine contemporary mythology into new theatrical territory makes it one of the significant plays of the post-devolutionary era.

Since 1998, Thomas has produced only one full-length play for the stage, though he has also been involved in a number of collaborative theatre events. This is mostly the consequence of his involvement with television, though, as suggested already; there is an understandable desire to be free of the weight of endless national identity discussions. This is not to suggest that Thomas no longer cares about the future of a fledgling Welsh culture: his was, for example, one of the most public voices raised in support of the Arts Council Chair under threat from the Welsh Assembly Government's need to use the arts as one the few ways that it could actually wield power in pursuit of nation-building. (http://www.theatre-wales.co.uk/index.asp) On the other hand, *Stone City Blue*, produced by Clwyd Theatr Cymru in 2005, has been seen by most as Thomas's theatrical break with the identity of Wales. Well into the decade after devolution Thomas's work for theatre seems to be heading in another direction as evidenced by its opening directions:

> Winter in a city. Berlin, Paris, Cardiff, Antwerp

> It could be anywhere

> For the lovers, the losers, the lost and the beautiful the journey into night is just beginning.

> The streets are alive, restless, expectant, something will happen, must happen

He knows this and so does she

He's in a hotel room, anonymous, functional, corporate

She, somewhere in the city, checking her face in a compact

She is alone; he's waiting...

(Cited at http://www.theatre-wales.co.uk/index.asp)

'It could be anywhere', though including 'Cardiff' is less an end to a concern for Wales as an adoption of an attitude to the new Welsh nation that sees it as postmodern and European as more fashionable places in which to have a bout of existential angst. Though again rejected by many of the English critics, some at least have seen *Stone City Blue* as a vital new stage in Thomas's development as a significant writer for the stage:

Whatever it was that stopped Ed Thomas writing in 1998, whatever killed the old playwright with his obsession with the unreliability of memory, the need to reinvent, the vision of a New Wales, whatever that was has given birth to the new Ed Thomas.

The Ed Thomas of Stone City Blue still deals in self-referential characters and familiar places but instead of meditating on national identity he now looks inward and tries to come to terms with his own personal identity – or identities, since there are four characters on stage albeit with one narrative.

(http://www.theatre-wales.co.uk/plays/index.asp)

By 2006, then, it is possible to argue that Wales's most significant theatrical voice of the last two decades has moved on, in the manner of many of his Scottish contemporaries. This is not an even picture by any means, and Wales's claims to be a new culture gradually becoming more at ease with itself is fundamentally undermined by the endless bickering over the relationship between the Wales Assembly Government and the arts community. If many of the artists are trying to move on, then the debates about the arts and the public sphere in Wales still lag some way behind the confidence in Scotland epitomized by its radical approach to the idea of a 'national' theatre.

In a country that has been so often defined by debates over language, it is perhaps strange to have, so far, given it relatively little attention. This is not to deny the importance of Welsh-language theatre in the recent history of all theatre in Wales but, rather, to suggest that, very often, it has been either the relative downplaying of the significance of language as a theatrical strategy or the use of both languages as a device that have been the most powerful contributions to the way that theatre has approached language as a key feature of Welsh national identity. However, mainly in the heartlands of north-west Wales, though, increasingly in Cardiff as well, there has also accumulated a body of work in Welsh that is significant in the total project of national self-definition.

In its own company details, Bara Caws make particular mention of its membership of Offspring – an organization of theatre companies from European minority cultures. The leading small-scale touring, Welsh-language company, therefore, foregrounds not so much its difference within the UK, but its membership of a significant international community from which Wales can draw strength and look to a future in a much wider sense than that of the performing arts. This, on the whole, tends to typify the attitude of those who seek to make contemporary theatre in Welsh, though the National Theatre debate has, at times, become an unfortunate exception.

Not only Bara Caws but Arad Goch, the leading producer of Welsh-language work for young people, and the Welsh-language new writing work of Sgript Cymru tend to add up to a Welsh language theatre scene that is innovative and vibrant, though, small and still rooted very firmly in a traditional heartland. That the latter is no longer an absolute is testament to the huge expansion of Welsh-medium education in the urban south and the consequent growth of an audience for touring work. In recent times this has meant the opportunity to see touring Welsh-language productions at Cardiff's mainstream venues and the production of new work in Welsh by younger writers such as Sera Moore Williams. There is little doubt that this is sustainable and it is likely that work for the theatre in the Welsh language is likely to become a more significant part of the way that the medium contributes to a growing sense of Wales rather than less. This, of course, brings its own tensions such as those around the role of National Theatre that have already been discussed, but if these can be overcome there is undoubtedly a generation of young theatre makers who see the Welsh language as, at least, a significant part of their repertoire and who will continue to seek ways in which to use it.

If the post-devolutionary history of theatre in Wales is, as I said at the start of this chapter, one that is rooted in internal conflict and dispute, it is important to finish by remembering the optimism that can be gleaned from such a situation as well as despair at the endless sound of clashing egos. Here there has been space to allude to only the most significant of the rows and it has meant no mention even of the considerable vitriol surrounding the production of Dic Edwards' *Franco's Bastard* in 2002 and what was seen as its attack on nationalist ideological posturing (stink bombs landed on the stage during one showing in Chapter Arts Centre in Cardiff). What seems clear, though, is that the role of the theatre in public debate, in general, and in shaping the future direction of Wales, in particular, is far from dead. One must not overstate this, of course. One thing that the Welsh Assembly Government is clearly right about is that the arts in Wales (just like the rest of the UK) needs to expand its audience base and a lot of the chattering does take place amongst a narrow range of participants. Nevertheless, the strength of feeling involved in some of the disputes, the extended coverage given to them in the press and the excellent and well-used website devoted exclusively to theatre in Wales are signs of life at least. If such signs can avoid the trap of parochialism then Wales has the potential to be, like Scotland, a truly significant voice among those small European nations that act as such valuable correctives to those closer to the heart of the global cultural marketplace.

BIBLIOGRAPHY

Please note that where reference is made to a newspaper article and no page number is used, it is because it has been accessed via that publication's Internet archive.

Aaron, Jane (2005), 'Bardic Anti-colonialism' in Chris Williams and Jane Aaron (eds.) *Postcolonial Wales*, Cardiff, University of Wales Press.

Aaron, Jane and Chris Williams (eds), (2005), *Postcolonial Wales*, Cardiff, University of Wales Press.

Adams, David (2004), 'So what's this National Theatre debate?' *New Welsh Review* 65, spring.

Adams, David (1996), *Stage Welsh*, Llandysul, Gomer.

Adams, David (1998), 'Edward Thomas: Negotiating a Way Through Culture' in Walford Davies, Hazel (ed.), *State of Play, 4 Playwrights of Wales*, Llandysul, Gomer.

Adams, David (1999), 'Retrospective' in Rowlands, Ian, *A Trilogy of Appropriation*, Cardiff, Parthian.

Alexander, Karen (2000), 'Black British Cinema' in Robert Murphy (ed.), *British Cinema of the 90's*, London, BFI.

Allen, Paul (2002), 'Is British drama racist?' *The Guardian*, 17 April.

Andrew, Geoff (2002), 'Interview with Lynne Ramsey', *The Guardian*, 28 September.

Anthony, Andrew (1999), 'Terribly nice, awfully flat', *The Observer*, 4 April.

Archibald, David (2003), 'It's not about me', *The Guardian*, 15 August.

Armstrong, Richard (2005), 'Social Realism', Screenonline, http://www.screenonline.org.uk/ film. Last accessed, 25 June 2005.

Ashcroft, Bill, Gareth Griffiths and Helen Tiffin (2001), *Post-Colonial Studies, The Key Concepts*, London, Routledge, 2001.

Barton, Ruth (2004), *Irish National Cinema*, London, Routledge.

Barton, Ruth (1999), 'Feisty Colleens and Faithful Sons, Gender in Irish Cinema', *Cineaste*, volume XXIV, nos. 2–3.

Basnett, Susan (2000), 'The politics of location' in Elaine Aston and Janelle Reinellt, *The Cambridge Companion to Modern British Women Playwrights*, Cambridge, Cambridge University Press.

Bennett, Ronan (1995), 'Lean Mean and Cruel', *Sight and Sound*, 5, 1, January.

Berry, David (1994), *Wales and Cinema, The First Hundred Years*, Cardiff, University of Wales Press.

Berry, David (1997 a.), *Ffocws*, vol. 4, no. 1, p.3.

Berry, David (1997 b.), 'Darkman' in *Orson* (Chapter Arts Centre Film Notes), November 1997.

Blandford, Steve (1997), 'Making House of America: An Interview with Ed Thomas and Marc Evans', in Steve Blandford (ed.), *Wales on Screen*, p.68.

Blandford, Steve (2004), 'Being Half of Everything', *New Welsh Review* 65, autumn.

Blandford, Steve (2005), 'BBC drama at the margins: the contrasting fortunes of Northern Irish, Scottish and Welsh television drama in the 1990's' in Jonathan Bignell and Stephen Lacey (eds.) *Popular Television Drama*, Manchester, Manchester University Press.

Bradshaw, Peter (2000), 'London Film Festival's small-screen finale', *The Guardian* 17 November, http://www.guardian.co.uk/reviews/story/0,,398802,00.html. Accessed 9 May 2005.

Bradshaw, Peter (2002), 'Bend It Like Beckham', 12 April.

Bradshaw, Peter (2003), 'Young Adam', *The Guardian*, 26 September.

Bradshaw, Peter (2004 a.), 'Ae Fond Kiss', *The Guardian*, 17 September.

Bradshaw, Peter (2004 b.), 'My Summer of Love', *The Guardian*, 22 October.

Brewster, Scott and Virginia Crossman (eds.), (1999), *Ireland in Proximity, History, Gender, Space*, London, Routledge.

Brooks, Xan (2000), 'Billy Elliot brings Hollywood to Britain', *The Guardian*, http://film.guardian.co.uk. Last accessed 28 June 2005.

Brooks, Xan (2001), 'Sexy Beast', *Sight and Sound*, vol. 11, 2, February.

Brown, Irina (1999), 'Fade to Tears' in Ian Rowlands, *A Trilogy of Appropriation*, Cardiff, Parthian.

Brunsdon, Charlotte (2000), 'Not Having It All: Women and Film in the 1990s' in Robert Murphy (ed.), *British Cinema of the 90's*, London, BFI..

Brunsdon, Charlotte (2004), 'The Poignancy of Place: London and the Cinema', *Visual Culture in Britain*, 5.1.

Burke, Gregory (2001), *Gagarin Way*, London, Faber and Faber.

Carlson, Susan (2000), 'Language and identity in Timberlake Wertenbaker's plays' in Elaine Aston and Janelle Reinelt, *The Cambridge Companion to Modern British Women Playwrights*, Cambridge, Cambridge University Press.

Cavendish, Dominic (2002), 'Great Scots', *Daily Telegraph*, 8 August, http://www.telegraph.co.uk/arts/main. Accessed March 2006.

Cavendish, Dominic (2006), 'Home is where the art is', 27 February, http://www.telegraph.co.uk/arts/main. Last accessed March 2006.

Chadha, Gurindher (2002), 'Call that a melting pot?', *The Guardian*, 11 April.

Chambers, Lilian Ger Fitzgibbon and Eammon Jordan (eds.), (2001), *Theatre Talk: The Voices of Irish Theatre Practitioners*, Dublin, Carysfort Press.

Chibnall, Steve (2001), 'Travels in Ladland: The British Gangster Film Cycle 1998–2001' in Robert Murphy (ed.), *The British Cinema Book* (2nd edition), London, BFI.

Chrisafis, Angelique (2001), 'Revenge of the provinces', *The Guardian*, 8 December.

Church Gibson, Pamela (2000), 'Fewer Weddings and More Funerals: Changes in the Heritage Film' in Robert Murphy (ed.), *British Cinema of the 90's*, London, BFI.

Coulter, Colin (1999), *Contemporary Northern Irish Society*, London, Pluto Press.

Coveney, Michael (2004), 'Will you still need me?: As it hits 40, Liverpool's once unmissable Everyman has got to get its act together.' *New Statesman*, 20 September. http://www.findarticles.com/p/articles/mi_m0FQP/is_4706_133/ai_n6247289. Last accessed 3 December 2004.

Cullen, Greg (1997), 'The Graveyard of Ambition' in Anne-Marie Taylor (ed.), *Staging Wales, Welsh Theatre 1979-1997*, Cardiff, University of Wales Press.

Dowling, Tim (2003), *The Guardian*, 13 November 2003, http://film.guardian.co.uk/features/featurepages/ Last accessed 23 June 2005.

Evans, Marc (2002), 'Looking Forward, Looking Back' in Ed Thomas, [*selected*] *work '95-'98*, Cardiff, Parthian.

Evans, Rian (1998), 'A Profile of Ian Rowlands', *Western Mail*, 18 May.

Fannin, Hilary, Stephen Greenhorn, Abi Morgan and Mark Ravenhill (1998), 'Introduction' to *Sleeping Around*, London, Methuen.

Fevre, Ralph and Andrew Thompson (ed.), (1999), *National Identity and Social Theory, Perspectives from Wales*, Cardiff, University of Wales Press.

Fisher, Mark (1998), 'Review of *Passing Places*', *The Herald*, 16 April.

Fisher, Mark (2002), 'The Plurality of Scottish Theatre', *International Journal of Scottish Theatre*, vol. 3 no.1.

Foley, Jen (2004), 'Ken Loach and Paul Laverty interviewed' http://www.bbc.co.uk/films/2004/09/10/ken_loach_paul_laverty_ae_fond_kiss_interview.shtml. Accessed 18 April 2005.

French, Philip (1999), 'Something for the weekend', *The Observer*, 6 June.

French, Philip (2001), 'All good people go to haven', *The Observer*, 18 March.

French, Philip (2002 a.), 'Last of a dying breed', *The Observer*, 13 January.

French, Philip (2002 b.), 'Bend It Like Beckham', *The Observer*, 14 April.

French, Philip (2002 c.), 'Frears finds the heart of London's underground', *The Observer*, 15 December.

French, Philip (2003), 'Not bonny – but plenty of Clyde', *The Observer*, 28 September.

Fuller, Graham (2002), 'Over the Edge, Into the Abyss', *Film* Comment, September/October. http://www.filmlinc.com/fcm/9-10-2002/greengrass2.htm. Accessed April 2006.

Fuller, Graham (ed.), 1998, *Loach on Loach*, London, Faber and Faber, p.111.

Gardner, Lyn (2000), 'The Force of Change', *The Guardian*, 10 November.

Gibbons, Fiachra (2000 a.), 'Truth and nail' *The Guardian*, 10 April 2000.

Gibbons, Fiachra (2000 b.), 'Windfall rescues regional theatre', *The Guardian*, 26 July 2000.

Gibbons, Fiachra (2001 a.), 'Meet me in Margate', *The Guardian*, 9 March.

Gibbons, Fiachra (2001 b.), 'Hytner looks to new identities for National', *The Guardian*, 26 September.

Gibbons, Fiachra (2001 c.), 'Playwright savages 'gutless' theatres', *The Guardian*, 21 December 2001.

Gibbons, Fiachra (2003 a.), 'A museum for migrants', *The Guardian*, 9 June 2003, http://www.19princeletstreet.org.uk/press/guardian/html. Accessed April 2006.

Gibbons, Fiachra (2003 b.), 'The Guardian profile: Nicholas Hytner', *The Guardian*, 26 September.

Gibbons, Fiachra (2006), 'Life's a terrible torture that's been sent to try us', *The Guardian*, 10 February http://film.guardian.co.uk/features. Accessed March 2006.

Gilbey, Ryan (2002), 'Reasons to be cheerful', *Sight and Sound*, 12, 10, October.

Gilbey, Ryan (2003), 'Written on the body', *Sight and Sound*, 13, 9, September.

Godiwala, Dimple (2005 a.), 'Editorial introduction: Alternatives within the mainsteam: British black and Asian theatre', *Studies in Theatre and Performance* 26:1.

Godiwala, Dimple (2005 b.), 'Genealogies, archaeologies, histories: the revolutionary "interculturalism" of Asian theatre in Britain', *Studies in Theatre and Performance*, 26: 1.

Greig, David (2002 a.), 'Reaping the harvest of Scottish theatre', *The Independent*, 9 August.

Greig, David (2002 b.), *Plays: 1*, London, Methuen, pp. 243–5.

Greig, David (2003), 'A tyrant for all time', *The Guardian*, 28 April.

Hallam, Julia (2000), 'Film, Class and National Identity' in Justine Ashby and Andrew Higson (eds), *British Cinema, Past and Present*, London, Routledge.

Harvie, Jen (2003), 'Nationalizing the "Creative Industries"', *Contemporary Theatre Review*, volume 13 (1), February.

Harvie, Jen (2005), *Staging the UK*, Manchester, Manchester University Press.

Hattenstone, Simon (2003 a.), 'I wrote it as therapy', *The Guardian*, 7 April 2003.

Hattenstone, Simon (2003 b.), interview with Peter Mullan at the National Film Theatre, 4 November, http://film.guardian.co.uk/print/0,3858,4795691-101730,00.html. Accessed 26 April 2005.

Hayward, Susan (2000), 'Framing National Cinemas' in Hjort, Mette and Scott Mackenzie (eds.), *Cinema and Nation*, London, Routledge.

Hickling, Alfred (2004), 'We don't have to whinge any more', *The Guardian*, 2 June.

Higgins, Victor (2000), *Arts*, December.

Hill, John (1996), 'British Television and Film: The Making of a Relationship' in Hill J. and Martin Mcloone *Big Picture, Small Screen. The Relations Between Film and Television*, University of Luton Press.

Hill, John (1998), 'Every fuckin' choice stinks', *Sight and Sound* 8, 11, November.

Hill, John (1999), *British Cinema in the 1980s*, Oxford, Oxford University Press.

Hill, John (2000), 'Failure and Utopianism: Representations of the Working Class in British Cinema of the 1990s', in Robert Murphy (ed.), *British Cinema of the 90's*, London, BFI.

Hill, John (2001), 'Contemporary British Cinema: Industry, Policy, Identity', *Cineaste*, vol 26, no. 4, p.33.

Hill, John (2005), 'Divorcing Jack' in Brian McFarlane (ed.), *The Cinema of Britain and Ireland*, London, Wallflower Press.

Hjort Mette and Scott Mackenzie (eds.), (2000), 'Introduction' *Cinema and Nation*, London, Routledge.

Holdsworth, Nadine (2003), 'Travelling Across Borders: Re-Imagining the Nation and Nationalism in Contemporary Scottish Theatre', *Contemporary Theatre Review*, vol. 13(2).

James, Lennie (2004), 'Who do you think you are?', *The Guardian*, 11 February.

James, Nick (1999), 'Farewell to Napoli', *Sight and Sound*, vol. 9, 5, May.

Jenkins, Mark (2004), *More Lives Than One (Selected Work)*, Cardigan, Parthian..

Jones, Marie (2000), *Stones in His Pockets and A Night in November*, London, Nick Hern Books.

Jordan, Glenn (2005),'We Never Really Noticed You Were Coloured': Postcolonialist Reflections on Immigrants and Minorities in Wales' in Aaron, Jane and Chris Williams (eds.), (2005), *Postcolonial Wales*, Cardiff, University of Wales Press.

Jordan, Neil (1996), quoted on http://www.filmeducation.org/filmlib/MichaelCollins.pdf. Last accessed 14/12/04.

Kaye, Nick (ed.), (1996), *Art into Theatre: Performance Interviews and Documents*, Amsterdam, Harewood Academic Publishers.

Kemp, Philip (1995), 'Shallow Grave', *Sight and Sound* 5, 1, January.

Kemp, Philip (1998), 'Divorcing Jack' *Sight and Sound*, volume 8, issue 10, October.

King, Barnaby (2000), 'The African-Caribbean Identity and the English Stage', *New Theatre Quarterly* (62), vol 16, no. 2, May.

Kolawole, Helen (2003), 'Look who's taking the stage', *The Guardian*, 26 July.

Kureshi, Hanif (1986), *My Beautiful Launderette and The Rainbow Sign*, London, Faber and Faber.

Laverty, Paul (1997), *Carla's Song*, London, Faber and Faber.

Lawrenson, Edward (1999), 'Orphans', *Sight and Sound*, 9, 5, May.

Lawrenson, Edward (2000), 'Cosmic Dancer', *Sight and Sound*, vol. 10, 10, October.

Lawrenson, Edward (2004), 'Afterlife', *Sight and Sound*, 14, 9, September.

Lawson, Mark (2001), 'Sick-buckets needed in the stalls', *The Guardian*, 28 April.

Leigh, Danny (2000), 'Get Smarter', *Sight and Sound*, vol 10, 6, June 2000, p.23.

Lewis, Lisa (2004), 'Welsh-language production/Welsh-language performance: the resistant body', *Studies in Theatre and Performance* 24: 3.

Linehan, Hugh (1999), 'Myth, Mammon and Mediocrity: The Trouble with Recent Irish Cinema', *Cineaste*, volume XXIV, nos. 2–3.

Llewellyn-Jones, Margaret (2002), *Contemporary Irish Drama and Cultural Identity*, Bristol, Intellect.

Lojek, Helen (1999), 'Playing Politics with Belfast's Charabanc Theatre Company' in J. P. Harrington and Elizabeth J. Mitchell (eds.), *Politics and Performance in Contemporary Northern Ireland*, Amherst, University of Massachusetts Press.

Louvish, Simon (1999), 'Solomon and Gaenor', *Sight and Sound*, 9, 5, May.

Luckett, Moya (2000), 'Image and Nation in 1990's British Cinema' in Robert Murphy (ed.), *British Cinema of the 90's*, London, BFI.

Lury, Karen (2000), 'Here and Then: Space, Place and Nostalgia in British Youth Cinema of the 1990's' in Robert Murphy (ed.), *British Cinema of the 90's*, London, BFI.

Mackenzie, Scott (1999), 'National Identity, Canadian Cinema, and Multiculturalism' *Canadian Aesthetics Journal*, vol. 4, summer, http://www.uqtr.ca/AE/vol_4/scott.htm. Accessed April 2006.

Macmillan, Joyce (2003), 'Flying the Flag', *On Tour*, London, The British Council.

Macnab, Geoffrey (2001), 'About Adam', *Sight and Sound*, volume 2, issue 5, May.

Martin Jones, David (2004), 'Two Stories, One Right, One Wrong. Narrative, National Identity and Globalization in *Sliding Doors*.' Cineaction, 64.

McArthur, Colin (1982), *Scotch Reels : Scotland in Cinema and Television*, BFI, London.

McArthur, Colin (1993), 'In Praise of a Poor Cinema', *Sight and Sound* 3, 8, pp 30–2.

McDonagh, Martin (1999), *The Beauty Queen of Leenane* in *Plays: 1*, London, Methuen.

McIlroy, Brian (1999), 'Challenges and Problems in Contemporary Irish Cinema: The Protestants', *Cineaste*, volume XXIV, nos. 2–3.

McLoone, Martin (1999), 'Reimagining the Nation: Themes and Issues in Irish Cinema', *Cineaste*, volume XXIV, nos. 2–3.

McLoone, Martin (2000), *Irish Film, The Emergence of a Contemporary Cinema*, London, British Film Institute.

McLoone, Martin (2001), 'Internal Decolonisation? British Cinema in the Celtic Fringe', in Robert Murphy (ed.), *The British Cinema Book* (2nd edition), London, British Film Institute.

McPherson, Conor (1998), 'If you're a young Irish playwright, come to London. If you can put up with being defined by your nationality, the opportunities are huge.' *New Statesman*, 20 February. http://www.findarticles.com/p/articles/mi_m0FQP/is_n4373_v127/ai_20484956/print. Accessed 11 November 2004.

Mitchell, Gary (1999), *Trust*, London, Nick Hern Books.

Mitchell, Gary (2000), *The Force of Change*, London, Nick Hern Books.

Mitchell, Gary (2003), 'Balancing Act', *The Guardian*, 5 April.

Monk, Claire (1997), 'Darklands' in *Sight and Sound*, volume 7, number 11, November.

Monk, Claire (2000 a.), 'Men in the 90's', in Robert Murphy (ed.), *British Cinema of the 90's*, London, BFI.

Monk, Claire (2000 b.), 'Billy Elliot', *Sight and Sound*, vol. 10, 10, October.

Monk, Claire, (2000 c.), 'Underbelly UK. The 1990s underclass film, masculinity and the ideologies of 'new' Britain.' in Justine Ashby and Andrew Higson (ed.), *British Cinema, Past and Present*, London, Routledge.

Morgan, Sally (1999), 'The ghost in the luggage. Wallace and *Braveheart*: post-colonial 'pioneer' identities', *European Journal of Cultural Studies*, vol. 2 (3).

Morris, Nigel (1998), 'Projecting Wales' in *Planet* 126, December-January.

Mullan, Peter (2004), online interview for FilmFour at http://www.channel4.com/film/reviews/feature.jsp?id=111965. Last accessed 30/1/05.

Murphy, Robert (2000), 'The Path Through the Moral Maze' in Robert Murphy (ed.), *British Cinema of the 90's*, London, BFI.

O'Hagan, Andrew (1996), 'The boys are back in town', *Sight and Sound*, 6, 2, February.

O'Regan, Tom (1996), *Introducing Australian National Cinema*, London, Routledge.

O'Sullivan, Charlotte (1999), 'Notting Hill, *Sight and Sound*, vol. 9, 6, June.

Osborne, Deidre (2005), 'Writing black back: an overview of black theatre and performance in Britain', *Studies in Theatre and Performance*, 26: 1.

Osborne, John (1976), *Look Back in Anger*, London, Faber and Faber.

Owen, Gary (2005), *Plays: 1*, London, Methuen.

Paxman, Jeremy (1998), *The English. A Portrait of a People*, London, Michael Joseph.

Peretti, Jacques (2000), 'Shame of a Nation', *The Guardian*, 26 May 2000, http://film.guardian.co.uk/Feature_Story/feature. Last accessed February 2006.

Perrins, Daryl (2000), 'This Town Ain't Big Enough For the Both of Us' in Steve Blandford (ed.), *Wales on Screen*, Bridgend, Seren.

Perry, George (2001), 'About Adam' http://www.bbc.co.uk/films/2001. Last accessed 14/12/2004.

Petrie, Duncan (1996), 'Peripheral visions: film-making in Scotland' in Wendy Everett (ed.), *European Identity In Cinema*, Exeter, Intellect.

Petrie, Duncan (2000), *Screening Scotland*, London, British Film Institute.

Petrie, Duncan (2001), 'Devolving British Cinema: The New Scottish Cinema and the European Art Film', *Cineaste*, vol. 26, no 4.

Petrie, Duncan (2004), *Contemporary Scottish Fictions, Film, Television and the Novel*, Edinburgh, Edinburgh University Press.

Pettitt, Lance (2000), *Screening Ireland*, Manchester, Manchester University Press.

Pink, Daniel (1999), 'The Brand Called UK', *Fastcompany*, issue 22., February 1999. http://pf.fastcompany.com/magazine/22. Last accessed 25 June 2005.

Powrie, Phil (2000), 'On the Threshold Between Past and Present' in Justine Ashby and Andrew Higson (ed.), *British Cinema, Past and Present*, London, Routledge, pp. 316–326.

Prichard, Rebecca (1998), *Yard Gal*, London, Faber, 1998.

Ravenhill, Mark (2004), 'A Tear in the Fabric: the James Bulger Murder and New Theatre Writing in the "Nineties"', *New Theatre Quarterly*, volume 20, no. 4, November.

Rebellato, Dan (2002), 'Introduction', *Plays: 1*, David Greig, London, Methuen.

Rebellato, Dan (2003), 'And I Will Reach Out My Hand With A Kind of Infinite Slowness And Say The Perfect Thing': The Utopian Theatre of Suspect Culture, *Contemporary Theatre Review*, vol. 13 (1).

Renton, Jennie (2005), 'Interview with Gregory Burke', *Textualities*, http://textualities.net/ writers/features-a-g/burkeg01.php. Last accessed March 2006.

Rockett, Emer (2005), 'Ordinary Decent Criminal' in Brian McFarlane (ed.), *The Cinema of Britain and Ireland*, London, Wallflower Press.

Romney, Jonathan (2004), 'New blood! (And the death of an old pro)', *The Independent*, 1 August.

Roms, Heike (1998), 'Caught in the Act: On the Theatricality of Identity and Politics in the Dramatic Works of Edward Thomas' in Hazel Walford Davies (ed.), *State of Play, 4 Playwrights of Wales*, Llandysul, Gomer.

Roms, Heike (2004), 'Performing Polis: theatre, nationess and civic identity in post-devolution Wales', *Studies in Theatre and Performance*, 24: 3.

Ros, Nic (2004), 'Editorial: Performance in post-referendum Wales', *Studies in Theatre and Performance*, vol. 24, 3.

Ryan, Susan and Richard Porton (1998), 'The Politics of Everyday Life: An Interview with Ken Loach', *Cineaste*, 24, 1, accessed at http://www.lib.berkeley.edu/MRC/ LoachInterview.html, 29 March 2005.

Saunders, Graham (2002), *'Love me or kill me' Sarah Kane and the theatre of extremes*, Manchester, Manchester University Press.

Saunders, Graham (2003), '"Just a Word on a Page and there is the Drama", Sarah Kane's Theatrical Legacy', *Contemporary Theatre Review*, vol. 13 (1), February.

Schoene, Berthold (2002), 'The Union and Jack: British masculinities, pomophobia and the post-nation' in Glenda Norquay and Gerry Smyth (eds), *Across the Margins: Cultural Identity and Change in the Atlantic Archipelago*, Manchester, Manchester University Press.

Scullion, Adrienne (2000), 'Contemporary Scottish Women Playwrights' in Elaine Aston and Janelle Reinellt (eds), *The Cambridge Companion to Women Playwrights*, Cambridge, Cambridge University Press.

Scullion, Adrienne (2001), 'Self and Nation: Issues of Identity in Modern Scottish Drama by Women', *New Theatre Quarterly*, 17:4, November.

Sherlock, Ceri (2004), 'The performative: body – text – context and the construction of a tradition', *Studies in Theatre and Performance*, 24: 3.

Sierz, Aleks (2001), *In-yer-Face Theatre, British Drama Today*, London, Faber.

Sierz, Aleks (2004), 'Me and My Mates: the state of English Playwriting, 2003', *New Theatre Quarterly*, vol.20, no.1, February.

Sinclair, Ian (2001), 'The Cruel Seaside' *Sight and Sound*, 11, 3, March.

Sinclair, Ian (2002), 'Heartsnatch hotel', *Sight and Sound*, 12, 12, December.

Smith, Paul Julian (1997), 'Carla's Song', *Sight and Sound*, 7, 2, February.

Spencer, Liese (1999 a.), 'What are you looking at?' *Sight and Sound*, 9, 10, October.

Spencer, Liese (1997), 'House of America' in *Sight and Sound*, volume 7, number 9, September.

Spencer, Liese (1999 b.), 'Hello Mr Chips', *Sight and Sound*, 9, 11, November.

Stafford, Roy (2004), 'Representation issues in British Cinema: Asylum Seekers and Refugees', http://www.itpmag.demon.co.uk/Downloads/AsylumRep.pdf. Last accessed 12 August 2005.

Sullivan, Caroline (1999), Review of *Everything Must Go*, 25 February at http://www.theatre-wales.co.uk/reviews/index.asp. Accessed January 2006.

Taylor, Paul (2005), 'Playing With Fire', *The Independent*, 23 September 2005, http://enjoyment.independent.co.uk/theatre/reviews/article314626.ece. Accessed April 2006.

Teare, Jeff (ed.), (1998), *New Welsh Drama*, Cardiff, Parthian.

Teare, Jeff (ed.), (2001), *New Welsh Drama, Volume 2*, Cardiff, Parthian

Thiesse, Anne-Marie (1999), 'Inventing national identity', *Le Monde diplomatique*, June, http://mondediplo.com/1999/06/05. Last accessed April 2006.

Thomas, Edward (2002), *selected work '95-'98*, Cardigan, Parthian.

Thompson, Ben (1997), 'Twin Town' in *Sight and Sound*, 7, 4, April.

Trotter, Mary (2000), 'Women Playwrights in Northern Ireland' in Elaine Aston and Janelle Reinelt (ed.), *The Cambridge Companion to Modern British Women Playwrights*, Cambridge, Cambridge University Press.

Tunney, Tom (1998), 'Tom Tunney cooks up a hardboiled movie menu', *Sight and Sound*, 8, 5, June.

Turner, Jenny (2001), 'Born Romantic', *Sight and Sound*, 11, 3, March.

Verma, Jatinder (1999), 'Sorry, No Saris!' in Vera Gottlieb and Colin Chambers (eds.), *Theatre In a Cool Climate*, Oxford, Amber Lane.

Walford Davies, Hazel (2004), 'Mark Jenkins in Conversation with Hazel Walford Davies', in Jenkins, Mark (2004), *More Lives Than One (Selected Work)*, Cardigan, Parthian.

Walford Davies, Hazel (ed.), (1998), *State of Play, 4 Playwrights of Wales*, Llandysul, Gomer.

Watts, Robert (2000), Review of *Flesh and Blood*, 1 November at http://www.theatre-wales.co.uk/reviews/index.asp. Accessed January 2006.

Westwell, Guy (2004), 'Goldfish Memory' *Sight and Sound*, volume 14, issue 11, November.

Williams, Charlotte (2002), *Sugar and Slate*, Aberystwyth, Planet.

Williams, Chris (2005), 'Problematizing Wales: An Exploration in Historiography and Postcoloniality' in Chris Williams and Jane Aaron (eds.), *Postcolonial Wales*, Cardiff, University of Wales Press.

Internet Sources

The following are Internet sources used in the body of the text that are not attributable to an individual author.

http://enjoyment.independent.co.uk/theatre/news/article334858.ece.

http://icwales.icnetwork.co.uk/0900entertainment. Last accessed June 2005.

http://news.bbc.co.uk/1/hi/uk/213484.stm, (13 November 1998). Last accessed June 2005.

http://news.bbc.co.uk/1/hi/uk/4611682.stm.

http://www.artscouncil.org.uk./nextstage/national.html. Last accessed November 2004.

http://www.artscouncil.org.uk/documents/information/php74fniH.doc. Last accessed November 2004.

http://www.billybragg.co.uk/words/words9.html. Last accessed November 2004.

http://www.channel4.com/film/reviews/film.jsp?id=106460. Last accessed January 2006.

http://www.dubbeljoint.com/. Last accessed November 2004.

http://www.elementalfilms.co.uk. Last accessed May 2005.

http://www.generationterrorists.com/quotes/trainspotting.html. Last accessed March 2005.

http://www.prolificfilms.freeserve.co.uk/Questions.htm. Last accessed February 2006.

http://www.sheffieldtheatres.co.uk/index. Last accessed February 2006.

http://www.tag-theatre.co.uk/index. Last accessed March 2006.

http://www.theatre-wales.co.uk/index.asp. Last accessed 30 January 2006.

http://www.theatre-wales.co.uk/index.asp. Last accessed 30 January 2006.

http://www.theatre-wales.co.uk/news/index.asp. Last accessed January 2004.

http://www.theatre-wales.co.uk/plays/index.asp. Last accessed 30 January 2006.

http://www.theatre-wales.co.uk/reviews/. Last accessed 30 January 2006.

http://www.timesonline.co.uk/article/. Last accessed February 2006.

http://www.timesonline.co.uk/article/0,,2090-1310869_1,00.html. Last accessed 18/10/04.

http://film.guardian.co.uk/features/featurepages/0,4120,1322073,00.html, ('Austen allegro' *The Guardian*, 7 October 2004). Last accessed 13 July 2005.

INDEX

Aaron, Jane   13, 14, 39
Abbott, Paul   17
Abigail's Party   132
About Adam   50
Adams, Gerry   130
Ae Fond Kiss   17, 76-7
Afterlife   84
Allen, Kevin   72, 93
Allen, Woody   100
Anderson, Benedict   12, 68, 152
Anderson, Lindsay   43
Arad Goch   180
Architect, The   153
Arms length principle (Arts Councils)   168
Art and Guff   172
Art cinema   66, 78, 93
Art-house   31, 40, 57, 67, 70, 72, 77, 83, 95
Arts Council of England   115, 120
Arts Council of Scotland   148-9, 160
Arts Council of Wales (ACW)   167-8, 170-1
Arts Council   105, 125
Asante, Amma 102-4
Assimilation   114
Asylum seekers   10, 41, 42, 43
Asylum   16, 38, 42
Atwood, Margaret 174
Auerbach, Shona   84
Augé, Marc   149
Austen, Jane   40, 41
Auteur   30
Avan, Ghizala   77
Avant-garde   166, 174

Bacon, Francis   71
Baker, Don 54
Bakhtin   134
Baksh, Shabana   77
Ballykissangel   62, 134
Bara Caws   180
Bardolatory   38
Barton, Ruth   47, 49, 50, 51, 53, 55
Bassey, Shirley   95
Bateman, Colin   57-8
Battle of Algiers, The   61
Bayley, Stephen   88
Beautiful Mistake   92
Beauty Queen of Leenane   137
Beckett, Samuel   143
Bend It Like Beckham   40, 41
Bergman, Ingmar   102
Berlin Film Festival   98
Berry, Dave   88, 95
Bhaba, Homi   152
Bhaji on the Beach   40
Big Telly   143
Billy Elliot   28-30, 75, 78, 102
Binchy, Maeve   49
Bio-pic   52
Birmingham Six   137
Birthday Girl   43-4
Birthistle, Eva 76
Black Hawk Down   61
Blair, Tony   26, 111
Blairite   28
Blanchett, Cate   38

Blasted 116-117
Bloody Sunday: A Day in History 60-61
Blue Heron in the Womb 175
Blue Juice 32
Bogside 60
Boilerhouse 145
Bold Girls 158-9
Bolger, Dermot 136
Bollywood 37, 40, 113
Bombay Dreams 113
Bonnaire, Sandrine 67
Boorman, John 56
Borges, Jorge Luis 138
Born Romantic 84
Boxer, The 55
Boy Soldier 88
Boyle, Danny 66, 68, 70, 94
Boyle, Jimmy 158
Bradfield, James Dean 92
Bragg, Billy 105, 118
Branagh, Kenneth 121-2
Branwen 91
Brassed Off 25, 26, 27-8, 31, 95
Braveheart 66, 68, 69, 71-2, 151, 157
Brenton, Howard 176
Bride and Prejudice 40
Bridget Jones: The Edge of Reason 25
Bridget Jones's Diary 21, 25
Brigadoon 20, 85
Bristol Old Vic 122
Britart 26
Brith Gof 164-5, 167
British Broadcasting Company (BBC) 17, 76, 79, 80
British Empire 52
Britpop 26
Brookes, Mike 166
Bunuel, Luis 80
Burke, Gregory 147, 156
Burke, Kathy 31, 34
Burroughs, William 83
Burton, Richard 173
Bush Theatre 108
Bush, George W. 73, 111
Butterworth, Jez 43, 118
Byrne, John 150
Cabezas, Oyanka 73
Cagney, James 55
Cahill, Martin 56
Caine, Michael 45
Calderwood, Andrea 79.

Cale, John 92, 97
Caledonia Dreaming 145, 150, 153
Caligula 151
Callas, Maria 167
Callow, Simon 20-1
Capaldi, Peter 67
Capitalism, 28, 120, 121, 127
Capra, Frank 30
Captain Corelli's Mandolin 23
Carla's Song 73
Carlyle, Robert 73
Carney, John 51
Carnival 113
Carry On films 43
Carville, Daragh 141
Cassel, Vincent 44
Caton-Jones Michael 66, 68
Celtic nations 27, 89
Celtic periphery 11
Celtic Tiger 8, 48, 61, 135, 140
Cerdd dant 164
Chadra, Gurinder 39-41, 44
Channel 4 60, 69, 87, 88
Chaplin, Ben 44
Charabanc Theatre Company 141
Charles, Prince of Wales 26, 95, 175
Cheney, Dick 111
Cheviot, the Stag and the Black, Black Oil, The 150
Circle of Friends 49
Class 21, 22, 23, 25, 30, 45, 46, 81, 84, 90, 104, 129, 156
Classless society 43
Clean Break Theatre 107
Clifford, John 150
Clockwork Orange, A 71
Closer You Get, The 49
Clowns 126
Clwyd Theatre Cymru 168, 178
Coen brothers 70
Cohen, Leonard 83
Cold Feet 84
Collins, Michael 52, 53
Colonial 10, 46, 89, 90, 102, 130, 140, 158, 174-5. 178
Colonialism 17, 50, 63, 69, 73
Colonization 134
Colour of Justice, The 110
Coming Up Roses 88
Confessions of a Teenage Drama Queen 101
Conlan, Gerry 54

Connolly, Billy 80
Considine, Paddy 43
Contras 73
Convictions 141
Cool Britannia 26, 35, 117
Cool Cymru 172-4
Cosby Show, The 109
Cosmonaut's Last Message to the Woman He Once Loved in the Former Soviet Union, The 153
Cosmopolitanism 11, 139
Costa-Gavras 61
Costello, Deidre 27
Court Room No.1 142
Court Room No.20 142
Courtenay, Tom 45
Crazy Gary's Mobile Disco 172
Creative industries 121
Crucible Theatre (Sheffield) 122
Crying Game, The 52-3, 54
Cullen, Greg 170, 176
Culturebox 115
Cumming, Alan 67
Curtis, Richard 22-5, 84
Dal: Yma Nawr (Still: Here/Now) 93
Daldry, Stephen 28-30
Dalier Slyw 170, 172
Darklands 93, 95-7
Davies, Russell T. 17
Davies, Terence 31, 80, 83
De Jongh, Nicholas 108
De Palma, Brian 167
Dear Frankie 84
December Bride 56-7
Deconstruction, 11
Demos 26
Deren, Maya 78
Devolution 7, 10, 11, 13, 15, 18, 20, 30, 31, 33, 39, 44, 62, 65, 66, 68, 69, 73, 74, 75, 76, 77, 78, 80, 81, 83, 84, 88, 91, 95, 100, 105, 108, 115, 116, 118, 120, 125, 146, 149, 150, 151, 155, 157, 161, 163, 164, 166, 168, 169, 171, 172, 175, 177, 178.
Dhupa, Venu 114
Diana, Princess of Wales 37, 175
Diaspora 69, 87, 93, 147, 156
Dirty Pretty Things 17, 43-44
Disco Pigs 51
Divorcing Jack 57-8, 60
Diwrnod Hollol Mindblowing Heddiw (A Totally Mindblowing Day Today) 93

Dogma group (Denmark) 93
Dolly West's Kitchen 139
Donald, Simon 150
Douglas, Bill 31, 66, 77, 80, 83
Dr Who 158
Driver, Minnie 49
Dromgoole, Dominic 108
Druid Theatre Company 136
Dubbeljoint Theatre 142
Eadie, William 78
Ealing Studios 88, 102, 154
Earthfall 167
East is East 41
Ecclestone, Christopher 57, 69
Edgar, David 111, 176
Edwards, Dic 176,180
Edwards, Peter 103
Eisteffod 89, 164
Ejifor, Chiwetel 43
Eldridge, David 118
Elemental Films 82
Elizabeth 37-8
Elmina's Kitchen 108-9
Emlyn, Endaf 91-2
Englishman Who Went Up a Hill and Came Down a Mountain, The 100,154
Ethnicity 17, 20
Europe 152
European Union (EU) 8, 9, 44
Europudding 67
Evans, Caradoc 95
Evans, Gwynfor 87
Evans, Marc 55, 92-4, 97-8, 101
Everything Must Go 173
Face 36
Fannin, Hilary 106,107
Farrell, Nicholas 111
Fast Show, The 143
Father Ted 102, 137
Featherstone, Vicky 147
Federation of Scottish Theatres 147
Feminist 116,140,158
FHM 36
Fiction Factory 176
Fiennes, Joseph 99,122
FilmFour 57, 81, 88
Fitzgerald, Tara 28, 99
Flesh and Blood 173
Fonda, Jane 59

Force of Change, The 130-1
Forced Entertainment 122
Forsyth, Bill 65, 67, 154
Four Days in July 61
Four Weddings and a Funeral 20-22, 84
Fox, Kerry 69
Francis, Karl 88-9, 91
Franco's Bastard 180
Frazer, Laura 57
Frears, Stephen 17, 39, 43
Frost, Sadie 99
Full Monty, The 25-8, 30, 31, 75, 95,102
Further Than the Furthest Thing 158
Gadael Lenin (Leaving Lenin) 92
Gandhi 39
Gangster No.1. 36
Ganz, Bruno 67
Gargarin Way 156
Grandage, Michael 122
Gas Station Angel 177-8
Gay identity 119
Gender identity 29, 91
Gender 25, 29, 33, 46, 54, 60, 103, 116,
   118, 130, 147, 158
General The 56
Genre 36, 48, 53, 55, 56, 66, 67, 69, 83, 94,
   96, 151
George, Terry 54
Get Carter 36
Giant Steps 170
Gibb, Andrea 84
Gibson, Mel 66, 68, 94
Giedroyc, Coky 84
Glasgow Film Production Fund 65, 69, 73
Glendower (Glyndwr), Owain 94, 175
Globalization 11, 39, 97, 101, 152, 155, 156,
   178, 180
Glover, Sue 145, 159
Goddard, John-Luc 59
Godfather The 53
Gododdin 165
Goldfish Memory 50-1
Good Friday Agreement 8, 135,142
Gorman, Damien 142
Gottlieb, Vera 149
Gough, Steve 91
Grant, Hugh 22-5, 26
Greengrass, Paul 60-61
Greenhorn, Stephen 106, 107, 145, 151, 152
Greig, David 145, 147, 150, 151, 153, 160, 161

Griffin, Helen 173, 174
Griffiths, Rachel 58, 102
Griffiths, Trevor 149, 176
Gruffydd, Ioan 93, 102
Guantanamo Detention Centre 110
Guiding Star 119
Guildford Four 54
Gulp 170-1
Gupta, Tanika 113
Haern 165
Hall, Lee 28
Hannah, John 21
Happiness 170
Hardy, Robin 95
Hare, David 9, 110, 176
Harris, Zinnie 145, 159
Harrower, David 145, 151, 161
Harvey, Jonathan 119
Harvie, Jen 12, 113, 121, 165
Hawes, James 99
Head 100
Hear My Song 49
Hedd Wyn 89-91
Hegelian 156
Hegemony 100, 113, 155, 167
Heggie, Ian 150
Hemmings, David 45
Here Come the Huggets 34
Heritage 97, 134, 142, 156
Heritage cinema 37, 38, 89, 90
Hidden Agenda 61
Higgins, Michael 47
Hill, John 21, 26-7, 39, 47, 58, 74, 88
Hillsborough 119
Hodge, John 66, 68
Holding Room 142
Home 148, 159
Horror 55, 93
Hough, John 143
House of America 92, 93, 97-8, 155, 176
Howells, Kim 95
HTV 102
Hughes, Declan 136
Human Traffic 79, 94, 100, 101
Hunger strikes 54
Hutton Inquiry, The 110
Hybrid 14, 40, 89, 100, 101, 112, 113, 133,
   171
Hybridity 11, 32, 40, 41, 91, 92, 93
Hynes, Gary 136

Hytner, Nicholas 108, 109, 113
Identity 7, 9, 10, 17, 25, 28, 30, 32, 33, 36,
    37, 40, 41, 42, 43, 45, 46, 48, 49, 54, 56,
    67, 68, 76, 77, 89, 90, 91, 92, 100, 101,
    102, 103, 104, 105, 107, 112, 115, 116, 118,
    121, 125, 129, 132, 138, 145, 146, 147,
    150, 153, 155, 156, 159, 160, 166, 168,
    173, 175
Ifans, Rhys 23, 93, 99
Immigration 9, 17, 41, 42, 43, 44
Imperialist 117, 158, 175
In the Name of the Father 53, 54, 55
In This World 43
In Which We Serve 21
INLA (Irish National Liberation Army) 137, 138
Internationalism 11
In-yer-face Theatre 107, 116, 117, 120, 136, 172
IRA (Irish Republican Army) 52, 54, 56, 131,
    132, 138
Iraq war (2003) 40, 111
Irish Film Board 59
Iron 158
Isaacs, Jeremy 88
Ivory, James 21
Jackson, Eddie 142
Jacobi, Derek 122
Jaffrey, Said 39
James, Henry 23
James, Lenny 112
James, Stephanie 104
Jenkins, Marc 173
Jennings, Alex 111
Jobson, Richard 85-6
Johnson, Joyce 98
Jones, Catherine Zeta 32
Jones, Marie 132, 133, 135, 141, 142
Jones, Patrick 173
Jones, Tom 95
Jordan, Neil 52, 53
Jordon, Glenn 103
Joyriders 126
Judges Room 142
Jury Room 142
Kabosh 143
Kailyard 94, 100, 156
Kane, David 83
Kane, Sarah 116, 153
Kapur, Shekhar 37
Kar-wai, Wong 86
Kassovitz, Mathieu 44

Kelly, Gerard 76
Kennedy, John F 59
Kerouac, Jack 98
Kerrigan, Justin 100, 101
Khan, Ahmed 77
Khan-Din, Ayub 41
Kidman, Nicole 44
Kiernan, Kitty 53
Kieslowski, Krzysztof 86
Kingsley, Ben 37
Kinnock, Neil 178
Kirwan, Dervla 57
Knight, Steven 44
Korsun, Dina 43
Kubrick, Stanley 71
Kureishi, Hanif 39
Kusturica, Emir 80
Kwei-Armah, Kwame 108-9, 112
La Haine 97
La Ronde 106
Ladd, Eddie 166, 167
Ladybird, Ladybird 74
Larkin, Philip 43
Last Great Wilderness, The 83
Last Orders 45-6
Last Resort, The 17, 42-3, 45
Laverty, Paul 73, 74, 75, 76
Lawrence, Stephen 36
Leenane Trilogy, The 136, 137
Leftfield 69
Leigh, Mike 43, 61, 132
Lenczewski, Rysard 42
Lessing, Doris 174
Letts, Tracey 116
Lewis, Gwyneth 93
Lieutenant of Inishmore, The 137, 138
Little Britain 44, 143
Liverpool Everyman 121, 122
Liverpool Playhouse 121
Livingstone, Ken 8
Lloyd Webber, Andrew 113
Loach, Ken 16, 25, 30, 31, 44, 61, 66, 70,
    72, 74-77, 102
Loaded 36
Loane, Tim 141
Local Hero 67
Lochhead, Liz 145, 150, 160
Lock, Stock and Two Smoking Barrels 32, 36,
    66, 99
Lohan, Lindsey 101

Lonely Are the Brave   37
Long Good Friday, The   36
Look Back in Anger   46
Lottery   , National (UK)   65
Love Actually   20, 24–5, 50
Loyalist   127, 128
Luckett, Moya   38
Lury, Karen   32
Lyceum Theatre (Sheffield)   122
Lyn, Euros   93
Lynch, Martin   142
Mabinogion, The   91, 164
Macdonald, Andrew   66, 68, 94
Macgregor, Ewan   28, 32, 69, 83, 94
Macgregor, Rob Roy   69
Mackenzie, David   83
Mackintosh, Steven   32
Made in Wales   170, 172
Magdalene Sisters, The   59–60, 81–2
Main Hall   142
Major, John   20, 22, 118
Making the Nation   145
Male Toilets   141
Malik, Terence   86
Mandela, Nelson   53
Mandelson, Peter   23
Manic Street Preachers, The   92, 173
Marginality   85
Marginalization   152, 159, 178
Mark, Karl   173
Marriage of Convenience   175
Marxist   74, 156
Mary, Queen of Scots, Got Her Head Chopped Off   160
Masculine identity   29, 78
Masculinity   26, 28, 29, 80, 81, 116, 117, 118, 119, 128, 130, 140, 156, 158, 172
Matchmaker, The   49
Matthews, Cerys   92
Maxwell, Douglas   161
McArthur, Colin   67, 94, 100
McCafferty, Owen   141, 142, 143
McCartney, Nicola   142, 145, 159
McDonagh, Martin   135, 136
McDougall, Peter   80, 158
McGovern, Jimmy   60–61
McGrath, John   149, 150
McGuiness, Frank   138
McKee, Gina   35
McIlvaney, William   80

McLoone, Martin   11, 47, 48, 52, 55, 57, 101
McLucas, Cliff   165
McPherson, Connor   135, 136, 138, 139, 140–1
Meadows, Shane   30–1
Melodrama   52
Merchant, Ismail   21
Meshes of the Afternoon   78
Metropolis   32
Metropolitan centre   20, 97, 120, 121
Metropolitan   36, 53, 97, 172
Metz, Christian   14
Michael Collins   52–3
Michell, Roger   66
Miles-Thomas, May   82–3, 85
Millions Like Us   21
Mimicry   171
Miners' strike (1984–5)   28
Miramax   75
Mirren, Helen   45
Misogyny   27
Mitchell, Gary   127, 130, 133, 140, 142
Mockney   45, 99
Modernism   143
Mojo Mickybo   143
Moore Williams, Sera   180
Morgan, Abi   106, 107
Morrison, Tony   174
Morton, Samantha   79
Morvern Callar   78–9
Mulgan, Geoff   26
Mullan, Peter   16, 59–60, 66, 73, 74, 77, 80–2, 83
Multicultural   26, 41, 77
Multiculturalism   11, 23, 103, 104, 113
Multiracial   114
Munro, Rona   145, 158, 159
Muriel's Wedding   102
Murphy, Robert   11, 20, 66
Mutabilitie   139
My Beautiful Launderette   39
My Name is Joe   73–74, 80
Nagy, Phyllis   116
Nairn, Tom   7
National cinemas   14
National Endowment for Science, Technology and the Arts (NESTA)   82, 167
National identity   8, 9, 11, 15, 16, 21, 22, 23, 24, 25, 26, 30, 32, 33, 37, 38, 39, 42, 46, 48, 49, 51, 67, 71, 79, 84, 88, 91, 98, 108,

109, 110, 111, 113, 115, 116, 126, 147, 150,
    152, 153, 154, 157, 165, 175, 178
National Lottery   48
National Theatre (Scotland)   146, 147, 148,
    160, 161
National Theatre (Wales)   166, 167, 169, 180
National theatres   14, 15-16
National unity   46
Nationalism   8, 9, 10, 11, 38, 46, 52, 54, 60,
    71, 81, 93, 95, 96, 117, 119, 130, 131, 147,
    152, 156, 166, 174, 175
Nationhood   150, 175
Nations   152
Neeson, Liam   69
Neilson, Anthony   118, 145, 161
New authenticity   134
New Labour   26, 28, 30, 33, 38, 42, 74, 75,
    93, 98, 108, 109, 110, 111, 113, 115, 116,
    126, 147, 150, 152, 153, 154, 157, 165,
    175, 178
New South Wales   175
Night in November, A   132, 133-4
Nil By Mouth   34-5
Northern Ireland Assembly   125
Norton Taylor, Richard   110
Noson, Iawen   164
Notting Hill   20, 22-3, 66
Nottingham Playhouse   114
Noyce, Philip   54
Nunn, Trevor   139
NVA   145
O Dreamland   43
O'Sullivan, Thaddeus   55, 56-7
Offspring   180
Old Labour   27, 111
Oldman, Gary   34-5
On the Edge   51
Once Upon a Time in the Midlands   31
One Life Stand   82
Ordinary Decent Criminal   50, 55-6
Orientalised   94, 113
Orphans   66, 80-1
Osborne, John   46
Outlying Islands   154
Owen, Gary   172
Paines Plough Theatre Co   106, 122, 147, 154,
    155, 172
Parker, Alan   89
Parralax Films   66
Passage to India, A   39

Passing Places   152, 155
Patriarchy   102, 140
Pavee Lackeen   61-62,
Pawlikowski, Pawel   17, 20, 42-3
Paxman, J   8, 105
Peace Process (Irish)   7, 48, 52, 53, 54, 57, 58,
    125, 126, 130, 132, 134, 137, 138, 143
Pearson, Mike   165, 166
Peebles, Alison   84-5
Penhall, Joe   118
Periphery   32, 48
Permanent Way, The   110
Petrie, Duncan   65, 66, 72, 75, 77, 80, 83, 84,
    158
Pinnock, Winsome   113
Play What I Wrote, The   121
Playing With Fire   111
Pontecorvo, Gillo   61
Postcolonial   10, 11, 12, 14, 17, 38, 40, 48, 51,
    61, 62, 89, 90, 100, 103, 112, 116, 118,
    120, 130, 134, 139, 140, 156, 166, 167,
    171, 174, 178, 179
Post-feminist   34
Post-industrial   25
Postmodern   59, 136, 137
Post-nation   13, 39
Powell, Enoch   41, 119
Prague   66, 67, 79
Prichard, Rebecca   107, 116
Prime Suspect   130
Protectionism   48
Prydain: The Impossibility of Britishness   166
Psychoanalytical   11
Puri, Om
Pyramid Project, The   122
Pyrenees   154
Quiet Man, The   135
Race   25, 40, 103, 104, 111, 118, 174
Racial identity   39-42
Rafelson, Bob   100
Raining Stones   74
Raj films   74
Ramsey, Lynne   66, 73, 77-80, 82
Rancid Aluminium   98, 99, 100, 177
Ratcatcher   66, 77-9, 83
Ravenhill, Mark   106, 107, 118, 119
Rea, Stephen   54
Reade, Simon   122
Reagan, Ronald   73
Realism   151

Redwood, John 104
Reed, Lou   97
Rees, Marc 167
Reeves, Saskia   57
Refugees   41, 42, 43
Regional identity   28, 31
Regional   25, 30, 31
Regionalism   20
Reid, Christina 126
Renoir, Jean   83
Republican 137
Resurrection Man   55
Rhydaymerau 164
Rhys, Matthew 93,102
Richards, Julian   93, 95–6
Richardson, Miranda   54
Ridiculusmus 143
Riefenstahl, Leni 167
Riff Raff   74
Rigg, Diana 122
Ritchie, Guy   66
River, Sol B 112
Riverdance   56
Road movie   67, 83, 93, 155
Rob Roy   66, 68, 69
Roberts, Julia   22–3
Rockett, Emer   56
Rockett, Kevin   47
Rolling Stones, The   59
Room for Romeo Brass   30-1
Roth, Tim   31–2
Rowlands Ian 174, 175
Royal Court Theatre 125, 136, 138
Royal National Theatre   17, 108, 109, 115,
   123, 138, 139, 172
Royal Ulster Constabulary (RUC) 130, 131
Rumsfeld, Donald 111
Run of the Country, The   49
Safar   170
Sammy and Rosie Get Laid   39
Sandanistas   73
Saving Private Ryan   61
Say Nothing 143
Scarface 167
Schepisi, Fred   45
Schnitzler, Arthur 106
Schoene, Berthold   13–14
Schwartz, Stefan   67
Scorsese, Martin   80, 100
Scott, Arms to Iraq Inquiry 110

Scottish Arts Council National Lottery Fund   73
Scottish Film Fund   67
Scottish Film Production Fund   65
Scottish National Party (SNP)   68,
Scottish Parliament 68, 156
Scottish Screen   59, 65
Scullion, Adrienne   15,158, 159, 160
Secret of Roan Inish, The   49
Sellars, Ian   66, 67, 77, 79
Semiology   11
Sense of Freedon, A 158
Seth, Roshan   39
7:84   150, 159, 160, 162
Sexual identity   39, 51, 84, 116
Sexuality   20, 29, 54, 118
Sexy Beast   36–7
Sgript Cymru   172
Shakespeare in Love   38
Shakespeare, William   80,139
Shallow Grave   66, 67, 69, 70, 72, 94
Shankill Butchers   55
Sharp, Alan   69
Sharp, Lesley   27
Sheffield theatres 122
Sheffield: City on the Move   25
Shepherd, Sam 98
Sheridan, Elizabeth   51
Sheridan, Jim   53–4
Sherlock, Ceri   91, 92, 164
Shetland Saga 159
Shining City 140
Shoot for the Sun   71
Shopping and Fucking   119
S4C (Sianel Pedwar Cymru)   87–8, 91, 92, 93,
   95
Sierz, Aleks 105, 107, 108, 116, 117, 118, 136,
   172
Sim, John   101
Sinn Fein 138
Site-specific work 164
16 Years of Alcohol   85
Sleeping Around 106, 107, 155
Sliding Doors   32–5
Smith, Chris 120
Smith, Othniel 170
Snowcake 98
Social realism   26, 85, 97, 97, 102, 143, 150
Socialism   81, 120
Soft Top, Hard Shoulder   67
Solid Air   82

Solomon and Gaenor 89-91
Some Explicit Polaroids 119, 120
Some Mother's Son 54-5
Southern, Terry 83
Spacey, Kevin 50, 56
Spencer, Edmund 138
State of the Nation 110, 111, 176
Stella Does Tricks 84-5
Stembridge, Gerald 50
Stephen Lawrence Inquiry 110
Stereophonics 104
Stereophonics, The 92
Stone City Blue 178-9
Stones in His Pockets 133-4, 135, 142
Straits 157
Straw, Jack 118
Strelnikhov, Artiom 43
Strictly Ballroom 102
Stuff Happens 9,110, 111
Sugarman, Sara 101, 102
Sunday 60-61
Super Furry Animals 92
Surrealism 80
Suspect Culture 145, 149
Swan Lake 29
Sweet Sixteen 75
Swift, Graham 45
Syal, Meera 113
Sydney Opera House 173
Synge, John Millington 136
TAG Theatre 145
Tait, Margaret 67, 77
Tara Arts 113
Tarantino, Quentin 36, 55, 70, 100
Tarkovsky, Andrei 86
Tartanry 94, 100, 156
Teare, Jeff 170
Thatcher, Margaret 28, 42, 54, 74, 87, 119
Thatcherism 20, 74, 116
The troubles (Ireland) 54, 57, 58, 60, 61, 126
Theatr Genedlaethol Cymru 168
Theatre Royal (Stratford East) 170
Theatr Y Byd 174
Thewlis, David 57
This Happy Breed 34
This Other England 154
This Year's Love 83-4
Thomas, Ed 97-8, 155, 176, 177, 179
Thomas, Owen 82
Three Birds Alighting on a Field 116

Tiger Bay 104
Tinderbox 141, 142
Titanic 52
Tomlinson, Ricky 31
Trainspotting 66, 67, 70-72, 81, 94, 95, 97, 100, 101
Transnational 33
Transnationalism 11
Traverse Theatre 151
Tregenna, Catherine 172
Tribunal Plays 110
Trimble, David 130
Trocchi, Alexander 83
Tron 175
Trust 128
Trycycle Theatre 110
Tuan John, Sean 167
Tucker Green, Debbie 112, 113
Twenty-Four Seven 30-1
Twin Town 72, 93-5, 96, 97, 98, 100
Twpathau 161
UDA 128, 130, 131
Un Nos Ola Leuad (One Full Moon) 91-2
Unionism 128, 131
Up 'n' Under 25
Upton, Judy 116
Valleywood 100
Velvet Underground, The 92, 97
Venus Peter 66
Verbatim Theatre 110
Verma, Jatinda 113
Very Annie Mary 101, 102
Waking Ned Devine 49
Wallace, Naomi 116
Wallace, William 68
Walsh, Enda 51
Walsh, Kieron 51
War Zone, The 31-2, 34
Warner, Alan 79
Way of Life, A 17, 102-4
Way, Charles 170, 176
Weir, The 138, 140
Welcome to Sarajevo 43
Welles, Orson 173
Welsh Assembly Government 68, 168, 169, 171, 173, 179
Welsh, Irvine 71
Wertenbaker, Timberlake 116
West Yorkshire Playhouse 114, 121
Westerns 37, 69

Weston, Joanna 168
When Brendan Met Trudy 51
White Powder, Green Light 99
Wicker Man, The, 95
Wildcat 149, 161
Williams, Charlotte 103
Williams, Chris 13, 39
Williams, Roger 171
Williams, Roy 112
Winstone, Ray 34–5, 37, 45
Winterbottom, Michael 35, 43, 57
Wire, Nicky 173
With or Without You 57–8

Withnail and I 172
Wonderland 35–6
Woods, David 143
Woof, Emily 27
Writing back 48
Yard Gal 107, 109
Young Adam 83
Yule, Eleanor 84–5
Z 61
Zellweger, Renee 25
Zero Degrees and Drifting 122
Zola, Emile 83